Edexcel A2 Psychology

Christine Brain Karren Smith Dawn Collis Liz Reeve
Ali Ghalib

STUDENT BOOK

Contents

A PEARSON COMPANY

About this book

This A2 Psychology Student Book provides all the content and assessment practice and guidance you need to study Edexcel's Advanced GCE in Psychology.

Written by a team of experts including experienced examiners and teachers, you can be sure that you have everything you need to succeed!

Key features of the Student Book

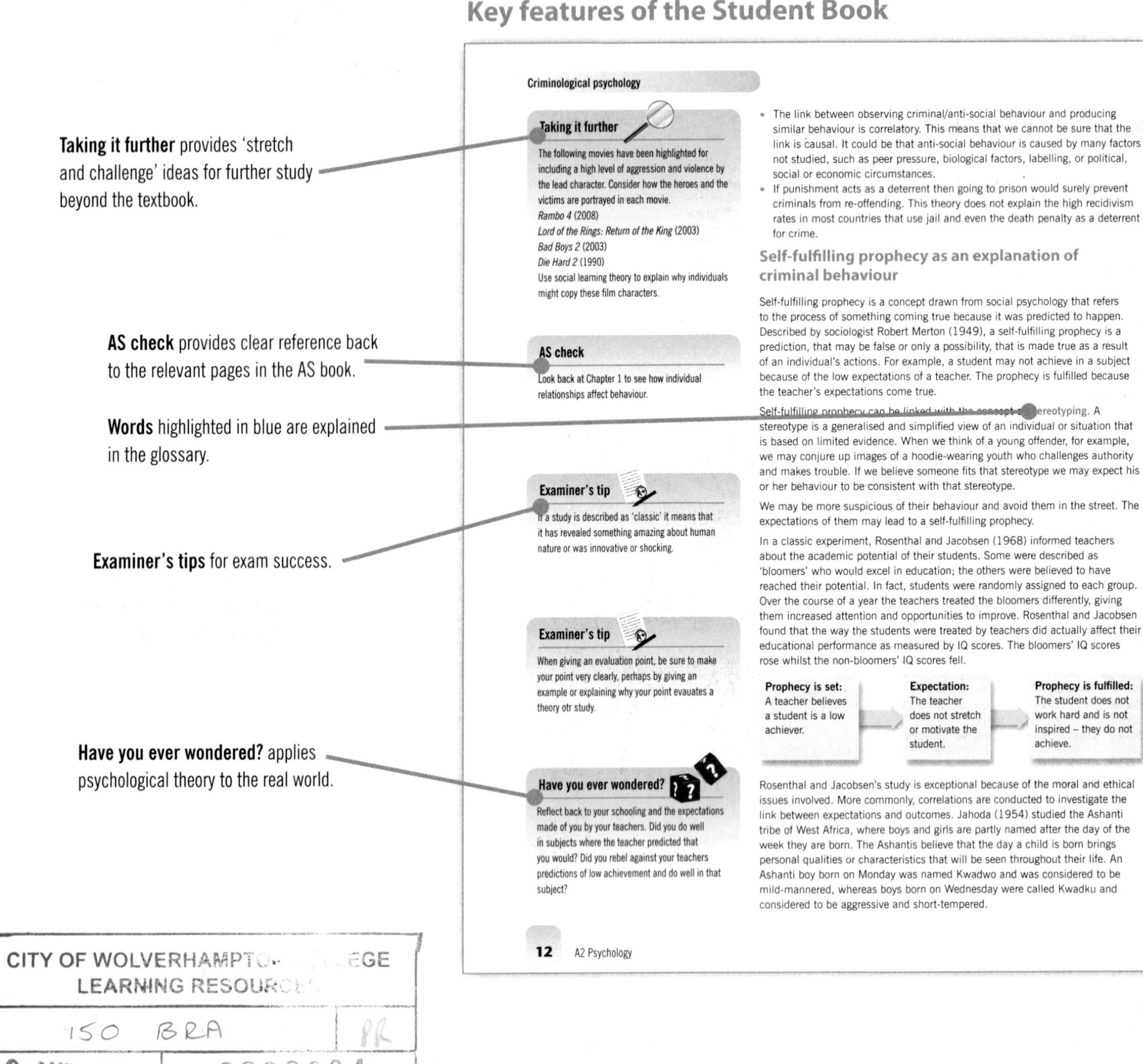

Criminological psychology

Taking it further

The following movies have been highlighted for including a high level of aggression and violence by the lead character. Consider how the heroes and the victims are portrayed in each movie.

Rambo 4 (2008)
Lord of the Rings: Return of the King (2003)
Bad Boys 2 (2003)
Die Hard 2 (1990)

Use social learning theory to explain why individuals might copy these film characters.

AS check

Look back at Chapter 1 to see how individual relationships affect behaviour.

Examiner's tip

If a study is described as 'classic' it means that it has revealed something amazing about human nature or was innovative or shocking.

Examiner's tip

When giving an evaluation point, be sure to make your point very clearly, perhaps by giving an example or explaining why your point evauates a theory otr study.

Have you ever wondered?

Reflect back to your schooling and the expectations made of you by your teachers. Did you do well in subjects where the teacher predicted that you would? Did you rebel against your teachers predictions of low achievement and do well in that subject?

- The link between observing criminal/anti-social behaviour and producing similar behaviour is correlatory. This means that we cannot be sure that the link is causal. It could be that anti-social behaviour is caused by many factors not studied, such as peer pressure, biological factors, labelling, or political, social or economic circumstances.
- If punishment acts as a deterrent then going to prison would surely prevent criminals from re-offending. This theory does not explain the high recidivism rates in most countries that use jail and even the death penalty as a deterrent for crime.

Self-fulfilling prophecy as an explanation of criminal behaviour

Self-fulfilling prophecy is a concept drawn from social psychology that refers to the process of something coming true because it was predicted to happen. Described by sociologist Robert Merton (1949), a self-fulfilling prophecy is a prediction, that may be false or only a possibility, that is made true as a result of an individual's actions. For example, a student may not achieve in a subject because of the low expectations of a teacher. The prophecy is fulfilled because the teacher's expectations come true.

Self-fulfilling prophecy can be linked with the concept of stereotyping. A stereotype is a generalised and simplified view of an individual or situation that is based on limited evidence. When we think of a young offender, for example, we may conjure up images of a hoodie-wearing youth who challenges authority and makes trouble. If we believe someone fits that stereotype we may expect his or her behaviour to be consistent with that stereotype.

We may be more suspicious of their behaviour and avoid them in the street. The expectations of them may lead to a self-fulfilling prophecy.

In a classic experiment, Rosenthal and Jacobsen (1968) informed teachers about the academic potential of their students. Some were described as 'bloomers' who would excel in education; the others were believed to have reached their potential. In fact, students were randomly assigned to each group. Over the course of a year the teachers treated the bloomers differently, giving them increased attention and opportunities to improve. Rosenthal and Jacobsen found that the way the students were treated by teachers did actually affect their educational performance as measured by IQ scores. The bloomers' IQ scores rose whilst the non-bloomers' IQ scores fell.

Prophecy is set: A teacher believes a student is a low achiever. → **Expectation:** The teacher does not stretch or motivate the student. → **Prophecy is fulfilled:** The student does not work hard and is not inspired – they do not achieve.

Rosenthal and Jacobsen's study is exceptional because of the moral and ethical issues involved. More commonly, correlations are conducted to investigate the link between expectations and outcomes. Jahoda (1954) studied the Ashanti tribe of West Africa, where boys and girls are partly named after the day of the week they are born. The Ashantis believe that the day a child is born brings personal qualities or characteristics that will be seen throughout their life. An Ashanti boy born on Monday was named Kwadwo and was considered to be mild-mannered, whereas boys born on Wednesday were called Kwadku and considered to be aggressive and short-tempered.

12 A2 Psychology

At the end of each approach you can consolidate your knowledge with exam-style questions in the Examzone section. Sample student answers to some of the questions, with Examiner's comments, are included in the Exam advice section (see page 181). These questions are marked *. The remaining answers may be found on www.edexcel.com/A2psychology-studentanswers.

Examzone

1 Define the following terms:
   i Recidivism
   ii Anti-social behaviour
   iii Crime (6 marks)

2 Outline how a field experiment is used as a research method to investigate witness effectiveness. (3 marks)

3 During your course you will have studied one field study into eyewitness testimony. Identify this field study and describe its findings. (2 marks)

4 Evaluate the field experiment in terms of validity or ethical issues. (4 marks)

5 Lilly is worried that her son is watching too much television. His behaviour has become aggressive and he is often told off at school for hitting other children. Use your knowledge of Social Learning Theory, research and the role of the media to explain Lilly's problem. (8 marks)

6 The probation service is looking into ways to treat offenders and lower recidivism. They are using token economies but realise this treatment programme is limited in the extent to which they rehabilitate offenders and lower recidivism. Describe another way of treating prisoners and evaluate the usefulness of this programme. (12 marks)

What you will learn about provides a clear overview of the chapter content.

Important psychological **key terms**. Each is clearly explained in a comprehensive glossary at the end of the book.

Psychology is brought to life through **photos and diagrams** that contextualise core content.

What you need to know gives an overview of the content and skills required for the assessment.

Introduction

4. Sport psychology

What you will learn about in this chapter

- The ways in which psychologists study sport.
- Factors affecting participation and performance.
- Ways of improving performance.

Key terms

- participation
- excellence
- intrinsic motivation
- extrinsic motivation
- arousal
- anxiety
- audience effect
- qualitative data
- quantitative data

◆ What is sport psychology?

Sport psychology aims to study the behaviour of people in sport. This includes why people choose to participate in sport, which sports they pursue and their progress within the sport. It looks at how mental state can influence performance as well as how sport can influence mental state. Sport psychologists apply understanding of these factors to help people in sport gain the greatest benefit from what they do.

◆ Who participates in sport?

Sport can be defined as: 'an activity governed by a set of rules that participants must abide by and where the individual is required to use physical skills they possess, or can learn'.

Children learn many skills through sport. Adults, too, enjoy the challenge and satisfaction of acquiring and improving skills. It is rare to find someone who has never participated in sport, but participation in organised sport does decline as we grow up. Children almost always participate in sport. However, during adolescence, participation does drop, particularly among females. So, although participation in sport does continue throughout adulthood, it is at a reduced level. There is evidence that someone is more likely to maintain an active participation in sport if their parents or carers have also participated in sport, or actively supported them during childhood.

◆ What determines the sport you choose?

- Opportunity: If facilities are limited, through either cost or location, this will influence choice.
- Personality: People who are happiest in company are more likely to choose a team sport, whereas a shy person may prefer a more solitary sport.
- Gender: Some sports are taken up much more by one gender than another.
- Encouragement: Children may be encouraged or discouraged to take up a particular sport by family or friends.
- Ability: Being good at a sport brings positive reinforcement.

▲ Personality is often a significant factor in determining whether someone prefers team or individual sports.

◆ How well will you do?

Many factors can influence how well you do in sport. Of particular importance are:

- Ability: Particular skills can mean you are better at one sport than another.
- Effort: Top sportspeople spend many hours practising skills and maintaining peak fitness. Many talented people do not put in this effort, so never reach the top.
- Personality: Some sportspeople show tremendous potential but 'bottle it' in competition, when the stress and tension affect their performance. Unless they are taught ways to control their stress levels, they will always underperform in competition.
- Coaching: An outstanding coach can raise performance significantly.

A2 Psychology 75

What you need to know

- Describe and evaluate two studies. One of these must be Loftus and Palmer's (1974) study of the effect of leading questions.
- The second study must be one of:
  - Yuille and Cutshall (1986) case study of eyewitness testimony
  - Charlton et al. (2000) naturalistic study in St Helena
  - Gesch et al. (2003) diet and anti-social behaviour in young adult prisoners.

Overview of Units 3 and 4

The A2 part of your course gives you the opportunity to study some issues of psychology in the real world. You will discover how the Approaches you learned about at AS come together to help explain human behaviour.

Unit 3

You will choose two out of the following four applications:

Criminological psychology

This looks at psychological explanations for criminal behaviour, problems with eyewitness testimony and treating offenders.

- Definition of the application
- Methodology: Experiments and evaluation of their use in criminological psychology
- Content: Causes of crime, eyewitness testimony, defendant characteristics and treating offenders
- Two studies in detail: Loftus and Palmer (1974) plus one other
- One key issue of choice
- Practical evidence: Content analysis/article analysis related to the key issue

Child psychology

This looks at the development of relationships in infancy and the impact of daycare on young children.

- Definition of the application
- Methodology: Observations, cases studies and cross-cultural longitudinal research
- Content: Bowlby, attachments, deprivation, privation, one developmental issue, one enrichment programme
- Two studies in detail: Curtiss (1977) plus one other
- One key issue of choice
- Practical evidence: Content analysis/article analysis related to the key issue

Health psychology

This considers the problems associated with the use of recreational drugs.

- Definition of the application
- Methodology: Animal studies and ethics
- Content: Actions, effects and treatment of drug abuse
- Two studies in detail: Blättler (2002) plus one other
- One key issue of choice
- Practical evidence: Content analysis/article analysis related to the key issue

Sport psychology

This looks at the reasons why individuals participate in sport, and why some people excel in training and flop on the big occasion, while for others the reverse is true.

- Definition of the application
- Methodology: Questionnaires and correlations
- Content: Participation, motivation, improving performance, anxiety and audience effects
- Two studies in detail: Boyd and Munroe (2003) plus one other
- One key issue of choice
- Practical evidence: Content analysis/article analysis related to the key issue

Unit 4

This comprises one additional application and a section called Issues and debates, where all the material you have covered is drawn together to develop an overview of the subject.

Clinical psychology

This covers explanations for mental illness, their diagnosis and treatment.

- Definition of the application
- Methodology: Research methods and issues of diagnosis
- Content: Defining, diagnosing, describing, explaining and treating mental disorders (schizophrenia and one other)
- Three studies in detail: Rosenhan (1973) plus two others
- One key issue of choice
- Practical evidence: Advice leaflet focusing on the key issue

Issues and debates

- Contributions of the approaches to society
- Ethics
- Research methods
- Key issues
- Debates (cultural issues, is psychology a science?, social control, nature/nurture)
- Applying knowledge to novel situations

1. Criminological psychology

What you will learn about in this chapter

- The nature of crime and anti-social behaviour, including theories that explain the causes of criminal behaviour.
- Laboratory and field experiments as research methods to investigate witness effectiveness.
- Research studies that examine the reliability of eyewitness testimony and criminal behaviour.
- How criminal psychologists treat offenders.
- A range of key issues in criminological psychology.
- How to conduct a content analysis or summary, drawing conclusions and linking to theories, research and concepts.

Key terms

- crime
- recidivism
- token economy
- anti-social behaviour
- stereotyping
- modelling
- eyewitness testimony

What is criminological psychology?

Criminological or criminal psychology is a specialised area that uses psychological knowledge to help understand criminal behaviour. It investigates the causes of crime by examining social and personality issues that can be contributory factors. It also deals with legal aspects of crime such as courtroom procedures, eyewitness testimony and policing techniques that are used to judge criminals. One of its key roles is to develop treatment programmes for offenders. These are used in the community or in prisons to rehabilitate offenders and prevent recidivism. Criminological psychology is also concerned with identifying offenders and predicting future crimes using profiling techniques.

Examiner's tip

Remember that it is anti-social – not unsociable – behaviour. These terms are often mixed up in the exam and have different meanings.

Crime and antisocial behaviour

A **crime** is a behaviour that violates social norms, moral values, religious beliefs or legal boundaries. Criminological psychology focuses on behaviour that breaks the law and as such is subject to punishment.

Social norms change over time, so any behaviour defined as criminal may change over time too. This is also true of legal crime. The Children's Act 2004, for example, has made smacking an offence similar to assault. Legal crimes often reflect the social norms and moral values of the society in which they are created.

Crime can be measured in different ways. Official statistics are produced by the Home Office based on the number of reported crimes. However, these can be unreliable because not all crimes are reported by the public, and some police choose not to report crimes that they feel will not lead to prosecution. The British Crime Survey is a national survey sent to random households asking questions about crime-related behaviour and what crimes they have been victims of. The Home Office estimates that less than half of all crimes recorded by the survey were actually reported to the police in 2007/8.

The purpose of the British Crime Survey is to uncover victimisation rates and perception of crime and risk of harm, so does not include crimes against children under 16, commercial crime such as fraud or victimless crime such as drug use. It also excludes murder.

Anti-social behaviour is defined by the Crime and Disorder Act (1998) as 'behaviour likely to cause alarm, harassment or distress to members of the public'. It can take the form of abusive language, excessive noise, littering, vandalism or drunken behaviour. Anti-social Behaviour Orders (ASBOs) were introduced in 1998 to widen police and court powers to improve the quality of life in communities where such behaviour was causing problems. Each ASBO is specifically made to fit the crime and offender. ASBOs have been criticised for being heavy-handed, arbitrarily used and considered a 'badge of honour' by recipients.

Taking it further

There are many people who are concerned about the use of ASBOs and their negative effects on the people convicted and communities involved. Research these problems on the Internet.

Methodology

What you need to know

- Describe and evaluate research methods (including laboratory and field experiments) used to study whether witnesses are effective.
- Explain the strengths and weaknesses of laboratory and field experiments in terms of their use in criminological psychology and in terms of reliability, validity and ethical issues.

AS check

You may have studied eyewitness reliability as a key issue. Details of this debate can be found on AS pages 58–59.

AS check

Look back at the research methods you studied, in particular laboratory experiments and field experiments (AS pages 40-41). You also need to be able to refer to other research methods such as the case study and survey.

AS check

You learnt about independent and dependent variables in the Cognitive Approach (AS see page 42).

Research methods used to study witness effectiveness

A witness is someone who experiences an incident, such as a crime or accident, and then later recalls the experience to a police officer. This is known as **eyewitness testimony**. It may be used to identify a suspect or build up a picture of an incident. If a suspect is found, the testimony may be relied upon later in court. Psychologists have questioned the effectiveness of witness testimony as many factors can affect a witness, such as how they are questioned by the police or whether they experienced stress during the incident. It is not usually possible to study real witnesses, because the experience might affect the testimony they give to the police or describe in court, so researchers use a range of research methods to study these factors on participants. The main ones covered here are laboratory and field experiments.

Laboratory experiments

Laboratory experiments are conducted in artificial environments where a researcher manipulates the **independent variable** and measures or records the **dependent variable**. The experiment is set up rather than occurring naturally.

In criminological psychology, laboratory experiments have been used to isolate the factors that might influence a witness and study the effect on their testimony. Elizabeth Loftus is a pioneer in eyewitness testimony research and many of her studies are laboratory experiments that investigate the influence of leading questions on recall by manipulating the type of question asked.

A typical laboratory experiment into eyewitness testimony will involve these steps:

1. Gather participants to take part in the study.
2. Show participants a video, film, slides or photograph of an incident.
3. Get them to recall it later in a memory test.

At some point, an independent variable(s) will be introduced. In Step 1, a researcher may vary the type of participant selected, for example by age, gender or experience. In Step 2, the video may vary so that some participants view a violent incident and some a non-violent incident. In Step 3, the researchers may investigate the influence of post-event information or questioning technique on witness recall.

Field experiments

Field experiments are similar to laboratory experiments in that they both have independent and dependent variables, but they are conducted in a more natural setting. Researchers will set up the experiment in an environment where the phenomenon being studied would naturally occur.

Eyewitnesses can experience incidents in any situation from a bank robbery to a car accident. A researcher considers the environment in which a particular incident might take place and attempts to recreate this in a realistic way. A field experiment will follow the same steps as a laboratory experiment, but Step 2 will be in real life rather than watching a video or photograph stills. Participants may be people in the setting at the time.

Reliability

Reliability refers to the consistency of the findings of research. High reliability is established by using **experimental controls** and being able to replicate research.

Laboratory experiments can control many factors so that only one or a few are studied directly. Such experiments can also be replicated again and again to check the consistency of the findings.

Loftus' laboratory experiments are a good example of high reliability because of the level of control over **participant** and **situational variables**. She showed participants the same video of a car accident and they all recalled using the same technique. Her studies have been replicated many times and have consistently found that, for example, leading questions do affect witness recall.

Field experiments are generally more difficult to control because many situational variables might occur in a natural setting, such as distractions from other people. It is therefore unlikely that a field experiment can be replicated exactly because these **extraneous variables** may affect the findings of the experiment. This would lead to inconsistent results and low reliability. Clever field experiments are able to control situational variables by choosing a contained and controlled environment in which to conduct the study. For example, a field experiment testing witness recall of a bank robbery may be able to control situational variables because it is set up in a bank.

AS check

You will have studied the effects of participant, situational and extraneous variables. (see AS page 43).

Validity

Validity is a term used to describe how well a study measures what it is supposed to.

Laboratory experiments of eyewitness testimony lack **ecological validity** because they are conducted in artificial surroundings that do not recreate the situation experienced by a real witness:

- They would not expect the incident to happen or be prepared to recall it.
- They might suffer stress and anxiety during the incident, particularly if it is violent or traumatic.
- They may discuss what they have seen with others
- Police will interview them and ask for their version of events.

In a laboratory experiment witnesses are prepared to view and recall from video footage or photograph stills. Under these conditions they are unlikely to be upset or distressed as they are aware that what they are witnessing is staged and not real. Participants are not interviewed by the police, but typically complete a questionnaire about what they have witnessed. This may result in less consideration over the testimony they give because participants know that it is a test and no one is going to rely on it as genuine evidence. Field experiments are less likely to suffer from these problems as participants are essentially experiencing the conditions of a real witness (although it is unlikely they will be interviewed by police).

Recalling a crime by completing a questionnaire does not reflect a realistic witness experience.

Laboratory experiments can also be criticised for lacking validity because participants may alter their testimony as they are aware of being part of an experiment. This is known as demand characteristics – participants alter their behaviour in response to the demands of the situation. If a participant guesses that the aim of a study is, for example, to test how stress affects witness recall, then they might recall less to meet the expectation of the research.

Being part of a laboratory experiment may also make a participant more or less cautious about their testimony compared to a real witness. Or, if the participant believes that the researcher knows what really happened in a video, they might be more likely to be misled by leading questions than a witness being interviewed by the police (who does not know what has happened).

In field experiments participants may be unaware that they are participating in a psychological study, so demand characteristics should not be an issue.

Research into the methodological issues of eyewitness testimony research

Wagstaff et al. (2003) examined real witness and victim descriptions of offenders and compared them to the actual offenders' details on arrest. They found very little evidence that factors such as weapon focus, age or level of violence had any effect on witness testimony. This shows that factors identified as having an effect on eyewitness testimony in laboratory and field studies may not have an effect in real life.

This is further supported by Yuille and Cutshall's (1986) case study of a real gunshop robbery and subsequent shootout in Canada. Real witnesses to the shooting were interviewed about the incident and this was compared to police records of other testimony. The researchers found that the witnesses had detailed memory of the event and were not misled by the researchers' leading questions. This case study casts doubt on the validity of laboratory research.

Ihlebaek et al. (2003) conducted a study that compared memory for a live staged robbery and video footage of the same robbery. The staged robbery was conducted in a field setting and the video footage in a laboratory setting. They found that participants who watched the video footage of the robbery recalled more details with greater accuracy than the live robbery.

Taking it further

Find out more about the British Psychological Society and the ethical guidelines for use with human participants at http://www.bps.org.uk/. Search for 'ethics' and download the code of conduct.

However, the number of errors in recall were the same in both conditions. This shows that, while laboratory experiments may find similar results to field experiments, they may overestimate witness recall. This is probably due to the level of attention participants give to the video compared with an unexpected incident.

Ethical issues

Protection of participants

Laboratory experiments often involve showing participants videos of crimes or incidents that it would be unethical to get them to experience in real life. Watching a video of a car accident, for example, is far less distressing than witnessing a real one. However, if a participant has a previous experience of a similar incident they might still find it upsetting. In this case, they should be given the right to withdraw.

In field experiments it is also important to protect participants because they are experiencing what they believe to be a real-life incident. A researcher conducting a field experiment would have to weigh up the nature of the incident they are intending to stage to make sure it does not cause excessive distress or concern.

Deception, right to withdraw and consent

To prevent demand characteristics and improve validity, a researcher may choose to deceive participants about the true aim of an experiment. Deception might be necessary, but it can result in participants feeling embarrassed, particularly if they are found to be a poor witness. If deception is used there will be a lack of informed consent, as participants will not be fully aware of the nature and consequences of the research.

Deception can be an issue for both laboratory and field experiments, although it is more likely that laboratory experiments will have gained participants' consent. If a field experiment stages an incident that a person might experience in their everyday lives, there is less need for consent. Similarly, a right to withdraw may not be a significant issue in a field experiment, if participants are likely to encounter the situation in everyday life. However, laboratory experiments almost always offer a right to withdraw, as participants are aware of being experimental subjects. If deception, right to withdraw and lack of informed consent are issues, it is good to debrief participants fully once the experiment is complete.

It is wholly inappropriate to conduct a field experiment that involves a serious incident, or a situation that may cause distress to potential participants. In such cases, the right to withdraw and informed consent are vital to protect participant witnesses from psychological harm.

Other ways of studying eyewitness effectiveness

Because of the ethical and methodological difficulties with conducting laboratory and field research on eyewitness identification, psychologists have adopted alternative research methods. Behrman and Davey (2001) analysed police records to compare line-up identifications with evidence found about the identified offender. This method used 271 actual cases involving multiple variables that can affect eyewitness identification. This study avoided some of the ethical issues with eyewitness research.

Neisser (1981) conducted a case study on the testimony of John Dean about the Watergate Affair. Neisser was able to compare John Dean's testimony with actual tape recordings made of meetings held in the Oval office of the Whitehouse.

Ethics will be considered again in Issues and Debates on pages 144-145 of this book.

AS check

You will have studied the ethical issues of consent, right to withdraw, protection of participants, deception and debriefing in the Social Approach (see AS page 10).

Examiner's tip

These issues of reliability, validity and ethics can be used later when you have to evaluate Loftus and Palmer's (1974) laboratory experiment on eyewitness testimony and Charlton et al's (2000) naturalistic experiment into media aggression in St Helena.

Content

What you need to know

- Explain criminal/anti-social behaviour from different approaches.
- Describe and evaluate the social learning theory as an explanation for criminal/anti-social behavior, and one other explanation from a different approach.
- Explain criminal/anti-social behaviour using the theories you have studied.

AS check

Social Learning Theory is briefly described here in relation to criminal behaviour, but it would be useful to refer back to AS pages 136-137 for more detail of operant conditioning and Social Learning Theory. Also review Albert Bandura's (1961) study of learning from aggressive role models on AS pages 142-143.

Theories of criminal behaviour

Explaining criminal behaviour can inform how to control or prevent it. Sociologists explain criminal behaviour as a product of social, economic and political issues. Whilst these are important, psychology seeks to explain behaviour in terms of the individual: biological reasons, personality, learning and upbringing.

Social learning theory

Social Learning Theory explains criminal behaviour in terms of **modelling** behaviour seen through watching others or via the media. Criminal behaviour is learnt through attention, retention, motivation and reproduction. A person needs to be able to observe criminal behaviour directly or indirectly in real life or via the media so that it can be remembered and reproduced. This is the **cognitive** element of the theory and can mean that the behaviour is not copied immediately but can emerge much later, which can make it difficult to prove the link.

◆ Motivation

Bandura (1977) outlined three important factors which determine whether we decide to copy:

1. **Vicarious learning**: If a behaviour is punished it is less likely to be repeated and, if rewarded, more likely to be repeated. However, vicarious learning is not direct reward or punishment, but is how an individual learns by watching *others* being rewarded or punished. Observing a successful criminal is therefore more likely to be a motivation to copy than observing an unsuccessful one. If an individual views the crime as victimless (such as shoplifting) they are also more likely to copy it.
2. External motivation: Once a criminal act has been acquired through social learning, the rules of operant conditioning apply. If the behaviour is rewarded (i.e. is successful), it is more likely to be repeated.
3. Self-reinforcement: This refers to the self-motivational factors associated with a crime. A behaviour is more motivating if some internal need is satisfied, such as the excitement of car-jacking.

◆ Role models

Central to social learning theory is that we copy behaviour that we observe. Criminal behaviour has to have been observed in role models already engaging in criminal activity. These may be family members, friends and peers or the social environment we live in. We are more likely to copy individuals with social status.

The role of the media

The opportunity to witness anti-social behaviour in real life may be limited. However, the opportunity to witness media violence and crime is less restricted. Violence and criminal acts are frequently on television – between 70% and 80% of programmes are estimated to contain acts of aggression. This becomes increasingly concerning when people watch approximately 38 hours of TV a week, with children between two and seven watching up to 25 hours a week (Rideout et al., 1999).

Research and surveys have found a link between TV viewing hours and the incidence of criminal convictions. Bandura's (1961) study predicts that boys are more likely to copy aggression from television, particularly if observing a male role model. Studies have shown that advertisements aired on Saturday mornings, when children are likely to be watching, are far more likely to contain aggression if they feature boys rather than girls (Macklin and Kolbe, 1984).

Recent experimental research has found that playing violent video games increases arousal and aggression levels. Anderson and Dill (2000) found that participants who played violent games were more likely to administer a loud and prolonged blast of noise to an opponent than those who played non-violent games. Barlett et al. (2007) conducted a similar experiment using *Mortal Combat: Deadly Alliance* with the amount of graphic blood set from zero to the highest level. They found that more blood led to more aggressive thoughts.

Motivation to copy from the media

- Anti-social or criminal behaviour on television or video games is not likely to be punished – in fact many 'heroes' are heralded for 'getting rid' of bad guys. Television victims are rarely seen; families are not seen crying at the funeral and graphic scenes of death are restricted to highly certificated movies. The motivation to copy from television may be greater than real life.
- The 2008 school killings in Finland were linked to song lyrics of a popular cult band. Music bands are high earning and celebrated, so it is possible that their song lyrics were translated into anti-social actions by their followers.
- Video games are, according to this theory, the most likely of all media to create anti-social behaviour and aggression because killing is rewarded and bodies disappear without consequence from the screen.

Evaluation

- Only a handful of incidents have been directly linked to media violence. However, we only have to observe children's play to witness re-enactments of their favourite superhero moves.
- Bandura's (1961) laboratory experiment provided causal evidence that children copy violent behaviour.
- Watching criminal behaviour or aggression on TV is maybe more likely to make us fear being a victim than produce criminal behaviour.
- Individuals with a predisposition to anti-social/criminal behaviour are maybe more likely to seek out similar individuals or media. They are anti-social through association rather than through copying.
- It is very difficult to establish a link between observational learning and criminal behaviour because of a lack of control over the experience of viewing anti-social behaviour and the time lapse possible before the behaviour is displayed.
- Bandura's (1961) study suggests that individuals, particularly boys, copy anti-social behaviour (physical and verbal aggression) from watching adult role models. His research also showed how animated aggression was copied.

"TV violence made him do it. Says he'll name shows if we drop the charges."

▲ We copy anti-social behaviour from the media.

The American National Television Violence Study (1997) found that 66% of children's viewing contained physical violence, compared with 57% of adult viewing.

See pages 22-23 for details of Charlton's (2000) study on the link between television and aggression. They found no evidence of negative media influence.

Taking it further

You might know of some tragic cases of individuals who have committed murder that have allegedly been a result of the influence of television, music, literature or video games. Research some of the following:

- Columbine High School Massacre (1999)
- Red Lake High School Massacre (2005)
- Jokela School Shooting (2007)
- Virgina Tech Massacre (2007)

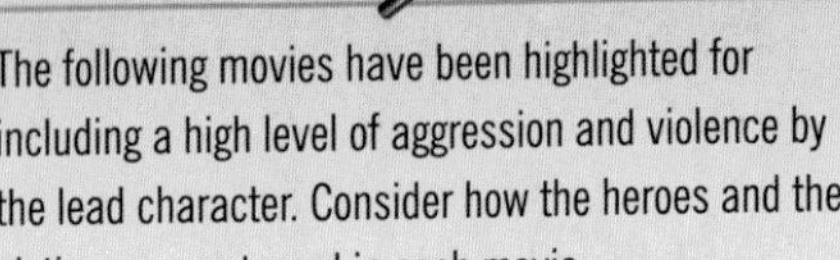

Taking it further

The following movies have been highlighted for including a high level of aggression and violence by the lead character. Consider how the heroes and the victims are portrayed in each movie.

Rambo 4 (2008)
Lord of the Rings: Return of the King (2003)
Bad Boys 2 (2003)
Die Hard 2 (1990)

Use social learning theory to explain why individuals might copy these film characters.

AS check

Look back at Chapter 1 to see how individual relationships affect behaviour.

Examiner's tip

If a study is described as 'classic' it means that it has revealed something amazing about human nature or was innovative or shocking.

Examiner's tip

When giving an evaluation point, be sure to make your point very clearly, perhaps by giving an example or explaining why your point evauates a theory otr study.

Have you ever wondered?

Reflect back to your schooling and the expectations made of you by your teachers. Did you do well in subjects where the teacher predicted that you would? Did you rebel against your teachers predictions of low achievement and do well in that subject?

- The link between observing criminal/anti-social behaviour and producing similar behaviour is correlatory. This means that we cannot be sure that the link is causal. It could be that anti-social behaviour is caused by many factors not studied, such as peer pressure, biological factors, labelling, or political, social or economic circumstances.
- If punishment acts as a deterrent then going to prison would surely prevent criminals from re-offending. This theory does not explain the high recidivism rates in most countries that use jail and even the death penalty as a deterrent for crime.

Self-fulfilling prophecy as an explanation of criminal behaviour

Self-fulfilling prophecy is a concept drawn from social psychology that refers to the process of something coming true because it was predicted to happen. Described by sociologist Robert Merton (1949), a self-fulfilling prophecy is a prediction, that may be false or only a possibility, that is made true as a result of an individual's actions. For example, a student may not achieve in a subject because of the low expectations of a teacher. The prophecy is fulfilled because the teacher's expectations come true.

Self-fulfilling prophecy can be linked with the concept of **stereotyping**. A stereotype is a generalised and simplified view of an individual or situation that is based on limited evidence. When we think of a young offender, for example, we may conjure up images of a hoodie-wearing youth who challenges authority and makes trouble. If we believe someone fits that stereotype we may expect his or her behaviour to be consistent with that stereotype.

We may be more suspicious of their behaviour and avoid them in the street. The expectations of them may lead to a self-fulfilling prophecy.

In a classic experiment, Rosenthal and Jacobsen (1968) informed teachers about the academic potential of their students. Some were described as 'bloomers' who would excel in education; the others were believed to have reached their potential. In fact, students were randomly assigned to each group. Over the course of a year the teachers treated the bloomers differently, giving them increased attention and opportunities to improve. Rosenthal and Jacobsen found that the way the students were treated by teachers did actually affect their educational performance as measured by IQ scores. The bloomers' IQ scores rose whilst the non-bloomers' IQ scores fell.

Prophecy is set: A teacher believes a student is a low achiever.
→ **Expectation:** The teacher does not stretch or motivate the student.
→ **Prophecy is fulfilled:** The student does not work hard and is not inspired – they do not achieve.

Rosenthal and Jacobsen's study is exceptional because of the moral and ethical issues involved. More commonly, correlations are conducted to investigate the link between expectations and outcomes. Jahoda (1954) studied the Ashanti tribe of West Africa, where boys and girls are partly named after the day of the week they are born. The Ashantis believe that the day a child is born brings personal qualities or characteristics that will be seen throughout their life. An Ashanti boy born on Monday was named Kwadwo and was considered to be mild-mannered, whereas boys born on Wednesday were called Kwadku and considered to be aggressive and short-tempered.

... studied police arrest records and found that males born on Wednesday had a significantly higher arrest rate (22%) than males born on Monday (6.9%). This finding can be interpreted using self-fulfilling prophecy, as children bearing the name of Kwadku were expected to be violent and were treated with greater suspicion than the mild-mannered Kwadwo.

Flouri and Hawkes (2008) used information gathered about children born in one week during 1970. They found that daughters whose mothers predicted they would stay in school longer had greater career success and confidence than daughters predicted to leave school earlier. This could be interpreted as a self-fulfilling prophecy. However, mothers who are likely to encourage education may be better off financially and therefore able to pay for extended education. Self-fulfilling prophecy cannot explain why the same expectation and outcome was not true of boys in this study.

Madon (2004) found that a self-fulfilling prophecy was stronger if more than one person held the same expectation. She found that parents who overestimated their child's alcohol use showed a positive correlation to actual alcohol use a year later. Either parents were excellent predictors of future alcohol use, or their expectation was a prophecy that came true. Madon found that when two or more people shared the same negative prediction of alcohol use (that their children would drink high levels) the correlation was stronger.

Evaluation of self-fulfilling prophecy

- The expectations held of an individual can only have an influence if they are not too dissimilar from how individuals view themselves. Similarly, if an individual has a low **self-concept**, they may be more inclined to accept a negative expectation.
- However, research such as Madon's (2004) study, highlights the strong influence of negative expectations. Self-fulfilling prophecy may be stronger for negative expectations than positive ones.
- It is highly unlikely we will ever be able to experimentally prove that self-fulfilling prophecy causes anti-social behaviour because of the moral and ethical issues involved in such research. Rosenthal and Jacobsen's experiment resulted in the IQ score of students actually falling or rising according to the academic judgment made of them by teachers. To create criminals by treating them differently would be immoral and would seriously contravene the BPS ethical guidelines.
- Correlational studies show the link between expectations and outcome, but this link cannot be accepted as causal. There may be many other factors that influence anti-social behaviour that the study did not directly measure. Madon's findings may be due to heavily-drinking parents predicting a similar fortune for their children. It might be that these children are simply copying a parent's behaviour rather than responding to expectations.
- Psychologists would certainly support sociological theories of criminal behaviour being a result of political, economic, education, and cultural and **sub-cultural factors**. There are stronger influences on behaviour than a self-fulfilling prophecy.
- An equally robust psychological theory that explains criminal behaviour is Social Learning Theory. Bandura's (1961) research demonstrates how children model aggressive behavior, so it is the experiences they observe rather than how they are treated that cause criminal/anti-social behaviour.

Taking it further

The Anti-social Behaviour Order was introduced in 2003 to help control anti-social behaviour in problem communities. Those issued with an ASBO are as young as 10 years old and their behavioural contract and personal details can be published and distributed to the local community. Think about how ASBOs can be self-fulfilling and about the stereotypes associated with ASBOs.

Other option

From Lombroso's (1876) research into the physical features of criminals to Raine et al.'s (1997) **PET scans** of murderers' brains, psychologists have sought to understand the biological factors associated with criminal behaviour. However, most of this research is inconclusive and a genetic basis for criminality has not yet been fully established.

Other option

Personality theories suggest that a person's character determines how they behave and respond in certain situations. For example, a person predisposed to be sensation-seeking will be more likely to be aggressive or need greater levels of excitement. These individual differences may contribute to a criminal tendency. Further information about personality theories of criminal behaviour can be found in *Criminal behavior* by Cassel and Bernstein.

Studies of eyewitness testimony

What you need to know

- Describe and evaluate three studies of eyewitness testimony, including a laboratory experiment, a field experiment and one other.

Eyewitness testimony can be affected by many factors before, during or after witnessing an incident. This section explores two studies that have each investigated a different factor. A third study is suggested and you could also use the laboratory experiment by Loftus and Palmer (1974) (see page 20).

Is threat or unusualness the cause of weapon focus? (Pickel, 1998)

Aim

To investigate whether **weapon focus**, the inability to recall peripheral details of an incident due to the narrowing of attention, is due to the unusualness of a weapon or the threat it poses.

Kerri Pickel conducted two laboratory experiments to discover whether poor witness recall was due to the presence of a weapon causing high levels of stress, or whether the weapon was distinctive and unusual, making witnesses look longer at this and not anything else.

Experiment 1 procedure

In Experiment 1, 230 psychology undergraduates in an American university were shown a two-minute video reconstruction of a hair salon incident. They saw the exterior of the hair salon and then footage of the interior where a female receptionist sat behind a counter. A man entered and approached the receptionist, who handed him money over the counter. The man then left and was seen to get into the passenger seat of a waiting car, which drove away.

An **independent measures design** was implemented and participants were randomly allocated to one of five conditions, which varied according to the item the man was holding in his hand as he spoke to the receptionist. The items were categorised according to their unusualness and threat:

1 A pair of scissors – high threat, low unusualness in a hair salon.
2 A handgun – high threat, high unusualness.
3 A wallet – low threat, low unusualness.
4 A raw chicken – low threat, high unusualness.
5 Empty – this was used as a control condition.

After watching the video, participants completed a filler task for 10 minutes. They then filled in a questionnaire requiring them to remember details about the receptionist and the man, including what he was holding in his hand and what they thought he was doing in the hair salon.

▲ Pickel (1998) used various props to test whether threat or unusualness affected witness recall.

Results

Independent researchers recorded the number of features about the receptionist and man from the salon that participants were able to recall. Because the female receptionist was shown in the video for some time before the man entered the salon, it was found that recall of her was very similar across all conditions. However, recall of the man did differ significantly between the experimental conditions.

Results

Scissors	Handgun	Wallet	Raw chicken	Nothing
8.14	7.83	8.53	7.21	9.02

◀ Experiment 1: Mean recall of the number of features about the man.

Clearly the handgun and raw chicken resulted in the poorest recall of the man, whilst the wallet and scissors had less effect in comparison. This could be interpreted as both high unusualness and high threat items producing low recall. However, comparing the results for handgun and scissors (both high threat) produces a different outcome, so threat alone cannot result in poor memory. Both the raw chicken and handgun are unusual in the context of a hair salon, so it must be unusualness that leads to poor recall, rather than threat.

Experiment 2 procedure

To check the validity of these findings, Pickel conducted a second experiment using 256 participants, this time in the context of an electrical repair shop. The procedure was identical but what the male was holding was changed:

1. A large screwdriver shown in a stabbing motion – high threat, low unusualness
2. A butcher's knife – high threat, high unusualness
3. A pair of sunglasses – low threat, high unusualness
4. A Pillsbury doughboy figure – low threat, high unusualness
5. Empty – this was used as a control condition.

A Pillsbory doughboy was a 8-inch character of a dough chef created to promote a baking company.

Knife	Screwdriver	Sunglasses	Pillsbury doughboy	Empty
6.71	7.00	7.82	6.55	8.36

◀ Experiment 2: Mean recall of the number of features about the man.

These findings replicate those of Experiment 1. The Pillsbury doughboy and butcher's knife are unusual in the context of an electrical repair shop and produced the lowest level of recall.

Conclusion

The ability of participants to recall the features of the man was significantly affected by the unusualness of the object he was holding. Both experiments show how 'weapon focus' diminishes the detail of witness testimony because there is a narrowing of attention on an object that is out of context.

Note that the term 'weapon focus', according to this experiment, is inappropriate, because the effect can occur with items that are not weapons – threat is not the cause of the narrowing of attention.

Evaluation

Strengths

- As in most laboratory experiments, there was a high level of control exercised over situational variables. All participants viewed the same footage (excluding the IV changes), for the same period of time, without distractions, and then answered the same questions. The experiment is replicable and its results are likely to be highly reliable.
- Pickel employed independent researchers to score and analyse the questionnaires, to ensure there was no researcher bias in the interpretation of the results.

Taking it further

Read about eyewitness identification in the Jean Charles de Menezes case. Guns were used by the police in this case. http://news.bbc.co.uk/1/hi/uk/4177082.stm

Weaknesses

- The study was conducted in an artificial environment not realistic of a real eyewitness event. Participants were expecting to view an incident and would have given more attention than a real witness.

- Real witnesses do not view a crime on a video recording. In real life there will be many distractions and their emotional state at the time would affect recall.
- The researchers wanted to test unusualness and threat, but it is unlikely that participants felt any threat from a video recording.
- Participants knew they were part of an experiment. This could have caused demand characteristics, although this would have been controlled to some extent by using an independent measures design.

A field experiment on eyewitness recall and photo identification (Yarmey, 2004)

Aim

Compared with the amount of laboratory research into eyewitness testimony there is less research conducted in the field. Yarmey set out to test eyewitness recall and ability to identify a target person from a photographic line-up in a field experiment.

Procedure

A sample of 590 men and women was selected by opportunity in public places. Each was approached by a female target who asked either for directions or for help in finding a lost piece of jewellery. Two minutes later the participant was approached by a female researcher and asked to participate in a study about person perception and memory. They were given a 16-question recall test that included questions about the physical characteristics and clothing of the female target. Participants were then given a set of six photographs, showing women similar to the female target, and asked to identify her. The photographs were randomly presented one at a time and participants were informed that the female may or may not be included in the set. The participants were thoroughly debriefed after the experiment.

This standard procedure was followed with all participants, but there were changes to the procedure to test different variables, including:

- Preparation: some participants were told to be prepared for a memory test by the female target herself and some were not.
- Retention time span: some participants were required to recall immediately and others four hours later.
- Line-up: some participants saw the target female in the photograph line-up, whilst others did not.

Participants were randomly allocated to the variations.

In addition to the field experiment, Yarmey asked 370 psychology undergraduates to predict how much eyewitnesses would be able to recall and the number of correct identifications.

Results

▼ Percentage of accurate recall.

Physical characteristics	Percentage recall	Clothing characteristics	Percentage recall
Height	60	Top clothing	60
Weight	44	Bottom clothing	65
Age	97	Jewellery	16
Hair colour	52	Footwear	18
Eye colour	21		

It is unsurprising that small characteristics, such as jewellery and eye colour, resulted in poor recall. Weight is often difficult to judge and footwear is often out of our visual field if a person is only a few feet away. Interestingly, when Yarmey compared the results to what the psychology students predicted, he found that they were largely incorrect. The students overestimated the recall for hair colour, jewellery and footwear and underestimated recall of age. Clearly, not being in the same situation as the witnesses resulted in the students having a lack of understanding of context and experience.

Common sense would suggest that preparation for a recall test at the time of the encounter with the female target would result in better recall. However, this was only the case for the recall of physical and clothing characteristics, particularly eye colour, not for the photograph identification.

It did not make much difference whether recall was immediate or after a four-hour delay, although inexplicably the witnesses seemed to recall hair colour and footwear better after a four-hour delay.

The photograph identification yielded a 49% correct identification rate when the female target was present in the line up, and there was a rejection rate of 62% when she was not present. This is fairly consistent with 'line-up' research, but the students over-estimated the number of witnesses who would correctly identify the target.

◆ Conclusion

Counter-intuitively, witness preparation did not improve eyewitness identification, and students significantly over-estimated how many witnesses would be able to identify the target correctly – an indication of why jurors put great faith in eyewitnesses during a court case. This is further supported by the students' over-estimation of witness recall generally.

◆ Evaluation

This field experiment is high in ecological validity because the witnesses were approached by the target in a realistic environment. However, an eyewitness is most commonly needed when an incident happens, which will probably be more exciting than a person asking for directions.

The witness participants would not have been aware of taking part in the study until the researcher approached them, so they would not have been paying particular attention to the target. This improves validity compared with a laboratory experiment where witnesses would have been deliberately focusing on the target.

Unlike a laboratory experiment, the study findings have good generalisability because the sample would be typical of any possible witness for varied ages, backgrounds and experience.

As a field experiment, it typically lacks control over the situational variables that may have affected the witnesses during the incident. A witness may have been too busy to pay attention or may not have known the direction asked, so would have spent less time with the target. However, many would argue that would be typical of a real witness and a real incident.

This research opens up the debate about the extent to which we should rely on witness testimony in court. Psychology students were not accurately able to predict the recall of the witnesses, so how would a layperson not trained in psychology fare as a juror?

Other option

Search the Gary Wells website, a source for articles on the reliability of eyewitnesses and debates about testimony being used in court. http://www.psychology.iastate.edu/~glwells/

Treating offenders

What you need to know

- How to treat offenders using a token economy programme to reinforce appropriate behaviour.
- How to treat offenders using anger management techniques to control aggressive thoughts and behaviour.

Have you ever wondered?

Does harsh punishment work? Would the boot camps recreated on television to solve the problem of anti-social youngsters work with real offenders? The Home Office commissioned just such a study on young offenders between 1996 and 1997. Find out more by visiting the website: http://www.homeoffice.gov.uk/rds/pdfs2/r163.pdf

▲ Token economy programmes can encourage positive relationships between prison staff and prison inmates.

In Project START, a TEP implemented in Springfield USA, the prison staff used the tokens to control prisoners unreasonably. This lead to rebellion and failure of the programme and produced negative feelings between staff and prisoner.

The Criminal Justice System has a range of treatments available to deal with offenders both in prison and in the community. Psychologists are concerned with the rehabilitation of offenders, changing behaviour to prevent re-offending.

Token economy programmes

Token economy programmes (TEPs) are used in prisons and community-based projects to encourage pro-social behaviour. Based on the principles of operant conditioning, they involve imposing a system of rewards that can be gained if a desired behaviour is performed. Prison management draws up a list of appropriate behaviours and, if an offender complies, they receive a token. Exchange rewards for tokens are negotiated with the offender – this is important as the reward is only effective if it is wanted.

Originally, TEPs were seen as a rehabilitative technique that could be used to encourage law-abiding behaviour. Today, they are generally viewed as a way of controlling behaviour rather than as a solution to crime. The system is useful in prisons because it provides a legitimate way of gaining access to privileges that would have otherwise been denied or only available by non-legitimate means. It also promotes positive social interaction between prisoners and prison staff.

Pearson et al. (2002) conducted a meta-analysis to review the effectiveness of behavioural techniques (e.g. token economy programmes) and cognitive-behavioural techniques (e.g. anger management). They examined the findings of 69 studies and concluded that cognitive-behavioural therapies helped reduce recidivism whilst behavioural treatments did not work. It seems that behaviour cannot be changed without a change in thinking.

Evaluation

- Although no specialist training is needed to implement a TEP, most experts recommend training for all staff as the system is open to abuse (see left).
- TEPs give prisoners a sense of control over their behaviour and the rewards they earn. However, some have argued that the programme can lead to **learned helplessness** where prisoners feel they have no choice but to comply otherwise basic privileges are withheld. We can also question whether TEPs violate human rights; at the very least they are patronising for adults.
- Whether tokens work is questionable. Their validity can be questioned as success could equally be due to improved staff-prisoner relationships, increased attention from staff or the benefit of clear rules set by the prison.
- TEPs need careful monitoring or they could become a form of contraband within the prison. Prisoners must be willing to engage with the programme fully and rewards or payments should be motivating. Ineffective tokens can easily be superseded by other sources of reinforcement within a prison, such as fear of a hardened inmate.
- A weakness is that the learnt behaviour may not generalise to the outside world. Society does work on a system of rewards for good behaviour and good work, but the rewards are subtler and less frequent than tokens.

Anger management programmes

Anger management is a cognitive-behavioural technique based on a model by Ray Novaco (1975). Novaco describes anger as a strong emotion with physiological, behavioural and cognitive elements. Anger management teaches relaxation techniques to deal with the physiological response to anger (e.g. increased heart rate), cognitive restructuring to retrain thought patterns, and time out or assertiveness training to deal with the behavioural element of anger. There are three steps:

1 Cognitive preparation
Offenders identify situations that provoke anger so they can recognise when an aggressive outburst is likely to occur. Thought patterns are challenged, for example if they become angry when laughed at, they might work through alternative conclusions such as that people are laughing at the behaviour and not them. They also consider the negative consequence of their anger on others.

2 Skill acquisition
New coping skills are learnt to help deal with anger-provoking situations, such as 'stop and think' or counting. Relaxation techniques are also learnt to help calm the physiological response. Assertiveness training can help deal with the issue constructively rather than violently.

3 Application practice
Offenders role-play a variety of scenarios to practise new skills to control anger. These are conducted in controlled environments so that the offenders feel safe and untrained individuals are not exposed to risk of harm.

Anger management programmes can be used in prisons or with ex-offenders who are serving a **probationary period** in the community. The courses are usually conducted in small groups and last for around ten sessions.

Evaluation

- Some offenders are not violent because of anger; they use violence for a specific purpose, such as intimidation or domestic control. In fact, some psychologists question that anger causes violence. Loza and Loza-Fanous (1999) studied 252 Canadian offenders in prison and examined the offences, recidivism and anger scores. They found no significant link between anger and violent or non-violent offences.
- There have been some reported successes. Dowden, Blanchette and Serin (1999) found that the programme was successful in reducing recidivism with high-risk offenders.
- Ireland (2004) studied 87 young male offenders, 50 of whom were assigned to anger management and the remaining 37 forming a control group who did not receive treatment. All 87 completed anger questionnaires prior to the study. After ten weeks they were questioned again; the experimental groups showed significant improvements in anger-related behaviour, but no changes were shown from the control group.

Examiner's tip

Remember that this is an option. You could pick social skills training, punishment or another treatment. The exam will not have a specific question relating to the method or evaluation of anger management directly (as they could for token economy) but could ask you to describe and evaluate a treatment you have studied or get you to apply your knowledge of your chosen treatment to a particular scenario.

The CALM anger management programme:

1. Assessing offenders' motivation to change behaviour.
2. Identifying physiological changes when becoming angry.
3. Recognising and understanding how irrational thoughts affect behaviour.
4. Learning good communication skills to deal with situations and taking responsibility for behaviour.
5. Practising skills in new situations.
6. Identifying risk situations to prepare for future experiences.

Other option: Social skills training

This is based on the principle that a lack of social competence may have contributed to offending. Social skills (e.g. body language, eye contact) enable successful human interaction to take place. Social skills training is a cognitive–behavioural technique that uses role play, modelling and reinforcement through feedback to encourage skill acquisition and the development of self-concept by changing thought patterns.

Other option: Punishment

Modern punishment techniques include fines, community service and prison, amongst many others. Imprisonment acts as a deterrent against committing criminal offences and also protects the public. Many politicians believe that prison is effective, but some psychologists believe that it just reduces respect for justice and creates better criminals.

For a review of whether prison works, follow the link to the Open University Learning Space: http://openlearn.open.ac.uk/mod/resource/view.php?id=227697. Some of the implications of imprisonment can also be explored by looking at the prison study at http://www.prisonexp.org/

Studies in detail

What you need to know

- Describe and evaluate two studies. One of these must be Loftus and Palmer's (1974) study of the effect of leading questions.
- The second study must be one of:
  - Yuille and Cutshall (1986) case study of eyewitness testimony
  - Charlton et al. (2000) naturalistic study in St Helena
  - Gesch et al. (2003) diet and anti-social behaviour in young adult prisoners.

AS check

You may have studied the reliability of eyewitness testimony as a key issue and you may remember Loftus and Palmer's study and other research into leading questions (see AS pages 58–59).

Loftus and Palmer (1974)

The reliability of eyewitnesses has been questioned by many research studies. One factor known to affect it from laboratory research is leading questions.

Aim

To investigate whether leading questions would influence the estimates of the speed of a vehicle recalled by eyewitnesses.

Experiment 1 procedure

In Experiment 1, 45 participants were shown seven video clips of different car accidents, in different orders, and asked to judge the speed of the car. They were then given a questionnaire instructing them to give an account of what they had witnessed, and to answer a series of specific questions. The participants all received the same specific questions, but one critical question in the questionnaire was changed. For nine participants the critical question asked 'About how fast were cars going when they hit each other?' and the remaining four groups of nine participants were asked the same question, but instead of 'hit' the verb was replaced with 'smashed', 'bumped', 'contacted' or 'collided'.

Verb used in the critical question	Mean estimate of speed (mph)
smashed	40.8
collided	39.3
bumped	38.1
hit	34.0
contacted	31.8

▲ Mean average of speed estimates made for each verb used.

Results

The results (left) show that the verb 'smashed' produced the fastest estimate of speed of the car before the traffic accident, and the verb 'contacted' produced the slowest. An overall difference of 9mph in estimates of speed was found associated with the verbs 'smashed' and 'contacted'.

Conclusion

Loftus and Palmer believed that these results could be due to one of two factors:

1. The verb used in the question altered the participants' memory of the film.
2. The participants did not know the answer so relied on the verb to make their judgement.

To test these conclusions, Loftus and Palmer devised a second experiment. If the verb used in the question did alter witness memory then it could also alter other details about the crime, such as whether there was broken glass from the car headlights after the collision.

Experiment 2 procedure

A sample of 150 participants was shown a one-minute film clip of a multiple-car collision (lasting only four seconds).

They were then asked to give a description of the film and answer a questionnaire about the accident. As with Experiment 1, the questionnaire contained a critical question. The participants were split into three groups of 50, each receiving a different critical question:

1 About how fast were the cars going when they smashed into each other?
2 About how fast were the cars going when they hit each other?
3 No critical question about speed of the cars was asked.

After a one-week period, the participants returned to answer 10 questions about the clip, without seeing it again. This time the main question was, 'Did you see any broken glass?'. The question was asked of all 150 participants, but there was no broken glass actually in the clip.

Results

Answer to question	Smashed condition	Hit condition	None (control condition)
Yes	16	7	6
No	34	43	44

Responses given to the question about broken glass.

In all the conditions, most participants accurately answered that there was no broken glass in the film. However, more of the participants in the 'smashed' condition did report seeing broken glass (32%) compared with the 'hit' condition ([illegible]). This demonstrates that the verb in the question did have an effect on recall rather than simply affecting judgement. Broken glass was not in the video, so the verb did imply a greater speed that changed memories for the accident.

Conclusion

Leading questions do have an influence on eyewitness testimony. They imply a specific response and may alter witness memory of an incident.

Evaluation

Strengths

- The laboratory experiments had a high level of control over the procedures:
  - The critical questions were all randomly hidden amongst other distracter questions so the participants were not able to guess the study aim and display **demand characteristics**.
  - For many of the films, the actual speed of the car was known to the researchers and they analysed whether actual speeds could have an effect on participants' estimates. For example, a car known to be travelling at 20mph was estimated on average to be travelling at 37.7mph, and a car travelling at 30mph was estimated on average to be travelling at 36.2mph. Loftus and Palmer found that the estimates were not significantly affected by the actual speed of the vehicles. This control ensured that the verb used, and not the actual speed, had an effect on participant estimates.
- The effect of leading questions has been confirmed by other similar studies. Loftus and Zanni (1975) found that the definite article 'the' had a stronger influence on recall than the indefinite article 'a' in the question, 'Did you see ... broken headlight?' – 15% replying 'yes' compared with 7%. This evidence supports Loftus and Palmer's study.
- An important strength of this study is its application for the police and justice system. The police need to avoid leading questions when interviewing a witness, and the justice system should consider the importance placed on eyewitnesses; if witnesses can be inaccurate they should not be relied upon in court without corroborating evidence.

AS check

If you studied Bartlett's reconstructive memory in the Cognitive Approach (see AS page 68), you may be able to interpret these findings in terms of his theory of memory. Participants could have used their schema for fast speeds and car crashes to reconstruct the memory and incorporate the broken glass.

Examiner's tip

You may have a strategy to remember how to describe a study, such as Name, Aim, Method, Results, Conclusion. However, a question may ask for a specific part of the study and it may also be expressed differently:

- Name/Identify the study.
- Aim/What did the researchers want to find out?
- Method/Procedure/What did the researchers do to investigate this?
- Results/Outcome/Findings.
- Conclusion/What did they conclude?/Finding/Outcome.

Note that findings and outcome cross both results and conclusion.

Weaknesses

- The most important weakness is that we cannot be sure that witness memory was actually altered by the questions asked. In Experiment 1, participants could have simply used the verb to make a guess about the speed of the car. In Experiment 2, the verb could have also implied a speed and participants may have simply guessed that there was broken glass as a result. Participants were displaying demand characteristics rather than a distortion of memory.
- The study was conducted in a laboratory setting, so can be criticised for lacking ecological validity. The findings cannot be applied to real-life witnesses. Yuille and Cutshall (1986) reported a case of real eyewitness testimony and found that leading questions had little effect on the accuracy of recall even five months after viewing a gunshop robbery.
- Real witnesses would not be prepared for the incident or subsequent recall. The participants of this study were, so were able to focus their attention on the films.
- There were no real consequences for the decision-making of these participants. Real witnesses would probably be more considered in their answers because they may influence a police investigation or courtroom decision. Real witnesses would not believe that the police were trying to deliberately manipulate their answers, which the participants may have thought about.

Charlton et al. (2000)

The social learning theory examined the influence of the media on criminal/anti-social behaviour (see page 11). Research in the laboratory has found that violent viewing leads to imitation, but most of this research can be criticised for lacking ecological validity and offering only short-term effects. Field experiments have also found significant links between TV violence and aggression, but many of these studies have used samples of participants known to be predisposed to violence, such as institutionalised young offenders.

Aim

To investigate the effects of television on children's behaviour, in particular whether TV affected pro-social and anti-social behaviour.

Procedure

Employing a **cross-sectional design**, the researchers studied the playground behaviour of 3 to 8 year-old children before and after the introduction of television on a small and isolated island in the South Atlantic. Video recorders were set up in the playgrounds of two schools four months prior to the introduction of television in March 1995, and once again five years later. The children's free-play during break times was recorded for a two-week period each time and the researchers compared the findings to establish whether behaviour had changed as a result of television.

Eight playground behaviours were categorised as pro-social or anti-social:

Pro-social:

- pro-social gestures or verbal comments made
- sharing, turn-taking or helping
- displaying affection or consoling others
- holding hands, arm-in-arm.

Anti-social:

- anti-social gestures or verbal comments
- kicking, punching, hitting
- seizing or damaging property
- non-compliant holding or forcing.

▲ Television was not introduced to St Helena until 1995.

Independent researchers in the UK watched the video footage and tallied how many times the children or a group of children displayed these behaviours. Two researchers watched the same video footage alone as many times as necessary, and only agreed tallied behaviours were recorded in the results. This is known as **inter-rater reliability**.

Results

Of 64 comparisons made between the behaviour of children in 1994 and 2000, only nine were statistically significant:

- Two showed decreases in anti-social behaviour amongst boys.
- Five showed increases in pro-social behaviour in both boys and girls.
- Two showed decreases in pro-social behaviour in boys.

Boys tended to display less hitting and pushing after television was introduced, but were also less willing to help and show affection. However, both boys and girls showed significant increases in pro-social behaviour overall.

Conclusion

Charlton concluded that the introduction of television had no negative effect on children's behaviour (in fact, quite the reverse). This finding shows longer-term effects and contradicts most laboratory research.

Evaluation

Strengths

- The study shows behaviour as a response to a real-life situation – the natural introduction of television. It has high ecological validity because children were observed in the natural setting of a playground, where they normally engage in social behaviour with their peers and are not constrained by parental rules. The supervisors interjected where they would have normally done so, and the children played as usual.
- The use of video recordings, although restricted in terms of a visual field, prevented researcher bias because recorded behaviours can be checked and cross-checked by independent observers. It also prevents observer fatigue. Having inter-rater reliability is a strength because it eliminates subjective interpretation of the children's behaviour.
- The use of hidden cameras also meant that the children would have behaved naturally, which may not have been possible if an observer was making notes in view of the children.

Weaknesses

- The study did not analyse the viewing habits of the children involved. Therefore we cannot be sure that any change in behaviour was an effect of television viewing.
- One reason for the findings, acknowledged by the researchers, is due to the close-knit community of St Helena. Most inhabitants knew the children and there was a culture of close supervision and parental control. These environmental influences could have inhibited the children from imitating aggression viewed on television, even if they wanted to.
- The island would have been conscious of promoting a good image of the inhabitants. It is possible that the children's behaviour in the playground was suppressed by supervising adults to ensure a positive image was maintained.
- Later research has suggested that the television viewed by the children of St Helena was not similar to mainland television programming. Popular children's programmes involving aggression was not broadcast in St Helena. This broadcasting censorship might explain why the children were more pro-social and less anti-social.

Taking it further

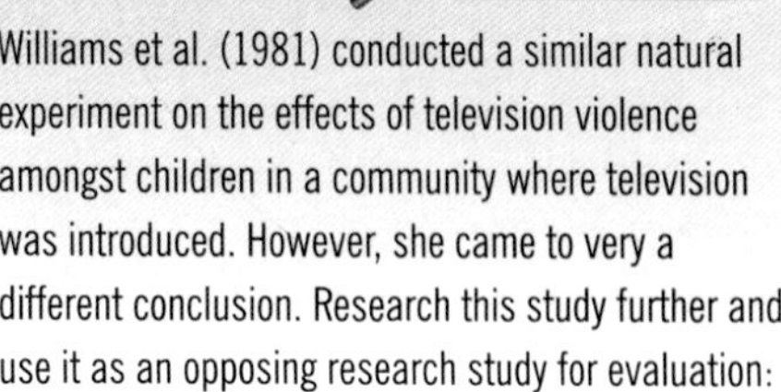

Williams et al. (1981) conducted a similar natural experiment on the effects of television violence amongst children in a community where television was introduced. However, she came to very a different conclusion. Research this study further and use it as an opposing research study for evaluation: http://world.std.com/~jlr/comment/tv_impact.htm

Other option

Yuille and Cutshall (1986) studied a case involving a gunshop robbery in Canada. The owner and robber were involved in a shoot-out and the robber was shot fatally. Months later, Yuille and Cutshall tracked down 15 of the original witnesses and compared their interview data to police reports. They found that witnesses had very accurate recall of the incident and were not misled by the researchers' leading questions. A detailed discussion of this study can be found in Gross R. D (1999) *Psychology, The science of mind and behaviour* or at http://www.simplypsychology.pwp.blueyonder.co.uk/Eyewitness%20Testimony.pdf

Other option

Gesch et al. (2003) supplemented some young offenders' diets with pills containing minerals, vitamins and essential fatty acids. Other young offenders received a placebo pill containing no supplements. The researchers and prison staff were unaware which pills offenders were receiving, but recorded that there were fewer reported offences by those who received additional supplements, which had dropped by approximately 30%. The full article can be found at: http://bjp.rcpsych.org/cgi/reprint/181/1/22

Evidence in practice

What you need to know

- Summarise information from two sources about the key issue you have studied or conduct a content analysis on a key issue.
- Draw conclusions from two sources you have selected or draw conclusions from the primary data collected from your content analysis.
- Explain the information gathered in terms of concepts, theories and research in criminological psychology.

The profile might include:
Type of body build
Age and gender of the offender
Likely occupation
Marital status
Hobbies
The motivation for committing the offence
Where the offender might live

Taking it further

Find out more about offender profiling at http://www.liv.ac.uk/psychology/ccir/op.html and http://homepage.ntlworld.com/gary.sturt/crime/offender%20profiling%20definitions.htm

Key issue: Offender profiling

Offender profiling is a psychological technique to aid police in criminal investigations. A psychologist uses case evidence and crime scene analysis to build up a picture of the type of person who would be likely to commit that crime in the way it was conducted. The profile can be used by the police to filter down a list of suspects to those most likely to have committed the offence. Profiling is based on the idea of criminal consistency.

Offender profiling has been criticised for being nothing more than educated guesswork showing more failures than successes. An incorrect profile can mislead an investigation and waste police time, as the real offender is overlooked because they do not match the profile being used. Profilers themselves range from academics and clinical psychologists to trained police officers, so the applications can be varied according to individual beliefs. The most serious indictment against offender profiling is the potential for harassment or worse. In the murder case of Rachel Nickell (1992), police officers used a profile to entrap and subsequently arrest Colin Stagg. It was later found that he was innocent of the crime but his life and reputation had already been destroyed.

It is difficult to judge the effectiveness of profiling because there are many factors that can affect the application of justice; police may not use the profile or the offender remains untraceable.

Introduction to the practical

This section explains an article related to the key issue of the use of offender profiling. It focuses on applying concepts, theories and research to understanding the article opposite; the process of selecting sources and summarising information can be found on pages 48-49.

Explaining the article

◆ Linking to offender profiling

This article clearly relates to the use of offender profiling to help police identify the serial killer. The first three experts mentioned in the article are applying their knowledge of psychological theory to understanding the criminal and all suggest possible characteristics of this offender.

◆ The issues with profiling

The article opposite clearly points to problems associated with the use of profiles to aid police investigations. Quite obviously the three expert profilers have difficulty in agreeing what kind of person the Ipswich murderer is and the motivation for the crimes. Glenn Wilson highlights the two key problems of understanding offender behaviour and the application of profile use by police.

Forensic psychologists tackle UK serial killer

With five dead bodies found in just 10 days, British police are describing the murders of prostitutes in the east of England as "a crime in action". The news late on Tuesday that two corpses had been discovered near Ipswich in Suffolk appears to confirm beyond doubt that police are looking for a serial killer. The bodies of Gemma Adams, Tania Nicol and Anneli Alderton were found between 2 December and 10 December. The bodies found on Tuesday, naked and dumped in woodland, are assumed to be those of Annette Nicholls and Paula Clennell, both of whom went missing recently. Keith Ashcroft, a forensic psychologist and expert in sex crimes, speculates that the murderer is deliberately "taunting" police. Meanwhile, Joseph Diaz, a criminologist, says that the fact the bodies were dumped in water suggests that the killer is of above average intelligence, because he knows physical evidence will be washed away. Diaz writes that the killer probably has a dominant mother, and is not in a stable relationship with a woman – possibly a virgin. David Canter says: "His first murder was likely to be a carefully considered attempt to hide some other crime: killing the victim because she was a crucial witness." But just how helpful are psychological profiles of killers? "Psychologists can paint a picture of a typical serial killer based on profiles of the limited number of serial killers available, but this will not necessarily be accurate, or help police," says Glenn Wilson, an expert in deviant personalities at the Institute of Psychiatry in London. "It may even lead detectives down a blind alley," he warns. "A psychological profile amounts to nothing more than a statistical probability and if police believe it is 100% accurate they run a very real risk of ignoring other evidence," Wilson says.

Over to you

Make a list of the key points in this article and draw conclusions from it.

Over to you

Describe the process of offender profiling as it might apply to this case.

You might like to consider the following concepts to help you:

- using behavioural and forensic evidence
- criminal consistency
- features of a profile.

Over to you

Using your knowledge of the problems with profiling, explain the concerns raised in this article. You might like to consider the following issues:

- the use of probabilities in catching offenders
- inconsistency in approaches to profiling
- experimental studies into the success of profiling
- problems with inaccurate profiles
- reliance on profiles by police.

◆ A further source

Some suggestions for another source relating to the use of offender profiling:

- BBC news coverage of the Ipswich murders: http://news.bbc.co.uk/1/hi/england/suffolk/6171571.stm
- Channel five ran a series of six documentaries called *Mapping Murder*, written and presented by David Canter and covering the use of offender profiling in famous cases. A copy of the series transcript can be found at http://www.i-psy.com/publications/publications_media_television.php

Other options

If you chose the key issue 'the reliability of eyewitness testimony' you can find sources related to this issue and link back to concepts and ideas from this issue as discussed in the AS book (see pages 58–59). Suggested sources and a fully-detailed practical can be found in the Edexcel *Getting Started* booklet, pages 35–37.

Alternatively, you may wish to conduct your practical on the key issue of whether criminals are born or made.

- Look for themes related to the biological basis for criminal behaviour (personality and genetics) to explain how criminal are made.
- Look for themes of family, learning and the media to explain how criminals are made.
- Link the ideas to biology and social learning theory.

You can find sources to summarise on the role of media violence or you may like to conduct a content analysis on how much violence is on TV.

- Look for themes of the media having an effect on behaviour through copying, and for arguments that go against the media affecting behaviour.
- Link to social learning theory.

Details on how to conduct a content analysis can be found in the Edexcel *Getting Started* booklet, pages 39–41. Remember to link your findings back to social learning theory and the key issue.

Summary

Criminological psychology explores a range of issues related to crime and criminal behaviour – from what causes criminality, issues surrounding the capture and treatment of offenders to factors affecting eyewitnesses.

Look back at the list of key terms for criminological psychology on page 5 and check you can define and use them all effectively.

Methodology

- Describe and evaluate the laboratory experiment and the field experiment as they are used to assess witness effectiveness.
- Consider the above research methods in relation to their use in criminological psychology and in terms of reliability, validity and ethical issues.

Note: You may be asked to draw upon your knowledge of other research methods and relate them to their use in criminological psychology.

Content

- Describe and evaluate two explanations of criminal/anti-social behavior, including Social Learning Theory.
- Describe and evaluate either the influence of personality theory or the influence of labelling and the self-fulfilling prophecy to explain criminal behaviour.
- Describe and evaluate one laboratory experiment investigating eyewitness testimony.
- Describe and evaluate one field study investigating eyewitness testimony.
- Describe and evaluate one other study of eyewitness memory.
- Describe and evaluate token economy programmes as a way of treating offenders.
- Describe and evaluate one other way of treating offenders, e.g. punishment, anger management or social skills training.

Studies

- You need to be able to describe and evaluate Loftus and Palmer's (1974) study of the effects of leading questions on eyewitness memory.
- There is a further choice of three studies of which you must be able to discuss one:
  - Yuille and Cutshall (1986): leading questions and eyewitness testimony
  - Charlton et al. (2000): St Helena experiment
  - Gesch et al. (2003): the influence of diet on anti-social behaviour.

Evidence in practice

- Describe one key issue in criminological psychology from the content you have studied in this application.
- Conduct a content analysis on the key issue you have described or summarise two articles on a topic you have studied in criminological psychology.
- From either the content analysis or the summary, draw conclusions and explain your findings drawing upon concepts, theories and research you have studied in criminological psychology.

Note: You should make sure that you have conducted one content analysis and one summary between your two applications. Whichever you choose for your applications, you should make sure you can describe the findings of the analysis and be able to link these findings back to concepts, theories and research studied in criminological psychology.

Examzone

***1.** Define the following terms:
  i Recidivism
  ii Anti-social behaviour
  iii Crime (3 marks)

***2.** Outline how a field experiment is used as a research method to investigate witness effectiveness. (3 marks)

***3.** During your course you will have studied one study into eyewitness testimony. Identify this study and describe its findings. (2 marks)

4. Evaluate the field experiment in terms of validity or ethical issues. (4 marks)

5. Lilly is worried that her son is watching too much television. His behaviour has become aggressive and he is often told off at school for hitting other children. Use your knowledge of Social Learning Theory, research and the role of the media to explain Lilly's problem. (8 marks)

6. The probation service is looking into ways to treat offenders and lower recidivism. They are using token economies but realise this treatment programme is limited in the extent to which they rehabilitate offenders and lower recidivism. Describe another way of treating prisoners and evaluate the usefulness of this programme. (12 marks)

2. Child psychology

What you will learn about in this chapter

- That early childhood experience affects later adult development.
- Observational techniques and the case study as research methods used to investigate childhood experiences.
- Bowlby's theory of attachment and its evolutionary basis.
- The classification of attachment types and their relationship to childrearing strategies.
- Whether a loss of attachment (deprivation) or a lack of attachment (privation) can affect later development and whether the effects of privation are reversible.
- Two explanations of autism and how it affects a child's development.
- Two studies: a case study of Genie (Curtiss, 1977) and Bowlby's study of 44 juvenile thieves (1946).
- The advantages and disadvantages of daycare for children.

Key terms

- attachment
- deprivation
- privation
- evolution
- daycare
- separation anxiety

◆ What is child psychology?

Child psychology is a branch of developmental psychology (lifespan development) that covers infancy, childhood and adolescence. It is particularly concerned with how the experiences we have in early relationships (with a caregiver) might affect our cognitive, social and emotional development. It also considers specific childhood experiences, such as neglect, daycare and learning difficulties.

◆ Attachment research

Children begin the process of attachment to a primary caregiver early in life. An attachment is an enduring love bond between child and caregiver that provides security and stability for the child. This special bond can be observed at around seven months old, when a child becomes distressed if they are separated from the caregiver – this is known as **separation anxiety**.

In animals, the process of attachment is clear to see; it can be observed as clinging to or following the first moving object seen (typically the caregiver). This is known as imprinting/bonding and is essential for the survival of the animal. However, attachment is more difficult to study in human babies, as they are immobile at birth.

Attachment research has explored how a child responds when an attachment that has formed is broken, or indeed is never formed. Research has also looked at the different types of attachment and how parenting styles in different cultures might create different attachment types.

◆ Deprivation and privation research

If attachment goes wrong in early childhood, the experience may have an effect on later development. Deprivation is the term given to the loss of an attachment that has been formed. This loss of attachment with a caregiver may occur through divorce, death or, more controversially, daycare. In more extreme cases, a child may suffer privation, when an attachment is never formed. Privation can occur if a child suffers neglect or abuse, or if a caregiver finds it difficult to bond with a child for reasons such as serious postnatal depression. Either experience can affect how a child develops socially, emotionally and intellectually. Research has examined these outcomes and whether the effects of deprivation and privation are reversible.

Examiner's tip

You will become more familiar with these key definitions as you follow this chapter. It might be useful to start a glossary of key terms now, so that when they are explored again you can put in examples and research to add more detail.

Taking it further

Two main figures in child psychology are Mary Ainsworth and John Bowlby. Find out about them and the history of attachment research at http://www.psychology.sunysb.edu/attachment/online/inge_origins.pdf – a long read, but worth it!

Methodology

What you need to know

- Describe and evaluate the observational research method (including both naturalistic and structured observations).
- Describe and evaluate the case study as a research method.
- Specifically, explain the strengths and weaknesses of both these research methods in terms of their use in child psychology, including reliability, validity and ethical issues.
- Describe and evaluate longitudinal and cross-cultural ways of studying development.

AS check

You will have studied many research methods that could also be used in child psychology, such as experiments, correlational studies and surveys. Try to understand how a variety of research methods could be used to study child development.

AS check

You should recall studying observations as a research method in the Learning Approach, but for a reminder refer to AS pages 128–129.

Time sampling: During a one-hour observation a researcher may only make recordings for a specific period of time. For example, they might record behaviour for 10 seconds in every minute. In the remaining 50 seconds they can make notes.
Event sampling: Observers record only specific events, or behaviour that is determined before the observation takes place – for example, when a boy plays with a girl's toy as an example of non-stereotypical behaviour.

Examiner's tip

We observe things all the time in psychological research. Experiments and case studies both involve observation, but it is not the main research method being used. The observation as a research method is defined by watching as its main characteristic. There is no IV manipulation as in an experiment, or in-depth study using a variety of methods. There is a subtle distinction between observation as a technique and observation as a research method.

Observations

Observations simply involve watching and recording behaviour as it is seen. This can be done in a variety of settings and ways. In child psychology it involves watching children in settings such as at home, nursery or school, or in a staged environment. An observer may record the behaviour live, video it for later analysis or use a one-way mirror so they are hidden from the child's view.

Observations collect **qualitative** in the form of detailed descriptions of what the child is doing and/or **quantitative** data such as the number of times a child plays with a toy. It is difficult to record every behaviour seen during an observation, particularly if it is live, so researchers may use time or event sampling (see left) or employ many observers to ensure that nothing is missed.

Observations can be **overt** or **covert**, i.e. the child may or may not know that they are being observed. However, the observation must not be covert in the sense that a parent or legal guardian does not know their child is part of a psychological study.

Observations of children are commonly **non-participant** studies, where the observer simply watches from a distance without being involved in the group being observed. **Participant observations** can be used with children, but not in the way typically used with adult participants, where a researcher joins the group. To study children, a participant observation might involve a researcher joining a school class as an Associate Teacher. In this way he or she can take part in activities alongside the children, but it is not the same as joint participation.

◆ Naturalistic observations

Naturalistic observations are conducted in a natural setting for the child being watched. A researcher wishing to investigate how children play together may choose a playground as this is where usual social interaction takes place. To explore the child-parent relationship, the observation may take place at home, where parent-child interaction is more natural.

◆ Structured observations

Structured observations typically take place in a staged environment. An observer records the behaviour of a child in a set-up situation. Mary Ainsworth used a structured observation to record the behaviour of a child when the mother left them alone or with a stranger. The episodes of this observation were staged so that the mother and/or stranger were present or not in the room for specific periods of time (this study is discussed in detail on page 34-36).

◆ Evaluation

▲ A structured observation takes place in a controlled situation, sometimes using a one-way mirror.

- Observations cannot establish cause and effect because there is no manipulation of an independent variable. So, if an observation shows that boys play with boys' toys more than with girls' toys, there is no evidence that might suggest the cause is parental role models, for example. Often observations are a precursor to experimental research, which could experimentally test whether children model their parents' behaviour.
- Observations can be unreliable because of researcher bias. An observer may record the behaviour of a child in one way and another researcher view the same in a different way. We all have fairly unique perceptions of a situation, but most observers are trained to be as objective as possible and often **inter-rater reliability** is established to overcome the problem of researcher bias.
- Naturalistic observations have high **ecological validity** because children are observed in natural surroundings and their behaviour is unaffected by observers, so they will not display **demand characteristics**. The results of a naturalistic observation will be true to life as the children are in the context where this behaviour naturally occurs. This is unlike a structured observation, which lacks ecological validity because it is a staged situation and artificial environment. The effects of being in an artificial environment may be dependent on the child's age. Being in a strange situation will not alter the behaviour of very young children dramatically, and they are also less susceptible to demand characteristics, as they are basically unaware of being observed.
- As with field experiments, naturalistic observations do not control extraneous variables that might crop up in real environments. Even in a school playground children's behaviour may be affected by the presence of a teacher or a playground skirmish. This makes naturalistic observations difficult to replicate, as identical conditions will be unlikely to be repeated. This criticism is not true of structured observations, where a highly standardised procedure and controlled environment can be used.
- Naturalistic observations with adult participants do not normally require consent, because participants are being watched in a public place where they would normally expect to be observed. This does not apply to naturalistic observations of children, where consent must be sought from a parent or legal guardian. It is not acceptable to watch children play in a school playground without parental consent – you could be arrested!

◆ Some ethical issues when children are participants

- Parental consent must be gained.
- A child's consent is not the same as an adult's, due to comprehension level and vulnerability.
- Children have a right to withdraw and researchers should have the competence to enforce this withdrawal if they suspect the child is experiencing difficulties.
- Children should be permitted to ask questions and be fully informed (unless justifiable deceit is supported by colleagues).
- All information is confidential.
- Information disclosed by the study that affects the child's well-being must be referred to an expert, who may follow this up with parents.
- Incentives, such as sweets, should not be offered in exchange for participation.
- The general ethical guidelines for use with human participants must be adhered to.

AS check

The case study as a research method is discussed in the Psychodynamic Approach on AS pages 72–73. Consider the general case study rather than the Freudian style case studies for this section.

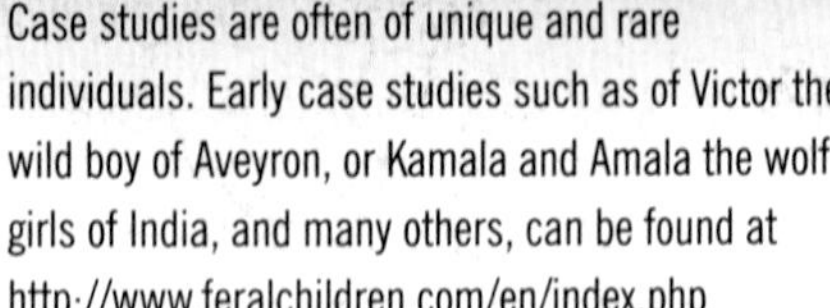

Taking it further

Case studies are often of unique and rare individuals. Early case studies such as of Victor the wild boy of Aveyron, or Kamala and Amala the wolf girls of India, and many others, can be found at http://www.feralchildren.com/en/index.php

Case studies

Case studies are detailed investigations of a single person or group of people. Case studies employ many techniques, such as experimentation, observation and interviewing, that add detail and richness to the study, as both qualitative and quantitative data is gathered and analysed about one case. Case studies are often used as a research method for rare and unique cases or when it would be inappropriate to use experimental methods, for example to study the effects of deprivation on child development.

Case studies in child psychology might look at rare instances of privation on the social, cognitive and emotional development of a child. In this instance, the child might be subject to *tests* to understand their level of cognitive ability (intelligence, perception, memory, etc.). Social development can be examined by *observing* the child's interaction with other children, and *interviewing* the child can be used to assess emotional development. Many research methods are used within a case study.

Evaluation

◆ Validity

- Case studies are considered one of the most valid research methods available to psychologists. They gather rich information using a variety of techniques that can be built up into a detailed record that is a valid assessment of that case.
- Different techniques are used to measure the same variable in different ways, and if they have the same outcome, the study is considered valid.

◆ Generalisability

- The findings of a case study may not be generalisable to others because they are one-off studies of unique individuals. The experiences and circumstances of the participant are exclusive to that person, so the findings are likely to be too.
- Reliability can also be affected by researcher bias as the researcher may interpret the behaviour of a child subjectively. Another researcher may not come to the same conclusion. This problem is magnified because the researcher often becomes closely connected with the child and may then lose their objective view. Case studies often establish reliability by using a range of different techniques to test the same concept. This is known as **triangulation**. Many researchers and those independent of the study are used to establish objectivity and prevent researcher bias.

◆ Ethics

- Case studies are often used in situations that it would not be ethical to study using other methods, such as the experiment. For example, it would not be ethical to deliberately isolate one child from its parents just to see how isolation affects development.
- Because case studies are often conducted on unique and rare individuals, it may be that they violate confidentiality, informed consent and the right to withdraw. The case of Genie exemplifies the ethical issues concerned with child case studies. Genie's care was entrusted to a group of researchers at a hospital. Without consent, she was subject to a range of tests and techniques to aid her development. Her case led to extensive media coverage, but she was unable to understand and therefore withdraw from this situation. Eventually she was re-homed when research funding ran out. Critics argue that this was blatant abuse of a vulnerable child, whilst others argue that her best interests were paramount. (This will be discussed further on page 46.)

Longitudinal research

As with all psychological research it is better to understand the development of behaviour in the long term rather than take a snapshot of it. Much of child psychology is concerned with development: how attachment, deprivation and privation affect a child's development; how daycare affects it; and how developmental issues such as autism affect a child. It therefore makes sense to conduct longitudinal research to understand such issues better.

◆ Evaluation

- Longitudinal studies are important because they show genuine development over the natural course of time. The alternative, for a similar purpose, is to use a **cross-sectional** study, which compares different age groups at the same moment in time. Cross-sectional research compares two different groups of people for the same characteristic, whereas longitudinal research studies the development of that characteristic within the same group. The advantage of longitudinal studies is that they avoid the **cohort effect** (the difference in social and cultural changes that exists between age groups because of a time/generational gap).
- Longitudinal studies are time-consuming and expensive. They are also very difficult to replicate because of obvious time constraints and generational differences that may affect the findings of a study if it is repeated later.
- A large sample is needed to ensure that genuine conclusions are drawn, and because participants may be lost for various reasons over the course of time.

Taking it further

'A Child of our Time' is a modern longitudinal study that began in 2000. Twenty-five millennium babies and their families are being followed to understand the factors that affect a child's development. Find out more about the study at http://www.bbc.co.uk/parenting/tv_and_radio/child_of_our_time/

Taking it further

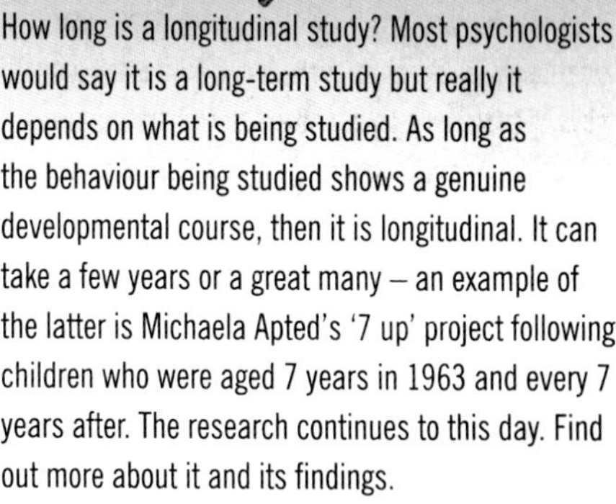

How long is a longitudinal study? Most psychologists would say it is a long-term study but really it depends on what is being studied. As long as the behaviour being studied shows a genuine developmental course, then it is longitudinal. It can take a few years or a great many – an example of the latter is Michaela Apted's '7 up' project following children who were aged 7 years in 1963 and every 7 years after. The research continues to this day. Find out more about it and its findings.

Cross-cultural research

Cross-cultural research is conducted to see if behaviour is universal. For example, we have found that language development occurs in the same stages in most cultures – all babies coo before they adopt a language and dialect, and all make grammatical mistakes at a similar age, for example. The stages of language development are therefore robust and universal. (An example of cross-cultural research is considered in detail on pages 36-37.)

Cross-cultural research can also give us important psychological insight into whether behaviour is due to biology or socialisation. Cultures differ in terms of the way they bring up or socialise children, so if behaviour differs we might conclude it is a product of socialisation and not genetics (which would show universality of behaviour).

◆ Evaluation

- **Ethnocentrism** might occur because a researcher may interpret the findings of cross-cultural research in terms of their own beliefs. However, others might argue that cross-cultural research discourages ethnocentrism because the research is not too confined to one culture.
- Cross-cultural research can be used to ensure the reliability of research findings, because if the same conclusions can be drawn in different cultures it is said to be reliable and also universal.
- This research is useful in understanding whether behaviour is innate (genetic) or learnt through socialisation. This can help psychologists understand the basis of behaviour and how it can be explored further. For example, attachment research has found that different cultures show different patterns of attachment (see page 37). Further research has explored how child-rearing styles vary between cultures, causing differences in attachment types.

Content

What you need to know

- Describe and evaluate Bowlby's theory of attachment, including the evolutionary basis of attachment.

AS check

In the Psychodynamic Approach you studied the importance of early childhood, particularly early relationships with parents. This theme is developed here to explore how early childhood experience can affect later adult development.

Bowlby went on to conduct research at the Tavistock Clinic for children to explore the effects of bond disruption on adolescents. This study is explored in detail on page 47.

▲ Mother-child attachments can be found among most mammals.

Bowlby's (1907-1990) theory of attachment

John Bowlby was commissioned by the World Health Organisation (WHO) to study the children of post-war Europe. The aftermath of World War Two had left children separated from their parents. Some were evacuated for lengthy periods, some lost parents during the war, and many others were separated from their mothers because of the need for women to work in factories and on the land.

Bowlby observed and interviewed children in hospitals and institutions to understand the impact of parent-child separation on children. His main finding was that a child's mental health was dependent upon a warm and continuous loving bond between caregiver and child. Children separated from their parents suffered a broken attachment that caused depression and difficulty in forming close relationships with others.

◆ Monotropy

Bowlby emphasised the importance of the relationship between a child and a single primary caregiver. He believed that this attachment occurred instinctively and was necessary for the child's survival. Of course other attachments may be formed, but this monotropic bond was the most significant for healthy development.

During their first six months, babies display **proximity-promoting behaviours**, such as crying, smiling and clinging. These encourage the formation of a bond between caregiver and child. They then begin to show distress and anxiety around strangers and develop a marked preference for the primary caregiver.

During the second six months, the baby's world becomes increasingly focused on the primary caregiver, treating them as a safe base from which to explore their world and a source of comfort when fearful or anxious. For Bowlby, if a child feels secure enough to show independent behaviour, they develop a positive internal working model of themselves as valued. He believed that this attachment during the first year of life is critical for healthy development. Attachments after this period are less effective in providing security for the child.

◆ Maternal deprivation hypothesis

Drawing these ideas together, Bowlby realised that a child who suffers deprivation (loss of attachment) during the first 24 months of life will develop an **internal working model** of themselves as unworthy. He coined the term **maternal deprivation**, not because he believed that the mother was the only person who could be a primary caregiver, but because at the time women typically took the role of carer. A child should have a continuous and mutually-loving relationship and, if this attachment is broken, it can have detrimental effects on a child's mental health, such as a lack of guilt and regard for the consequences of their own actions. Bowlby called this condition **affectionless psychopathy**. Bowlby also believed maternal deprivation could lead to lower intelligence, delinquency and depression.

Harlow and Harlow (1962) reared rhesus monkeys in isolation from the mother so that they suffered maternal deprivation. They found that the monkeys became aggressive and incapable of interacting with others of their own species. They were inadequate mothers to their own offspring.

◆ Evolutionary basis of attachment

Bowlby drew knowledge from the work of Konrad Lorenz (1935) to suggest that attachment had an **evolutionary** advantage. The essential idea is that a child must maintain proximity to a parent in order to survive. In our evolutionary past, there would have been many predators that would prey on the young. Attachment encourages closeness between caregiver and child so safety can be ensured.

Konrad Lorenz (1935) found that **precocial species**, who are mobile very soon after birth, imprinted on the mother within the first few days of life. Lorenz referred to this period of imprinting as a critical period, as the birds would attach to the mother (or closest moving object) within this limited period of time. Imprinting is instinctual as it is a pre-programmed behaviour, but if an attachment is not formed within this critical period, it would be unlikely to happen afterwards. Bowlby used the idea of a critical period to describe how human infants attach within a sensitive period, the first two years of life, to a proximal caregiver.

◆ Evaluation

- Bowlby's theory of attachment has been very influential in academic circles but, importantly, has also been applied to the real world. Hospitals now allow parents to stay with their child to prevent attachment disruption, daycare facilities adopt a keyworker strategy to provide a substitute caregiver in the absence of a working parent, and social services support parents who are struggling rather than remove children into foster care.
- Despite its positive contributions, Bowlby's theory suggests that even temporary separation between child and caregiver has damaging effects and this has led many working mothers to feel guilty for leaving their child. Bowlby's initial WHO report was used politically to remove the new female labour force and return them to the home, thereby freeing up employment positions for men returning from the war. In fact, some argue that a happy working mother is more able to provide quality interactions with a child than an unhappy non-working mother. It is the *quality* of interaction that is critical, not the quantity, as Bowlby emphasised.
- Bowlby's claim that a single caregiver was the most important figure for a child has been criticised. Instead it has been suggested that children have multiple attachments with caregivers other than the mother. These can be with the father, grandparents and siblings (Schaffer and Emerson, 1964), and are based on quality of interaction rather than quantity of care, which challenges Bowlby's concept of monotropy.
- The maternal deprivation hypothesis suggests quite serious consequences for even a small amount of separation. Some psychologists believe that these consequences are more likely a result of privation than of deprivation, and that Bowlby failed to distinguish between the two.
- The idea that human babies are pre-programmed to attach to a caregiver is very plausible, and there are plenty of animal comparisons that can be drawn to prove the evolutionary basis of attachment. However, the evolutionary basis of attachment does not place any value on the quality of attachment that is formed.
- Bowlby conducted his own research study on delinquent adolescents that supports his maternal deprivation hypothesis (see page 47).

AS check

Precocial species are born relatively mature and practically mobile from birth. For example, a baby chick is following its mother around only after a few hours of hatching.

Taking it further

Find out more about Konrad Lorenz and how he made newly-hatched goslings imprint on him (1937) at http://www.answers.com/topic/konrad-lorenz. Harlow investigated the social isolation of rhesus monkeys reared without their mother. Many of the experiments can be seen at http://uk.youtube.com/results?search_query=harlow%27s+monkeys&search_type=&aq=0&oq=harlow

Examiner's tip

Bowlby has been criticised for being sexist. This is a rather simplistic and inaccurate assessment of his research. He simply implied that the primary caregiver was likely to be the mother, a trend seen at the time of his research. Subsequent versions of his theory referred only to a 'caregiver' rather than a 'mother'.

Mary Ainsworth

What you need to know

- Describe and evaluate Ainsworth's research into attachment types.
- Describe and evaluate the strange situation as a research method to study attachment types.
- Understand cross-cultural issues relating to child-rearing styles and attachment types formed.

AS check

In the Learning Approach you studied the observation as a research method. Mary Ainsworth used a structured observation to investigate attachment types in a strange situation. Review this method on AS pages 128–129.

Mary Ainsworth became a colleague of John Bowlby when she moved from America to Britain. She was very influenced by the research Bowlby conducted and became interested in the individual differences in attachment types between caregiver and child. In the early 1950s, she moved to Uganda, where she conducted her Ganda study investigating mother-child relationships in six villages in Kampala. She visited 26 mothers and their infants regularly over many months, observing them for several hours at a time. She noticed the truth in Bowlby's theory of the mother being a safe base and was able to categorise relationships into one of three types:

- **Securely attached** – children were generally contented and pacified by the presence of their mother, using her as a safe base.
- **Insecurely attached** – children were less inclined to explore and cried frequently, even when with the mother.
- Not yet attached – children were indifferent to the presence of their mother.

She also found that securely-attached children had mothers who enjoyed breastfeeding and enjoyed the company of their children. She called this 'maternal sensitivity', as the mother responded to the infant's need to create a secure attachment.

Following her return to America in 1955, Ainsworth set about a similar study in Baltimore of 26 families. She regularly visited mothers and their children for up to four hours at a time, interviewing them and making detailed notes during her observations. Her findings were similar to those of the Ganda study, in that secure attachments could be found when mothers found contact with their children satisfying and they responded positively to their needs.

The strange situation as a research method

Psychologists have devised many subtle techniques to study attachment in infancy using observational methods. Ainsworth and Wittig (1969) developed one of the most widely-used techniques to measure attachment, called the **strange situation procedure**, which they used to study individual differences in attachment types. It involves a **structured observation** of parent-child interaction through a one-way mirror, following this sequence of three-minute episodes:

1. Mother and child are escorted into a small room that contains toys for the child to play with.
2. The child explores the room and play with the toys whilst the mother is present.
3. A stranger enters the room, greets the mother and talks to her and then tries to interact with the child through play.
4. The mother gets up and leaves the room, leaving child and stranger alone.
5. After a short period (determined by the child's distress) the mother returns to join the child and stranger. She consoles the child and the stranger leaves the room.
6. The mother leaves the observation room, leaving the child alone.
7. The stranger enters the room and attempts to interact and console the child in the mother's absence.
8. The mother returns to console the child.

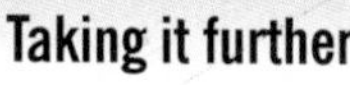

Ainsworth (1978) used the strange situation on children between 12 and 18 months old, focusing particularly on how the child responded to the stranger, the separation from the mother and the reunion with the mother. She found three distinct attachment types using this procedure: securely attached, anxious-avoidant and anxious-resistant. These are summarised below.

Taking it further

Observe the behaviour of a securely-attached child in the strange situation at http://www.youtube.com/watch?v=36GI_1PBQpM.

Attachment types and a child's behaviour

	Reaction to stranger	Reaction to separation from mother	Reaction to reunion with mother
Secure attachment (Type B)	Is indifferent to the stranger when mother is present but ignores the stranger when alone (stranger fear).	Becomes upset and distressed when mother leaves.	Is happy when mother returns in both first and second reunions and is quickly settled. The child easily calms and exploring resumes.
Anxious-avoidant attachment (Type A)	Plays with the stranger regardless of mother's presence. Does not check for mother's presence.	Is not distressed at mother's absence and can seek comfort from stranger.	Shows no interest in mother's return.
Anxious-resistant attachment (Type C)	Shows fear of the stranger and avoids the stranger with or without the mother being present.	Intense reaction to mother's absence. The child is clearly distressed.	The child wants the comfort of the mother but may push her away when approached. Resists comfort even if it is desired.

Ainsworth observed many child-mother interactions and found that 65% of American children were securely attached, 23% were anxious-avoidant and 12% anxious-resistant. Ainsworth and Bell (1969) explained the different attachment types found in the strange situation by examining the responsiveness of the mother to the child's needs. If a mother was sensitive, consistent and responsive to the child (reacting positively and appropriately to the child's signals) the child was more likely to develop a secure attachment. A child who was rejected by the mother felt unworthy and developed an insecure attachment (anxious-avoidant), as did a child whose mother was inconsistent (responsive and rejecting) with their parenting style (anxious-resistant).

Evaluation of the strange situation procedure and Ainsworth's research

- The strange situation can be criticised for causing unnecessary distress to the child. The child is separated twice from the caregiver, being left alone once. This procedure does not protect the child from harm according to the BPS guidelines. However, the purpose of this procedure is to study separation anxiety, stranger fear and reunion with the mother, which could not be achieved easily any other way in a controlled situation.
- It is a highly standardised procedure involving timed episodes and rigorous analysis of the observed behaviour. In this sense, it is a replicable and objective research method.
- The strange situation procedure and Ainsworth and Bell's theory do not take into account the individual differences of young children. The procedure itself could be measuring the temperament of a child rather than the attachment type itself. A child may be particularly anxious regardless of the mother's presence or absence.

Taking it further

Although the strange situation seems to examine only the attachment between mother and child, it can also be used to examine the attachment with the father. Look at this website to see father-child attachment: http://www.youtube.com/watch?v=Y6QtuU1L_A8&NR=1

Similarly, it is assumed that the attachment type is caused by maternal sensitivity, when this attachment could have been determined by the child's temperament instead. This criticism lies at the heart of the validity of the procedure. In this case, it could be argued that the strange situation is not a measure of attachment, but instead a measure of the characteristics of a child in a strange situation. Similarly, the basis on which attachment types are formed can also be questioned. Ainsworth believed that maternal sensitivity achieved a secure attachment type. If the strange situation is an invalid measurement of attachment then it also questions the validity of the link between parenting style and attachment type. The type of attachment could be caused by the temperament of the child, i.e. a parent may not be able to form a secure relationship with a difficult child.

- The strange situation procedure has been criticised for lacking ecological validity because the situation is unfamiliar to a child. The child could be responding to the situation they are placed in rather than the presence or absence of the mother. At home, a child may be happy to be left alone because they are in familiar surroundings.
- The strange situation has been criticised for its use with children accustomed to being separated from their primary caregiver on a regular basis, such as children who attend daycare. Children in daycare will suffer different amounts of stress at being left with a stranger compared with non-daycare children.

Cross-cultural issues in child-rearing styles

The strange situation has been used in different cultures to measure attachment types. In Israel, Germany and Japan, different patterns of attachment have been found:

Percentage of attachment types found in different cultures

	Percentage (%) of secure attachments (Type B)	Percentage (%) of anxious–avoidant attachments Type A)	Percentage (%) of anxious–resistant attachment (Type C)
Ainsworth (1978) Baltimore study (USA)	65	23	12
Sagi et al. (1985) Israeli study	37	13	50
Grossman et al. (1985) Germany study	33	49	18
Miyake et al. (1985) Japanese study	68	0	32

The findings from different cultures seem to suggest that there are far fewer secure attachments in Israel and Germany than in the USA. However, it would be a mistake to conclude that the caregivers are less maternally sensitive than in America. Instead, we should consider the cultural influences on child-rearing strategies that lead to these different attachment types.

Comparison of attachment types (Sagi et al., 1991)

	Family sleeping arrangement	Communal sleeping arrangement
Securely attached (Type B)	60%	26%
Anxious-resistant attachment type	8%	30%

◆ Israel

Israel has the highest percentage of anxious-resistant attachment types. Sagi studied children living in an Israeli Kibbutzim, a commune or collective community where childrearing is shared and children are often raised by a **metapelet** (non-biological community member). The anxious-resistant attachment type was found in Kibbutz children because the mother was regularly absent, and caregivers rotated shifts and could not give prompt attention to individual children. Kibbutz children have extended childcare, often experiencing communal sleeping arrangements.

This cultural difference affecting the attachment type is supported by a further study by Sagi et al. (1991), comparing Kibbutz children who experience family sleeping arrangements and communal sleeping. They found that children who slept with the family showed 'normal' attachment patterns compared with children who slept communally.

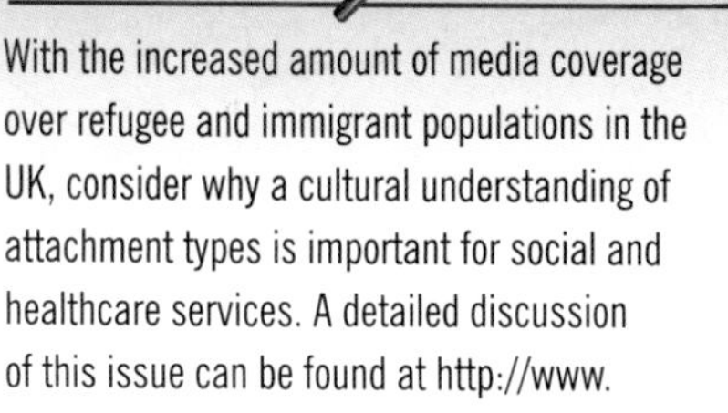

Taking it further

With the increased amount of media coverage over refugee and immigrant populations in the UK, consider why a cultural understanding of attachment types is important for social and healthcare services. A detailed discussion of this issue can be found at http://www.attachmentacrosscultures.org/about/about15.htm

◆ Germany

Grossman et al. (1985) found a greater number of anxious-avoidant (type A) attachment types. This does not mean that German mothers are insensitive to their children's needs. Grossman et al. conducted extensive observations of family life in Germany and concluded that the over-representation of anxious-avoidant attachment types was due to the cultural value placed on independence and early weaning.

◆ Japan

Miyake et al. (1985) found a higher number of anxious-resistant attachment types in Japan than the USA, but no anxious-avoidant attachment types at all. Miyake explained that traditional Japanese mothers do not leave their children with others and encourage dependency on them. Japanese children are kept close to pacify them and they rarely cry. In the strange situation procedure, these children would become very distressed. Durrett et al. (1984) observed that in modern Japanese families, mothers do go out to work and leave their children. The attachment types found amongst these modern families are similar to those found in the USA.

◆ Cross-cultural and within-culture variations in attachment types

Ijzendoorn and Kroonenberg (1988) conducted a meta-analysis of 38 cross-cultural studies that used the strange situation as a measure of attachment. In addition to examining attachment patterns between different countries, they also examined attachment types found within the same country but in different regions.

Surprisingly, they found that attachment types found within a country were as dissimilar as between different countries – for example, the difference in attachment classifications between Berlin and Bielefeld in Germany was as great as the difference between Berlin and an Israeli Kibbutz. It seems that studies conducted in one country resemble different countries more than they resemble themselves.

This meta-analysis points to the nature of samples used for each study rather than the consistency of the procedure. Some samples only included middle-class professional parents, whereas other studies, in the same country, included families who were of lower socio-economic status.

Conducting cross-cultural research using the strange situation has yielded some interesting findings and illustrates the impact of culture on attachment. However, some argue that the strange situation is not an appropriate tool for measuring attachment types in different cultures because we cannot determine whether it is the culture or the attachment type that is being measured – it is not a **culture-free** research method. It can also be seen as a distressing procedure, particularly for Japanese children who find it very unfamiliar and upsetting to be separated from their mother.

Deprivation

What you need to know

- Describe and evaluate research into deprivation/separation, both short-term and long-term.
- Understand how the negative effects of deprivation can be reduced.

▲ James and Joyce Robertson.

Hospitals in the 1950s

For reasons of sanitation parents were given little or no access to their children. For example:

- Guy's Hospital: parents could visit Sundays 2-4pm
- St Thomas's Hospital: no visits by parents for the first month, but parents could see children sleeping between 7-8pm
- West London Hospital: no visiting at any time
- London Hospital: parents of children under 3 years no visits, but parents could see children through partitions. Over 3 years, twice weekly.

Examiner's tip

Remember the effects of short-term deprivation using the abbreviation PDD for Protest, Despair, Detachment. Robertson and Robertson concluded that John suffered maternal deprivation, responding firstly with protest, then despair and finally detachment.

Deprivation is a term used to describe the loss of a formed attachment between a child and caregiver. According to Bowlby's maternal deprivation hypothesis, any disruption to the continuity of a loving and mutual bond can be potentially damaging to a child's emotional, intellectual and social development. In his own study, Bowlby found that separation from the mother can lead to juvenile delinquency and affectionless psychopathy (see page 47).

Short-term deprivation

Husband and wife James and Joyce Robertson both worked at Hampstead Wartime Nurseries and Hospital. Joyce Robertson had worked with children who had lost their parents during the War, and James Robertson was a researcher for Bowlby, observing children in nurseries and hospitals to study the effects of deprivation on children's behaviour.

In 1968, the Robertsons observed the behaviour of a 17-month-old boy, John, who was staying at a residential nursery whilst his mother had a second child. James recorded John's behaviour after being left by his mother for nine days.

In the first few days, John tried but failed to form attachments with the nursery staff. He began to **protest** and cry, but eventually became quiet and unresponsive to the staff and other children around him. He was often found to be hugging a teddy bear and rolling around in **despair**. When collected by his mother John ignored her and cried, showing **detachment** from her. The protest, despair and detachment that John experienced during his short-term deprivation would be the same experience for any child being separated from their primary caregiver.

◆ Discussion

- Studies of the effects of short-term deprivation are not well controlled, for ethical reasons, so most research involves observations of children who are in residential nurseries or care, which may have methodological problems.
- The majority of research into short-term deprivation that has found PDD as an effect was conducted when residential care staff were more concerned with duties (feeding, dressing) than caring for children's emotional needs. Today, much more importance is placed on children's emotional wellbeing.
- A child's response to short-term deprivation may depend upon individual differences, such as age and resilience to separation. John was a shy child and some of the other children were aggressive. This may account for why John, and some other children, suffered more from separation than others.
- Older children fare better than younger children. John was only 17 months old, and it is likely that an older child would not have such an extreme reaction to separation from their mother.

The Robertsons went on to provide short-term foster care to two girls in a similar situation to John. The substitute care provided by James and Joyce had a significant countering effect, as the girls did not show 'protest despair detachment' when separated from their mothers.

Daycare can also be seen as a form of short-term deprivation, as young children are separated from their mother for extended periods of time through the day. There are many studies into the effects of daycare on the social, emotional and intellectual well-being of children (see pages 44–45, 48)

Long-term deprivation

The effects of long-term deprivation are significantly, as the caregiver may not return to the child at all, so the attachment is broken permanently.

◆ Divorce

Divorce typically involves one parent leaving the family home, sometimes with little or no subsequent contact with their children. It might also involve family reordering, where the parent cohabits or remarries and the family is reconstituted as children gain stepbrothers and sisters.

Cockett and Tripp (1994) compared intact families with divorced and reordered families. They found that children in reordered families had problems at school and with their health, and the incidence of these issues increased with multiple reordering. Intact families with low conflict (parents who did not argue very much) fared better but, as the incidence of conflict increased, so did academic, social and emotional issues. Cockett and Tripp concluded that divorce and reordering had adverse effects on children, as did conflict but to a lesser degree. As conflict is a characteristic of divorce and reordering, it is likely that conflict rather than divorce and reordering was the significant factor.

◆ Death of a parent

The death of a parent rarely involves the type of conflict and disruption that is caused by divorce. In fact, it is more likely that a family will provide high levels of support for a child in such circumstances. It is also unlikely to cause the child to be angry as it is not a separation *choice* that a family makes.

Rutter's (1981) Isle of Wight study concluded that the *reason* for the separation was more important than the separation itself. Children who experienced the death of a parent fared better than children separated by high-conflict divorce or a parent suffering psychiatric illness.

Long-term deprivation has more serious consequences for a child but it is important to remember that research in this area is only correlational. Many other factors could produce a similar effect: the stress of financial worry and reordering, and moving school and losing friends, for example. Also, the findings of research associated with divorce could be used to try and keep families together in a dysfunctional situation when separation would have been better for the children.

Reducing the effects of deprivation

- James and Joyce Robertson demonstrated how adequate substitute care could minimise the protest, despair and detachment displayed by children experiencing short-term deprivation.
- Older children are more able to deal with short-term deprivation, and some psychologists such as Jay Belsky would argue that daycare should be kept to a minimum until a child reaches two years old.
- If separation is long-term, such as through divorce, children suffer fewer adverse effects if conflict is kept to a minimum or not witnessed by the children. Separation can be a sensible decision to avoid the adverse effects of conflict.
- To avoid an attachment being permanently broken, the non-custodial parent should try and maintain regular contact with their children.

Examiner's tip

There is a fine line between long-term deprivation and privation. An extended period of time constitutes long-term deprivation, but you may come across privation studies of institutionalised children that claim to show deprivation when, in fact, the children had never formed an attachment in the first place – that is privation, not deprivation.

Taking it further

There have been many studies conducted into the effects of divorce on children's development. Research some of these:

Hetherington (1993) - Virginia longitudinal study
Amato and Keith (1991) – meta-analysis
Jekielek (1988).

Taking it further

If you have found further research into deprivation, you might want to consider what the research tells us about the cause of problems with children's development and how this can inform how we should deal with deprivation better to reduce these effects. Use this research grid as a guide:

Research study conclusion	How this can be used to reduce the effects of deprivation
Example: Saler et al. (1992) found that children allowed to mourn the death of a parent suffered less depression.	Example: Allow children to mourn the death by talking openly about the bereavement, visiting the grave regularly and expressing their anger and sadness.

Privation

What you need to know

- Describe and evaluate research into privation.
- Discuss whether the reversibility of privation is possible using research.

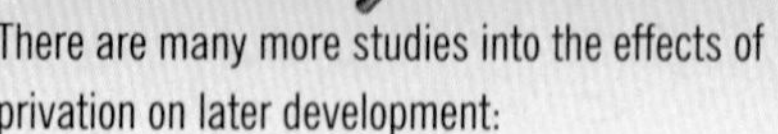

Taking it further

There are many more studies into the effects of privation on later development:

1. Freud and Dann (1951) Bulldogs Bank children http://www.annafreudcentre.org/war_nurseries5.htm
2. Hodges and Tizard (1989) study of institutionalised children http://www.holah.karoo.net/hodgesandtizard.htm and http://www.colchsfc.ac.uk/psychology/What%20does%20Hodges%20and%20Tizard.htm

Privation is when an attachment to a caregiver is never formed. These children are sometimes referred to as feral, which conjures up images of infants being found in the wild, whereas in reality they are often found in domestic situations, but have been severely neglected. It is known that privation can have very adverse effects on children's development socially, emotionally and intellectually. Psychologists are, however, still uncertain of whether the effects of privation can be reversed so that children can live 'normal' happy lives. A number of studies can be explored.

◆ Koluchová (1972) Czech twins

Koluchová (1972) reported a case of twin Czechoslovakian boys, Andrei and Vanya, who lost their mother shortly after they were born. After her death, they were placed in an institution for a year, then in the care of an aunt, before finally returning to their father and new stepmother at 18 months old. Their stepmother regularly beat them and locked them in a small dark room. The twins were eventually found at the age of six – mentally retarded, scared, severely undernourished and with little speech. They went to a children's home and, after two years of rehabilitation, were fostered by two sisters who provided exceptional care. When they were found, it was estimated that their IQ was around 40, though no tests to verify this could be used because of their poor development. By the age of 11, the boys had developed normal speech for their age, and by 14 had a normal IQ. At 20, the boys were in relationships and were working. It seems that the intensive loving care provided by the sisters had reversed the effects of privation for Andrei and Vanya.

◆ Rutter and the English and Romanian Adoptees (ERA) study team (1998)

This is a **longitudinal study** into the effects of early privation on Romanian orphans adopted by English families, compared with adopted children born in England. The Romanian children had all experienced Romanian orphanages of poor quality within a few weeks of life and were either adopted before six months old or between six months and two years. A sample of 111 Romanian adoptees were compared with 52 English adoptees, all aged four, on a range of measures.

Despite being developmentally delayed when they were adopted at six months, the Romanian adoptees had caught up in weight, height, head circumference and cognitive level with the English children. Children adopted at a later age had also made progress, but not as significantly as those adopted when younger. The negative effects of poor-quality orphanage care had affected these children psychologically and physically for a longer time, so recovery was slower. It was also found that a significant minority of Romanian adoptees suffered from attachment disorder; they were attention-seeking and non-selective in their choice of friendships and relationships. Later follow-up studies revealed that this pattern of attachment remained in many of the children when aged 11.

Reversibility of privation

According to Bowlby, early experience is critical for normal development.

In cases of privation, he predicted emotional disturbance and affectionless personality. However, it would seem that the effects of privation can, under certain circumstances, be overcome.

- Reversibility can depend upon the quality of care the children subsequently receive. Koluchová's (1972) Czech twins received excellent loving care and were able to recover. Hodges and Tizard (1989) found that children adopted from institutional care developed better than those children restored to their original families. They reported that adoptive care in this case was more intense, loving and supportive than the original family could provide.
- Age is also an important factor because the reversibility of privation depends upon the length of the isolation. The Czech twins were found at six years and made a good recovery, whereas Genie was 13 when she was found (see pages 46) and therefore could have been beyond the sensitive period for development (certainly for language development). Rutter and the ERA study team (1998) found that children adopted before six months made a better recovery by four years than those adopted later.
- It is difficult to establish whether privation is reversible from limited case studies that are unique and therefore lack reliability and generalisability.
- The Czech twins may have recovered from the effects of privation because they had formed attachments to each other.
- It is difficult to determine the quality of relationships formed before a period of privation. Genie's mother claimed to have formed an attachment with her daughter, so privation may not have been the cause of her issues. The Czech twins received good quality care in a children's home for 18 months following their mother's death. It was only after this that they suffered abuse at the hands of their father and stepmother. The attachments formed in the children's home could have stood them in good stead to endure later privation.
- Studies of privation are often complicated by many factors affecting individual children. Some children are more resilient than others so can deal better with a lack of attachment. Genie was believed to have been retarded at birth. This could account for the lack of reversibility in her case. Certainly neurological studies showed that she had similar sleep spindles (as measured by an EEG)to a child with learning difficulties. However, others would argue that the pace of her development in the first year of being found, indicated that she did not have a learning difficulty.

Examiner's tip 

Issues such as the reversibility of privation are not clear-cut. You will be assessed on your ability to discuss the issue, using and assessing evidence from research and your own understanding of the factors that may affect reversibility.

Other research into privation

Anna Freud and Sophie Dann (1951) studied and cared for six children raised in a concentration camp in Theresienstadt. Having lost their parents, the children were raised together by other prisoners of war, but care was infrequent and the ability to form attachments made difficult by the nature of the environment. The so-called Bulldogs Bank children came to the clinic where Freud and Dann worked and were initially aggressive towards adults. They were closely attached to one another and impossible to separate, but with time they began to form emotional attachments with the adult staff. The children may have recovered from some of the effects of privation because they had the opportunity to attach to each other for almost three years of life. This research suggests that the effects of privation from a caregiver can be somewhat buffered by attachments to other peers.

Hodges and Tizard (1989) examined the development of 65 children who had all spent time in institutional care during the first year of life. Some of the children were restored to their biological family, some were adopted, and some remained in the institution. They found that all children suffered to some extent from institutional care, which supports Bowlby's maternal deprivation hypothesis. However, those children who were adopted fared better than any other group. This research suggests that good-quality care received from adoptive families, who would put more effort into caring for the children, overcame some of the effects of earlier privation.

Autism

What you need to know

- Describe the characteristics of autism and 2 ways an artistic child's development is effected.
- Describe two explanations of autism. This section will look at 'mindblindness' and the 'extreme male brain' as explanations of autism.

Taking it further

Explore autism further by looking into the characteristics, causes and forms of treatment at http://www.nas.org.uk/nas/jsp/polopoly.jsp?d=10.

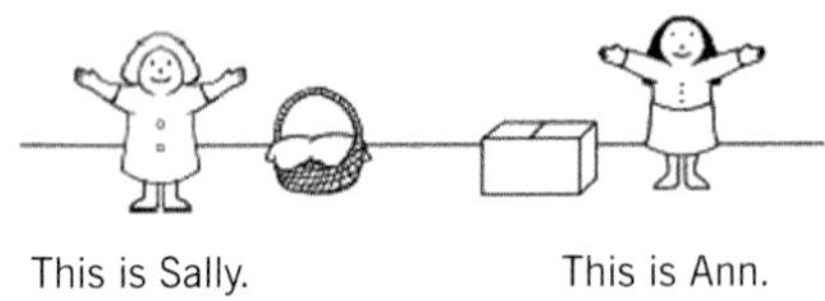

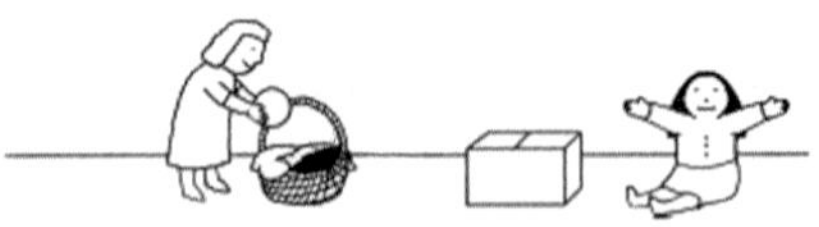

Sally has a ball. She puts it into her basket.

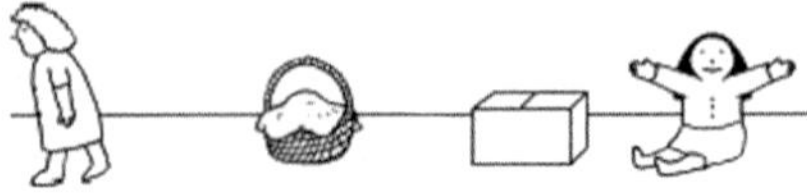

Sally goes out for a walk.
Ann taks the ball out of the basket.

Ann then puts the ball in the box.

Where will Sally look for the ball?

▲ The Sally-Anne task used by Simon Baron-Cohen and his colleagues to test for a theory of mind in autistic children.

Autism is a developmental disorder that affects approximately one in 1000 people, and is more prevalent in boys than girls. It is characterised by a lack of responsiveness to others and an inability to form attachments, even with parents. Other characteristics might include:

- ritualistic and repetitive behaviour
- highly-developed motor skills
- irregular responses to stimuli
- inappropriate emotional responses
- specialism in certain intellectual tasks
- inactivity or hyperactivity
- intolerance to change
- insensitivity to pain
- poor speech development
- lack of imagination

Autism is typically diagnosed between 18 months and four years. It is likely to be present at birth but is difficult to diagnose until a child is found to fall short of expected developmental milestones.

◆ Theory of mind

A cognitive explanation for autism, the theory of mind, was put forward by Simon Baron-Cohen (1997). He believed that the social problems that autistic children have could be explained by the way a child perceives themselves and others in their social world. To be socially competent we need to be able to 'mind read', not in the paranormal sense, but in the sense that we can understand that others think differently and have different intentions and feelings from ourselves. Think back to a conversation with a friend to understand that we spend a significant amount of time trying to read the thoughts, intentions and feelings of others. Baron-Cohen believed that an autistic child had 'mindblindness', the inability to read others' intentions, which would explain their lack of social interaction skills.

Baron-Cohen et al. (1985) adapted a study to test the theory of mind in 20 autistic children, 14 children with Down's syndrome and 27 typically-developing children. The Sally-Anne task (see left) was used on all of the children and they were asked three key questions:

1. Where is Sally's ball? (reality question)
2. Where was the ball to begin with? (memory question)
3. Where will Sally look for her ball? (belief question)

The last question was used to determine a theory of mind. If a child could understand that Sally would look in the basket where she left her ball, they would be able to understand that she possessed a mind that was distinct from their own. However, if they stated that the ball was in the box, they would not be able to understand that Sally had a different belief from them. Baron-Cohen found that most typically-developing children and children with Down's syndrome could answer the belief question, compared with only a minority of autistic children. The autistic children seemed not to have developed a theory of mind.

Baron-Cohen et al. (1995) also conducted a series of experiments to investigate how autistic children read others' mental state.

Every day we convey a huge amount of information about what we think and how we feel through our eye-direction. Children who are developing typically and children with learning difficulties frequently use eye-direction to judge and understand another person's mental state, whereas autistic children appear to be blind to this source of information. Autistic children cannot 'read minds'.

◆ Extreme male brain

Baron-Cohen et al. (2005) believe that the autistic brain is an extreme form of the typical male brain. Males and females are typically stronger at specific tasks:

Male-orientated tasks	Female-orientated tasks
Mental rotation	Language tasks
Targeting objects (arrows)	Empathy
Mathematical reasoning and systemising	Matching tasks
Disembedding figures from a whole object	Fine motor control
Geometry	Pretend play in childhood

They believe that these differences are caused by the presence of testosterone in the womb whilst a foetus is developing. At around eight gestational weeks, the male embryo releases testosterone and causes a male brain to develop distinctly different (in part) to that of a female brain. Baron-Cohen believes that autism is an extreme form of this male brain and research has indicated that, while boys are better at male-orientated tasks than girls, autistic children are far superior to males at these tasks. Knickmeyer and Baron-Cohen (2006) explain that these brain differences cause superior social and communication skills in females. Autism is a lack of such skills, and, as it occurs four times more frequently in boys, it could be that such brain differences can explain autism.

Falter et al. (2008) tested 28 autistic children and 31 typically-developing children on mental rotation and figure-disembedding tasks. They found that children with autism outperformed 'normal' children.

Baron-Cohen et al. (2003) put forward the idea that females are better empathisers (predicting and responding emotionally to others' needs and behaviours) and that males are better systemisers (understanding rules and constructing systems). Using a self-report method, they found that, in the general population, females scored more highly on empathy questions and males on systemising questions. Autistic children scored significantly lower on empathy and significantly higher on systemising than the general population, again lending support to the theory that autism is an extreme male brain condition.

AS check

In the Biological Approach you studied brain lateralisation in males (AS pages 106–7). This means that specific brain functioning in a male brain is located in one hemisphere, whereas it is represented in both hemispheres in females. You may also have studied the key issue 'Is autism an extreme male brain condition? (see AS pages 114–5).

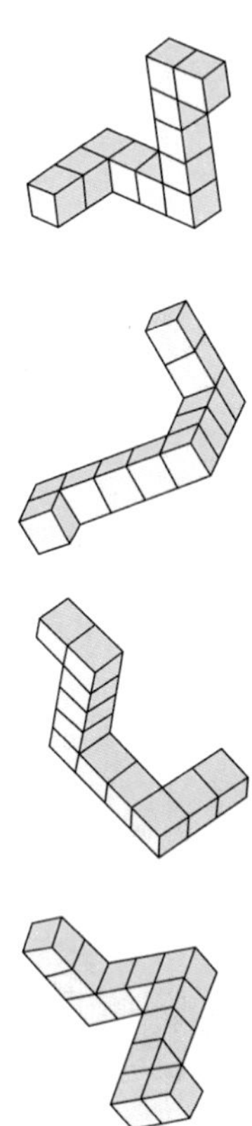

▲ Mental rotation tasks involve picking the correct object from a series of alternative perspectives. Which of these three objects is the same as the first?

Other options

You may consider the alternative option of describing and explaining severe learning difficulties. Learning difficulties are usually assessed as mild, moderate, severe or profound, based on measured intelligence level. The degree of difficulty experienced and care needed varies with each diagnosis. Children with severe learning difficulties can generally perform only basic functions and typically attend special schools as they are unable to deal with mainstream education. Severe learning difficulties are usually caused by a biological problem, such as genetic abnormality or the influence of adverse environmental effects on the developing foetus (drugs, radiation, pollution, etc.).

You may also consider the alternative option of describing and explaining ADHD (Attention Deficit Hyperactivity Disorder). ADHD is characterised by short attention spans and hyperactive behaviour. It is more common in males than females, and parents and schools can find behaviour difficult to manage. The causes of ADHD have been linked to food additives, irregular brain functioning in the reticular activating system and frontal lobes of the cortex, and genetics.

Daycare

What you need to know

- Describe and evaluate research into daycare.
- Describe and evaluate at least one study outlining the advantages of daycare and one outlining the disadvantages of daycare for children.

AS check

The Psychodynamic Approach described the effects of early childhood experiences on adult behaviour. The key issue of daycare follows a similar theme because some research implies that daycare can be harmful to children's social, emotional and intellectual development, whereas other research highlights the positive effects of daycare.

Daycare is when a child is looked after by a child-minder or daycare provider throughout the day, usually while parents work. In the UK, organised nursery provision is increasingly used by families where both parents work.

Bowlby would predict daycare to be a form of deprivation, as a child experiences short-term separation from the primary caregiver. This, according to his theory, would damage the attachment formed between them and cause lasting effects.

◆ Effects of daycare

Research into daycare has focused on several aspects of a child's development:

- **Social development:** refers to the ability of a child to interact with others, form health attachments and relationships with peers and family.
- **Emotional development:** refers to the ability of a child to cope with situations in a positive way; how confident and independent they are.
- **Cognitive development:** refers to the intellectual growth of a child.

◆ Positive effects of daycare

Sylva et al. (2004) conducted a longitudinal study (1997–2004) into the effectiveness of pre-school care for over 3000 children in the UK. The 'Effective Provision of Pre-School Education' project (EPPE) studied children between the ages of 3 and 7. The researchers created developmental profiles of the children each year, using SATs results and reports from pre-school staff, parents and schoolteachers. The pre-school provision ranged from homecare to day nurseries, playgroups and pre-school classes. The study also measured parental occupation and qualifications, social background and birth weight as factors that could affect development.

▲ Daycare is a common experience for children, but is it harmful or beneficial to them?

Sylva et al. found that assessments made during the pre-school experience showed that children benefited from pre-school care socially and intellectually, particularly if they started daycare before the age of three. High-quality provision, with highly-qualified staff, led to better social and intellectual development. The positive effects of daycare were still evident at the end of Key Stage 1, with higher scores in maths and literacy. The longitudinal study concluded that quality provision produced short-term advantages in social development and longer-term advantages in cognitive development.

◆ Evaluation of the EPPE project

- The study measured other factors that could have affected a child's development, to ensure that the effects of daycare were being measured and not an uncontrolled variable.
- The team used a range of measurements including interviews with parents, pre-school and school reports, and SATs scores, to measure the social and cognitive development of the children. This information was used to build up a detailed and valid profile of all the children at each stage in the study.

Taking it further

The full EPPE project report can be found at http://www.surestart.gov.uk/_doc/P0001378.pdf.

- As this was a longitudinal study, it was able to report on the long-term effects of daycare on development. It also meant that the same children could be followed during the course of the study and their initial assessment could be directly compared with later assessments.

◆ Negative effects of daycare

Belsky and Rovine (1988) drew on the findings from two major American longitudinal studies to investigate the effects of daycare during the first year of life on mother-child and father-child attachments in typical, non-risk families. They analysed attachment types from data using the strange situation (see page 34) when the children were aged between 12 and 13 months. They found that there was a higher incidence of avoidant (type A) mother-child attachment types (43%) among children under 12 months who had experienced more than 20 hours per week of non-maternal care than among children who experienced less than 20 hours. Boys whose mother worked full time, and therefore experienced full-time daycare (35 hours per week), had more insecure attachments with their father than did other boys.

◆ Evaluation

Clarke-Stewart (1989) criticised the use of the strange situation as a procedure to measure attachment types in children who experience extensive daycare. These children are familiar with being left by their parents with strange people, and so would not respond with the same stress as a child who had not received daycare. Children who experience daycare are routinely left with others and are more independent, which could be interpreted as avoidant behaviour. However, Belsky and Rovine countered this by arguing that children who experience daycare or who are home-cared do not differ significantly in the strange situation.

Factors affecting daycare

- **Quality of care:** Some research (Burchinal et al., 2000; Andersson, 1992) indicates that the quality of daycare is important. Low staff turnover, high staff:child ratios, staff training and qualifications, and a warm, nurturing and structured environment are the best conditions under which children thrive socially, cognitively and emotionally.
- **Duration of care:** Some research (Lamb, 1992; Belsky and Rovine, 1988) has highlighted that intensive daycare can be particularly damaging. However, Clarke-Stewart et al. (2004) would argue that the length of time spent in daycare has little effect on development.
- **Onset of daycare:** Belsky (1998) maintains that the first year of life is where main attachments are formed. Daycare during this first year can produce insecure attachments, particularly if it is for more than 20 hours per week.
- **Individual differences:** Increasingly researchers are examining the effects of daycare on individual children, as some children are more able to cope with separation than others. Daycare may provide independent and outgoing children with social skills, but shy children may be adversely affected by a constant milieu of social activity.
- **Background:** Research suggests that children from disadvantaged backgrounds benefit greatly from daycare as it offers stimulation and education that they may not receive at home. It also allows parents to work and improve their financial situation.

Examiner's tip

The factors discussed here can be turned into suggestions for how to improve daycare for children. For example, you might wish to argue that children should not start daycare until they are one year old. Where possible, try to support your suggestion for improved daycare with a research study as evidence.

See page 48 for further studies on the effects of daycare.

Studies in detail

What you need to know

- Describe and evaluate Curtiss's (1977) case study of Genie.
- Describe and evaluate Bowlby's (1946) study of 44 juvenile thieves.
- Describe and evaluate Belsky and Rovine's (1988) daycare research or Rutter et al.'s (1998) privation study, instead of Bowlby.

AS check

In the Psychodynamic Approach you considered case studies as a research method. It would be useful here to recap on the general description and evaluation of case studies on pages 72–73.

Examiner's tip

Case studies are treated differently from experiments, observations and surveys when we describe them. Instead of the typical description consisting of Name, Aim, Procedure, Results and Conclusion, a case study is described in terms of case detail and case analysis.

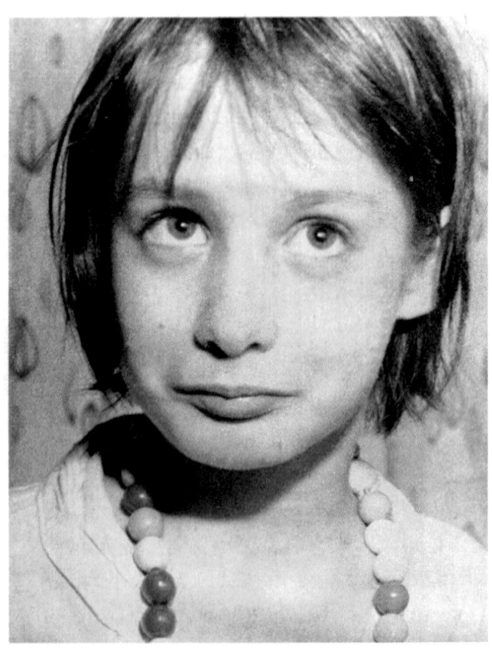

▲ Genie

Genie (Curtiss, 1977)

Genie was discovered in 1970. She was 13 years old and had spent her life locked in a room with nothing but a cot, a potty chair and cotton reels to play with. Her parents neglected her and her father often beat her for making sounds. She was fed baby food and spent most of her day tied to a potty chair. She was only on special occasions allowed to play with two plastic raincoats.

Both parents were charged with child abuse. Her mother, claimed that she was the victim of an abusive husband, and her father committed suicide before he was due to appear in court. Irene was never charged and the custody of Genie was given to Los Angeles Children's Hospital. Genie was fostered by researchers involved in her care at the hospital but, after funding for research ran out, Genie was returned to her mother, and finally to general foster care.

◆ The characteristics of a privated child

Genie was found with severe physical and intellectual retardation. She walked with a stoop and was almost entirely mute apart from a few utterances that were barely discernible as words. She was severely under-nourished and had stunted growth. She could not chew normal food and often urinated in her clothing. Any emotion displayed was often expressed inwardly; she displayed anger by biting and scratching herself.

After just a few days in the children's hospital, Genie started to show signs of progress. She began to help dress herself and use the toilet almost independently. She also began to form attachments to staff members, sometimes expressing distress and protesting when they left. After a few months she started to play and enjoyed day trips, although her language and eating behaviours were still delayed. It seemed that the signs of deprivation were beginning to reverse through intensive rehabilitation. However, this proved rather an optimistic prophecy. After repeatedly being fostered Genie was eventually found to regress to her initial state of emotional disturbance and verbal silence. Despite working with speech therapists, she never gained normal language – her grammar in particular never developed beyond that of a toddler.

◆ Evaluation

- Even with intensive rehabilitation and care, Genie never recovered from her initial privation. The reversibility of privation is questionable in this case.
- Genie's father claimed that Genie was diagnosed as being mentally slow before the age of two. If she was retarded at birth, that might explain why the effects of her privation could not be reversed. Neurological studies were conducted at the children's hospital, which concluded that she showed brain activity similar to that of a child who suffered retardation from birth. Others argued that the privation caused this type of brain activity.

- Case studies such as this are valid in that they are detailed and a rich source of information about the effects of privation. But the method can be criticised for lacking reliability and generalisability.
- The researchers can be criticised for putting the research ahead of the child. However, Genie did receive a high level of care during her stay at the children's hospital and whilst under the care of the researchers.

Forty-four juvenile thieves (Bowlby, 1946)

Bowlby spent many years observing children in hospitals and residential nurseries who had lost their parent during the war. He conducted his own research into the long-term effects of maternal deprivation on Europe's youth in the post-war era.

◆ Aim

To see if there was an association between delinquency and maternal deprivation.

◆ Procedure and results

Bowlby interviewed 44 juvenile thieves referred for treatment at the child guidance clinic where he worked. He compared these thieves with a control group of 44 juveniles referred to the clinic for emotional disturbance, but not involved in stealing. Along with social worker and psychiatric assessments based on interviews with the children and parents, Bowlby found that 14 of the thieves were classified as being 'affectionless', as they seemed to lack affection for others and showed no shame or responsibility for their actions. In the control group, no boys were classified as affectionless.

Of the 44 juvenile thieves, 17 had experienced prolonged separation of more than six months before the age of six. Only two of the control group had experienced similar separation. The most important finding was that, of the 17 thieves who had experienced maternal deprivation, 12 were also classified as affectionless, i.e. 12 out of the 14 boys who were classified as affectionless had also suffered deprivation.

◆ Conclusion

Maternal deprivation experienced when young affects later adult behaviour, causing such emotional issues as a lack of guilt and affection, and the potential therefore for criminality.

◆ Evaluation

- Case studies such as this are valid in the sense that they are detailed and a rich source of information about the effects of privation. Different methods were used to establish validity through triangulation. But the case study method can be criticised for lacking generalisability as its findings are unique to that case.
- Research into deprivation has highlighted the importance of understanding the cause of the separation, rather than focusing on the absence of a parent. Bowlby suggested that separation caused an affectionless character but did not explain the reasons for the separation in the first place. It might be that the factor that caused the separation led to problems later in life. This is a problem with correlational studies. They identify a possible link between two factors, in this case maternal deprivation and an affectionless character, but there may be reasons for this personality type other than the factor being studied.
- Only 17 of the thieves had suffered deprivation. This means that 27 had not suffered deprivation. Bowlby cannot conclude that maternal deprivation caused delinquency in the light of his findings.

Taking it further

A documentary about Genie can be found in parts on the following web pages:
Part 1: http://www.youtube.com/watch?v=iptOpjz0mwg&feature=related
Part 2: http://www.youtube.com/watch?v=nha-IGE_wjo
Part 3: http://www.youtube.com/watch?v=lxUBkKN0z_k&feature=related
Part 4: http://www.youtube.com/watch?v=lcEEvNFNETM&feature=related
Part 5: http://www.youtube.com/watch?v=rsRr9COltp0
Part 6: http://www.youtube.com/watch?v=3NGUP_JSRic&feature=related

Taking it further

Find out about a few of the juvenile delinquents Bowlby interviewed at http://www.simplypsychology.pwp.blueyonder.co.uk/Bowlby%2044%20Thieves.pdf

Other options

Belsky and Rovine's (1988) daycare study combined the findings of two American longitudinal studies to investigate the effects of daycare on children's development. Using the strange situation to determine attachment type, they concluded that children who experienced long hours of daycare (20 hours or more) in the first year of life had more insecure attachments. Further information can be found at http://www.ncbi.nlm.nih.gov/pubmed/3342709

Rutter and the English and Romanian Adoptees study team (1998) studied 111 Romanian children adopted by English families at or before the age of two. Compared with a control group of English adoptees, the Romanian children had caught up developmentally by the age of four due to enriched environments. More about this study can be found at http://www.ycc.ac.uk/yc/new/HUMSOC/psycho/unit1/rutter.htm

Evidence in practice

What you need to know

- Describe one key issue in child psychology and apply it to content you have studied.

Key issue: The effects of daycare

Bowlby would predict that children in daycare have less opportunity to form attachments, particularly if staff turnover is high and the attention is shared with other children, and suffer maternal deprivation. However, daycare can have positive effects, such as the opportunity to form peer attachments and develop social skills. Daycare environments are stimulating and structured to encourage cognitive abilities, and daycare providers have trained staff in care and education. For a detailed discussion of daycare, see pages 44-45.

Summary of studies into the effects of daycare

Research study	Positive effects of daycare
Andersson (1992)	Followed 119 Swedish children throughout their first 8 years of life. Andersson found that children who entered daycare early were rated by their teachers as more advanced socially than children of late entry or home cared. They had more friends and were more outgoing because daycare had provided early opportunity to develop social skills. However, it should be noted that Swedish daycare is particularly well-funded.
Burchinal et al. (2000)	Longitudinal study found that high-quality care (smaller groups and better qualified staff) showed positive effects on language and cognitive ability.
Howes (1988)	Longitudinal study found that high-quality care led to happier, more considerate and less shy children.
Campbell et al. and Ramey (2001)	Abecedarian Project followed 104 poor African American minority children who attended intensive high-quality daycare. They found that improved cognitive and academic ability persisted until the age of 21 years.
Research study	**No effects of daycare**
Clarke-Stewart et al. (1994)	Found no difference in the type of attachment formed with parents whether the child spent a little or longer hours in daycare.
Research study	**Negative effects of daycare**
Belsky and Rovine (1988)	Found that children who spent longer hours in daycare at an earlier age had more insecure attachments with their parents.
Ruhm (2004)	Found that daycare had a negative effect on later verbal ability, reading and maths skills at school.
NICHD Early Childcare Research (1991)	Found that children who attended high-quality daycare performed better academically at school, but entered school with more behavioural problems (aggression) than home-cared children.

◆ Introduction to the practical

You need to select, review and examine two sources linked to the key issue or topic you have studied. To guide you through the process, this section will follow an example of a source linked to the issue of daycare. You can use sources from newspapers, magazines, websites or TV programmes/videos. Stick to credible sources that you can trust to give you accurate information.

◆ Summarising sources

Follow these steps:

1. Read through the source to get the overall gist or meaning of the article and highlight the main points.
2. Make a list or draw a diagram of the key points.
3. Write a concise summary from your key points.
4. Ignore information that is not relevant to the overall meaning of the article.
5. Acknowledge the source you have used at the end of your summary.

Other options

You could study how the effects of deprivation could be alleviated (see page 39). Another key issue you might choose is whether autism has a biological explanation (see pages 42-43). You might wish to construct a 'for and against' argument for this issue.

Nursery children arrive at school with bad attitude – and it rubs off

The negative effects on children's behaviour of full-time nursery care also act upon their classmates when they start school, research suggests. Jay Belsky, the director of the Institute for the Study of Children, Families and Social Issues at Birkbeck University, London, who led the study, said: "Being in a classroom with a high proportion of children who have extensive childcare histories affects those with little or no early childcare experience. "So if your child had no childcare, but ended up in a class where lots of children had childcare, your child ends up being more aggressive. There is a contagious effect," he said.

Professor Belsky studied a US sample of 3,400 five-year-olds enrolled in 282 kindergarten classes – the equivalent of reception class in Britain. The children's parents were interviewed and their teachers completed a questionnaire to measure for each child the frequency of arguing, fighting, getting angry, acting impulsively and disturbing classroom activities. The children's competence in reading, maths and general knowledge were combined to give an overall score of academic achievement. These measures were taken in the autumn and again the following spring.

The researchers found that children placed in childcare of any kind, and for longer hours and at earlier ages, displayed significantly more problem behaviour. Those who had spent more time in nursery had better academic scores, although this effect wore off for children in nursery for more than 30 hours a week.

Beverley Hughes, the Children's Minister, said that it should not be assumed that findings from the US would apply equally to Britain. "Evidence from this country suggests that the impact on children of childcare is crucially dependent on quality and the length of time children spend in it," she said. "We know that when childcare is of high quality and led by well-qualified staff, and when children do not spend overly long in it, then the overall benefits are positive."

She conceded that British evidence suggested a small negative impact on social behaviour for some children from long hours in childcare.

◆ Linking ideas

The article presents the view that long hours in daycare has negative consequences. These findings can be linked to the following:

- deprivation
- maternal deprivation
- Ainsworth's strange situation
- Bowlby's (1946) 44 juvenile thieves study
- Bowlby's theory of attachment
- separation anxiety
- positive and negative effects of daycare on social, emotional and intellectual development
- Belsky and Rovine's (1988) daycare study.

◆ Methodology

Belsky's research findings documented in the article used **questionnaires** and **interviews** with parents and teachers of the children studied. The findings of such surveys are often criticised for being unreliable and subjective. Parents and teachers may have a biased view of a child or their behaviour, and this will influence their responses to questions. The researchers could also be biased as they may interpret the responses in a way that supports their views on daycare. This is known as researcher bias.

◆ Ethics

The research in the article was conducted by professional psychologists. However, the way in which the research is used by the article poses an ethical issue. As psychologists, we have a moral duty to present the findings of research in a responsible way. This article presents daycare in a negative way and it could be used to blame parents for the behaviour of their children. Also, consider how a parent who uses daycare might feel after reading the article.

Examiner's tip

You may be asked to describe and comment on the two sources used in the exam. Make sure you can say where the sources were from and how they are relevant to the topic.

Over to you

Write a short paragraph summarising the study from the key points you have made. Draw a conclusion from your main points.

AS check

How to conduct a survey and an evaluation of interviews and questionnaires is covered in the Social Approach (AS pages 8-11). You could use this knowledge to assess the credibility of the research by Belsky in the article.

Summary

Look back at the list of key terms for child psychology on page 27 and check you can define and use them all effectively.

◆ Methodology

- Describe and evaluate the observation (structured and naturalistic) and the case study as research methods used in child psychology.
- Consider these research methods in terms of their use in child psychology and in terms of reliability, validity and ethical issues.
- Describe and evaluate longitudinal and cross-cultural ways of studying children in psychology.

Note: You may be asked to draw upon your knowledge of other research methods and relate them to their use in child psychology.

◆ Content

- Describe and evaluate Bowlby's theory of attachment.
- Describe and evaluate Ainsworth's attachment research using the strange situation.
- Describe and evaluate cross-cultural research into attachment types and child-rearing styles.
- Describe and evaluate research into deprivation.
- Describe and evaluate research into privation and whether the effects can be reversed.
- Describe the characteristics of one developmental disorder (e.g. autism) and describe two explanations of the disorder and two ways it can affect a child's development.
- Describe and evaluate research into daycare, including one study that shows positive effects and one that show negative effects.

◆ Studies

- Describe and evaluate the study by Curtiss (1977) – Genie: a case study of extreme privation.
- Plus one of:
  - Bowlby's (1946) 44 juvenile thieves study
  - Belsky and Rovine's (1988) study of attachment type and daycare
  - Rutter and the ERA team's (1998) study of adopted children from Romania.

◆ Evidence in practice

- Describe one key issue in child psychology from the content you have studied.
- Conduct a content analysis on this key issue or a summary of two articles on a topic you have studied in child psychology.
- From either the content analysis or summary, draw conclusions and explain your findings, drawing upon concepts, theories and research you have studied.

Note: You must conduct one content analysis and one summary of two articles in your course.

Examzone

*1. Define the following terms:
   i Attachment
   ii Deprivation
   iii Privation (3 marks)

*2. Ainsworth classified different attachment types using the strange situation. Describe the behaviour of the children she observed in each attachment type, making it clear which type you are referring to. (6 marks)

3. Evaluate the use of the longitudinal method of studying children's development. (4 marks)

4. Nikita and Shaun have decided to separate and are considering divorce. They have a small child named Joel to consider, and are worried about any lasting effects their separation may have on him. Using your knowledge of research you have studied in child psychology, outline the advice you might offer Nikita and Shaun to reduce the effects of separation on Joel. (6 marks)

5. Nazam has been told that his son may have autism. Outline two ways in which his son's development is likely to be affected and describe two explanations for autism. (12 marks)

3. Health psychology

What you will learn about in this chapter

- The nature of substance misuse.
- How biological, social and psychological factors play a role in drug use and addiction.
- The role of biological, social and psychological factors in treating substance misuse.
- Research methods using humans and animals to investigate drug use.

Key terms

- substance misuse
- synapse
- tolerance
- physical dependence
- psychological dependence
- withdrawal

What is health psychology?

Health psychology aims to study how and why people behave in an unhealthy manner, and the methods that can be employed to persuade people to pursue a healthier course of action. It combines the study of the biological bases of behaviour, the way cognition affects the way we behave and the social aspects of behaviour. A key aspect of behaviour which can damage health is the taking of recreational drugs. Health psychology seeks to understand that behaviour.

Substance misuse

Substance misuse is the intake of drugs in quantities that are potentially damaging to physical or mental health. In this chapter, the substances you will learn about are all psychoactive (or recreational) drugs. That means that the chemicals affect the mind.

Biological aspects of drug use

A synapse is the junction between two neurons. Neurotransmitters are released by the neuron on one side of the gap and then taken up by the neuron on the other side. This is how messages are passed within the brain. Psychoactive drugs produce their effect by changing how this operates. If that effect is pleasant, the drug taker is likely to take the drug again. However, repeatedly taking the drug may cause physical dependence. At this point, not taking the drug produces unpleasant symptoms because the body can no longer function normally without the drug being present.

AS check

You learned about synapses and neurotransmitters in the Biological Approach (AS page 104).

Psychological aspects of drug use

People take drugs for the psychological effects they experience – drugs alter feelings, reactions and behaviour. Repeated use of a drug can lead to psychological dependence on it because the individual believes they cannot manage without the drug.

Social aspects of drug use

People often start using drugs for social reasons. Pressure from friends or peer group can be a powerful influence, as the drug-taking behaviour can be seen as normal in that situation and the individual doesn't want to feel left out. If drug taking always takes place in a particular social setting, it can also make breaking the habit much harder unless that social setting can be avoided.

These aspects of substance misuse will be examined in more detail in this chapter.

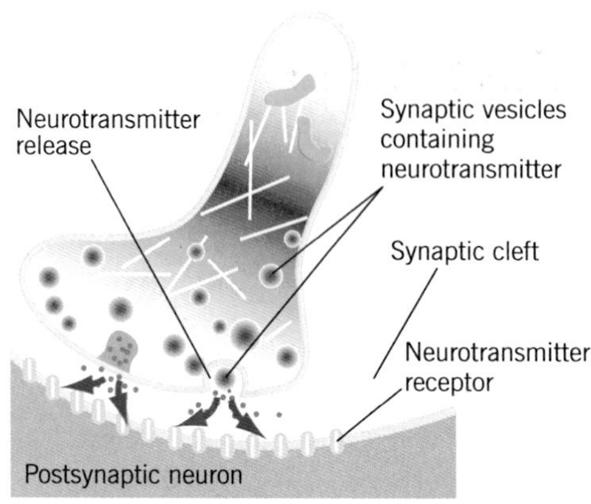

▲ Synaptic transmission.

Methodology

What you need to know

- Describe and evaluate the use of animals in laboratory studies when researching into drugs.
- Describe and evaluate two research methods using humans to study the effects of drugs.
- Evaluate, including practical and ethical strengths and weaknesses, research methods using animals.
- Evaluate, including issues of reliability and validity, research methods using humans.

Laboratory studies using animals

Animals are often used to investigate the psychological effects of drugs. These are usually laboratory studies so that conditions can be carefully controlled and the researchers can manipulate an independent variable and measure its effect on the dependent variable. Animals have been used to study the effects of drugs, levels of addictiveness, short and long-term consequences of drug use, as well as the effectiveness of some types of therapy. Most studies look at changes in behaviour as a consequence of the administration of a drug, though there are a few that test which areas of the brain are needed to produce the effects of a drug by the selective lesioning or **ablation** of specific parts of the brain.

The following study serves to raise many of the reasons why animal research is useful, but also why the results must be treated with great caution.

Schramm-Sapyta et al. (2008) investigated the possible origins of alcohol abuse. Adolescent male rats were placed in cages for 16 hours a day for three consecutive days with the only liquid on offer being alcohol (equivalent in strength to very strong beer). Afterwards the rats were given a choice between water and alcohol. Rats given alcohol as adolescents consumed more alcohol more frequently than rats not given such early exposure. The researchers concluded that, in rats, early exposure to alcohol is a predictor for later heavier consumption of alcohol.

Aversion therapy: the use of animal research

Research showed that rats made to feel sick when consuming sweetened water later avoided sweetened water. This demonstrated learning by association and provided evidence for aversion therapy to treat alcoholics. (You have already learned about aversion therapy in the Learning Approach AS page 138).

Evaluating the Schramm-Sapyta study

Showing a link between early exposure to alcohol and later alcohol consumption in rats is useful in pointing at an area where human evidence can now be gathered, to see if similar findings are likely. Allowing a sample of teenage humans to consume nothing but alcohol for three days is neither practical nor ethical, so the advantages of conducting such an experiment on rats are clear. If alcohol consumption is likely to have lasting negative effects, many would argue it is better that the study is conducted on rats instead of humans.

Evaluating the use of animal research

Practical strengths

- Animals for research are raised in controlled environments so the effects of prior experiences have been controlled.
- Conditions during the research can be more precisely controlled.
- Laboratory species tend to have much shorter life spans than humans, allowing life span effects to be more easily monitored.
- Animals that are genetically similar can be tested in different conditions, so removing the genetic variable.
- Animal research is usually cheaper (as the amount of a drug needed is less), time scales are shorter and adequate conditions and welfare are also less expensive than for humans.
- Results can be used to produce a model of how addiction may happen that can then be investigated in humans under less rigorous conditions.

Taking it further

Rats are a favourite laboratory animal. For something small, furry and not a primate they are very like humans in some important ways that makes them useful in psychological studies. Investigate the reasons why they are so useful. Online encyclopaedias are a good starting point.

Practical weaknesses

- There is no guarantee that what happens in rats will occur in humans, so findings from animal research can only be applied to humans with great caution.

- It cannot be used to explain the interaction between experiences, genetics and drugs found in human use.
- The financial benefits of using animals may be spurious if the results cannot be generalised.
- Cues present in the environment can make people respond more or less quickly to a drug and even make a normally 'safe' level of intake lethal. This cannot be investigated using animals.

Animal studies raise many ethical issues and it is important to be aware of the difference between the ethical standards required when dealing with animals and humans.

Ethical strengths

- Studies that are ethically impossible on humans can be conducted on animals, as animals can be seen as expendable.
- If there are long-term negative consequences of a drug, it is thought better for a non-human animal to be affected than a human.
- Provided the ethical guidelines for animal research are adhered to, then animal research tends to be more straightforward than similar research on humans.
- In Britain, the use of animals in laboratories is monitored and regulated by Home Office licence, so checks on the welfare of animals are more likely than on the welfare of human participants.

Ethical weaknesses

- A study may be ethically preferable but useless because of species differences, so animals may have suffered for no good purpose.
- Causing harm to non-human animals instead of humans is speciesism according to Ryder. If researchers are not willing to conduct the research on humans it should not be done.
- Ethical guidelines do not, according to some people, go far enough in protecting animals.

Should animal research be conducted?

When evaluating animal research it is important to consider both the arguments for and the arguments against such research. Negative aspects have to be weighed against the potential benefits such knowledge brings. There is no right or wrong answer in the question of whether to use animals instead of humans. It is an issue that divides people. What is important is to ensure you consider all the arguments both for and against when you are answering questions on this topic.

◀ Rats kept in a laboratory.

Examiner's tip

Remember that, to gain credit, studies must be related to the psychological effects of drugs; medical studies gain no credit. For example, an alcohol study looking at the potential risks for addiction (psychological) is fine, but one that looks at the dangers of cirrhosis of the liver (medical) would get no credit.

Taking it further

Some studies into the effects of psychoactive drugs destroy a very specific area of the brain to discover what role it has in mediating the effect of the drug. Find out more about research into drugs using lesioning and ablation on animals.

AS check

Laboratory studies have already been described and evaluated as a method in the Cognitive Approach (AS page 40) and the Learning Approach (AS page 131).

Taking it further

Attitudes towards drugs are constantly changing, as is our understanding of both the physical and psychological effects of a particular drug. Assess the reasons why some drugs are legal, others not, and why drug classifications vary. Be aware that reasons are not just medical or psychological.

AS check

Longitudinal studies have already been described and evaluated in the Psychodynamic Approach (AS pages 78-79).

Human research in health psychology

As the evaluation points on animal studies identified, one key problem is whether the results can be applied to humans. It is therefore essential that research on human participants is also used to provide evidence.

Laboratory studies

Many laboratory studies using human participants aim to investigate the effects of drugs on mental and physical processes. Data gained from such studies is used to further our understanding of the nature of a psychoactive drug. Objective, quantitative measurements include brain scans as well as behavioural measurements, such as speed of reaction time or accuracy in completing a cognitive task. Qualitative measurements are most likely to be the reports of the experience collected from participants.

There are also many laboratory studies that use participants who are regular drug users. Many of these people are addicts. These studies aim to understand the mechanisms of addiction, tolerance and withdrawal. They are also often the first stage in developing programmes used to treat substance misuse, for example Comer et al. (1997) used a laboratory-based token economy system to reduce drug taking in heroin addicts.

Evaluation

Strengths

- Participants can produce qualitative data by reporting how a drug makes them feel. This cannot be measured by quantitative methods.
- The well-controlled environment means that drug quantities and measurable effects can be seen to be objective and reliable.
- Data collected in laboratory studies on humans has given a much clearer idea of the effect of drugs on human performance compared with animal studies.
- Laboratory studies are the best way to systematically investigate the effects of a drug, as all other factors are held constant.
- Studies using drug addicts have allowed a better understanding of the mechanisms of dependence, tolerance and withdrawal, as mechanisms may be different in other species and field studies have too many uncontrolled variables.

Weaknesses

- What one participant means by a description may not be the same as someone else means, so it is impossible to know if qualitative data is reliable.
- A laboratory is a very different environment from a social situation so the experiences are very different, causing validity to be reduced.
- In the past, some laboratory studies have laid participants open to addiction, which is why people who are already addicted are used in modern research.
- It is possible that the responses of an addict to a drug may be very different from those of a non-drug user, so generalisation may be invalid.

Surveys

Another data-collection method that can be used in drug research is surveys. These may be interviews or questionnaires and they are often used as part of a longitudinal design where, in order to understand the nature of dependency and addiction, researchers follow a group of people over time. Longitudinal research is important if the repercussions of long-term drug use are to be understood, and questionnaires or interviews tend to be the only practical way of collecting data from the large sample often necessary in such research.

Questions may focus on possible causes of addiction, such as education, social situations and opportunities. They can also be used to investigate attitudes towards treating addiction, rates of relapse or recovery.

Some studies follow a sample from childhood through to middle age to see what factors are associated with becoming a drug user. Studies start by interviewing parents, move on to interviews with both parents and children then, as they move into adulthood, focus entirely on the children.

Evaluation

Strengths

- Data has high ecological validity because it relates to real experiences in the real world rather than the artificiality of the laboratory study.
- Researchers can ask about long-term effects, experiences or causes, so there can be a great deal of breadth and depth in the information.
- If questionnaires are used the sample size can be very large, so the conclusions drawn have a better chance of being relevant to the wider population.
- Qualitative data on respondents' perceptions provides a rich source of detailed information.

Weaknesses

- Large-scale questionnaires rely on mail-shots, which tend to produce a biased sample as busy people do not reply, so the results may not be representative of the wider population.
- People are not always honest in their replies, either giving socially desirable answers or being too embarrassed to own up to the truth.
- Responses about past experiences may be inaccurate if collected many years later, as memory is fallible.
- However, if participants are followed over many years to avoid forgetting, drop-out rates and intervening events may create distortions in the data collected.

Have you ever wondered?

How do researchers recruit participants for longitudinal studies? One particularly interesting one is the 'Woodlawn Study', which was started in 1973 and is still going strong. Use an internet search engine to find out about this project. Discuss the problems associated with such studies.

Content

What you need to know

- Two explanations of substance misuse, one from the Biological Approach and one from the Learning Approach.
- A comparison of the relative strengths and weaknesses of these two explanations.

Explanations of substance misuse

Both nature and nurture have a role to play in understanding substance misuse. The processes of dependency – how difficult someone finds it to cope without another fix – and withdrawal – the effects of coming off a drug – are similar for everyone. However, the experiences of dependency and withdrawal do differ between people and it seems likely that this is because nature and nurture modify these experiences.

Biological explanations

When an individual takes a drug that alters the availability of one or more neurotransmitters, it affects mood or behaviour. **Depressant** drugs slow the brain's activity by making transmission of messages between neurons less effective, whereas **stimulants** make the stimulation of one neuron by another easier.

Repeated use of any drug has the potential to change the chemical balances within the brain. This is because the level of neurotransmitters in the brain is regulated by feedback systems to prevent over- or under-production. When a person takes a **psychoactive drug** which artificially changes this level, the mechanisms in the brain adjust the level of natural production. The person then needs to carry on taking the drug so they can function normally, by maintaining neurotransmitter substances within the normal range for healthy functioning.

Evaluation

Strengths

- Withdrawal symptoms support the biological viewpoint that the brain is relying on the drug to function normally, as symptoms are of a severe deficit of the relevant neurotransmitter.
- There is a strong positive correlation between diagnosis of psychosis and heavy use of cocaine and/or amphetamines, suggesting that the drugs are inducing psychosis.
- Self-report evidence from drug users shows the development of psychological need correlates positively with physiological measurements of dependency.

Weaknesses

- There are large individual differences in whether a person becomes an addict. According to the biological explanation everyone is at risk of misuse developing yet, in the case of a common drug such as alcohol, for example, the majority of adults in Britain use the drug but only a minority misuse it.
- Cultural norms and peer-group influences play a major role in the likelihood of misuse occurring, as well as decisions about the drug of choice.
- If biological factors were what determine the amount required for a fix, overdosing because of **context dependency** would not occur. Overdosing on a normal-sized fix of heroin while in police custody is believed to be caused by the mismatch between the fix and context cues.

Nature

Our nature is determined by our biology, and is a result of our genes, the chemical balance in our body and the way these are expressed. There is evidence that some aspects of our personality are due to our genes. If so, people who are very strong-minded and find kicking a habit easy may be able to do this because of their genes.

Nurture

Experiences influence us even before we are born and right through our lives. Nurture refers to the way these experiences change and shape who we are and how we behave. Our parents and peers are of great importance. The social support we gain from those around us can make it much easier or harder to resist or take up drugs.

Have you ever wondered?

Alco-pops have caused great concern because of their high usage by young drinkers. They are more addictive than most other alcohol because of the combination of a high sugar content and alcohol in the form of spirits. Spirits are absorbed into the blood stream very quickly so give the brain the alcohol buzz very rapidly. The sugar gives a sugar fix, which is also very reinforcing. This means the drinker gets strong reinforcement from the effects of drinking an alco-pop very quickly.

AS check

The Learning Approach offers three explanations for substance misuse: operant conditioning, positive reinforcement (though this can also form part of the operant conditioning explanation), and social learning theory. See AS pages 136-137 for the principles.

Operant conditioning is also important in both starting and maintaining drug taking. Initially people usually start taking drugs because they enjoy the effect.

▲ The social context can be very important in decisions about drug taking.

◆ Learning explanations

Positive reinforcement is effective at explaining the early stages of drug taking – it is rewarding because it produces pleasurable and desired feelings, so the behaviour is likely to recur. This is short-term reinforcement, as the effect wears off relatively quickly. Another factor is the social approval of friends, which again positively reinforces the taking of drugs, and a further social factor may be that a young person feels more 'grown-up' because they are taking a drug.

Maintenance of drug taking and the development of substance misuse is seen as more to do with negative reinforcement. As the effect of the drug starts to wear off, it can be very unpleasant; taking more of the drug stops these negative experiences occurring. Drug taking is therefore negatively reinforced.

◆ Evaluation

Strengths

- It can explain why different cultures tend to see the misuse of different substances, as people will be more likely to try a drug seen as 'cool' in their culture in order to gain more social reinforcement
- Many drugs are known to produce a strong immediate effect which will positively reinforce use and help induce a 'taste' for the drug.

Weaknesses

- Not everyone succumbs to social pressure to participate (e.g. in heavy drinking), so operant conditioning cannot explain why some people resist social approval of drug taking.
- Some drugs produce unpleasant side effects when first taken which should put users off, yet many persist into addiction (e.g. nicotine).

Social learning theory

Social learning theory suggests that, if an individual observes a role model taking a drug, this can influence them to also take the drug. Whether the model appears to find the drug taking rewarding will also influence whether they are copied. It is just as likely that substance misuse is influenced by social learning as any other behaviour. However, as with any behaviour, other factors are likely to modify the impact of the model's behaviour.

Comparison of Biological and Learning explanations

Biological explanations help us to understand physiological dependence better than learning explanations because they show how changes in neurotransmitter levels cause addiction. In contrast, learning explanations are better at understanding psychological dependence as they deal with reasons people may find the prospect of coping without the drug very distressing.

Biological explanations show misuse can appear in someone who has no contact with other drug users as the explanation only requires exposure to the drug. Social learning requires contact with others to act as models.

Learning theory explains better why someone might start taking a drug because they will be influenced by the social context and reinforcement in the early stages. However, biological explanations explain chronic use better because they can explain why an addict needs to continue (due to the changes in the brain).

Both use the unpleasantness of withdrawal to explain addiction – the biological explanation through the impact of reduced levels of the neurotransmitters and brain mechanisms, and the Learning Approach because the effects produce a negative reinforcer that needs to be removed.

The Biological Approach explains why drug use and misuse are found in all cultures as everyone is equally susceptible regardless of culture. However, the Learning Approach is necessary to explain variability in the choice of drugs depending on culture and historical context, as this is influenced by those around us and what is available.

Examiner's tip

You might be asked in the exam to evaluate explanations by comparing them. Some candidates find these questions quite difficult but it is often just a matter of practice. One way to compare is to start by giving a similarity, then go on to explain in detail where the explanations start to differ. For example, both Biological and Learning explanations agree that withdrawal is very unpleasant. However, why this is so and what the repercussions are for an addict are very different.

How drugs work

What you need to know

- For heroin and one other drug (chosen from alcohol, cocaine, ecstasy, marijuana, nicotine), describe the mode of action, the effects, tolerance (or absence of tolerance), physical and psychological dependencies, and withdrawal.

AS check

You need to be clear how a synapse works (see AS page 104).

Neurotransmitters

The following will help you understand the action of psychoactive drugs.

Dopamine: Insufficient dopamine produces the symptoms of Parkinson's disease, while an excess is associated with paranoia. It is one of the neurotransmitters related to 'feeling good' as a pulse of activity through the dopamine system in the brain is linked to feeling happy, even euphoric. This is called the reward system.

Noradrenalin: Noradrenalin in the bloodstream is linked with adrenalin in the fight-flight mechanism. It is also found in the brain as a neurotransmitter, where it boosts attention and our ability to focus and is also linked to mood, with low levels of activity being linked to depression and vice versa.

Serotonin: This is closely linked to emotions and there is evidence that an incorrect level can make the individual feel depressed or angry and aggressive.

Endorphins: The body's natural opiates, they have two different effects. Firstly they are inhibitory neurotransmitters, occupying and therefore blocking receptor sites for pain. They also make us feel good through the stimulation of the dopamine reward cycle.

Acetylcholine: Lowered levels of acetylcholine are thought to be the reason for memory problems in old age and Alzheimer's disease as it assists the ability of synapses to modify and change (necessary if new memories are to be created). It makes synaptic transmission easier and stimulates the dopamine reward system.

GABA: This is the most important inhibitory neurotransmitter. It makes it more difficult for messages to be transmitted from one synapse to another. It slows neural activity so is referred to as a depressant.

Psychoactive drugs produce changes in the brain by affecting the action of neurotransmitters the chemicals used to transmit message across the synapses. The main ones you need to know about are described in the panel.

Heroin

Mode of action

Heroin mimics endorphin. During everyday activity a moderate amount of endorphin is naturally produced, causing the release of dopamine and facilitating the reward systems within the brain. If the body is put under stress and pain, receptors are stimulated and the level of endorphins is increased. These lock onto the receptor sites that transmit information about pain, blocking the brain's ability to register pain. Heroin acts like a massive release of endorphin into the brain. The heroin floods the endorphin receptors, stimulating the two actions of endorphins. Large quantities of dopamine are released, activating the reward system and producing feelings of well-being.

Short-term effects

Heroin rapidly produces a feeling of euphoria. The analgesic effect gives a feeling of calm and aches or pains will disappear. Heroin depresses most of the body's activity, so breathing becomes slower and shallower, heart rate slows and the user feels sleepy and very relaxed. Peripheral blood vessels dilate causing the user to feel flushed, warm and sweaty. When someone first takes heroin they are likely to feel that they want to vomit. However heroin depresses the activity of the vomiting centre in the brain, so the feeling of nausea gradually decreases as the effect of the heroin builds up.

Tolerance

Heroin's pain-killing effects and euphoria develop **tolerance** very quickly. Studies have shown dosage rates can increase tenfold in three to four months (Griffiths, Bigelow and Henningfield, 1980). Regular users take heroin at a level high enough to kill a non-user. The slowing-down effect on the body's mechanisms does not develop tolerance. Thus heart rate stays low, causing low blood pressure, breathing is depressed and, because the digestive system is underactive, the user may be permanently constipated. Sex drive is also likely to be very low.

Physiological and psychological dependencies

Physiological dependence develops very quickly. One fix can produce withdrawal symptoms if more is not taken within 12 hours. This does not mean the person is an addict immediately, as withdrawal symptoms at this stage are very mild. The brain rapidly gets used to the influx of heroin stimulating the dopamine reward system and flooding the pain receptor sites.

Soon, physiological dependence is established as the addict takes fixes to avoid the increasingly severe withdrawal symptoms. As tolerance builds the amount taken increases, dependency gets greater and withdrawal symptoms worsen.

As physiological dependence gets greater, psychologically the prospect of coping without a fix feels worse. Psychological dependence means the addict ceases to be concerned with maintaining contact with family and friends; the focus of life becomes finding the next fix. Even an addict with readily-available supplies can become progressively less satisfied with other aspects of life. When not in the immediate effects of a fix the addict tends to feel increasingly confused, anxious, restless and possibly paranoid, psychological symptoms that can only be alleviated by more heroin or treatment.

Taking it further

Portrayals of withdrawal on film tend to show the effects on those with a very heavy addiction, because the symptoms are the most dramatic. In all addictions the level of use influences the level of withdrawal symptoms. Look up on the Internet accounts of withdrawal by former addicts, to find out how accurate your own image of withdrawal is.

Withdrawal

Withdrawal symptom severity is directly related to addiction level. Symptoms start 6-12 hours after the last fix. Failure to take a fix causes the symptoms to increase and the addict becomes agitated and often very aggressive. Symptoms peak after 26-72 hours. Most symptoms are over in a week. First the person becomes agitated and restless, they alternate between feeling hot and cold and the skin develops goose bumps (the phase known as cold turkey). Breathing becomes short and jerky. They may then sleep for up to 12 hours. They will wake to cramps, vomiting, diarrhoea, sweating, shaking and twitching of the limbs. This gradually subsides.

Alcohol

Mode of action

Alcohol depresses activity in the brain by making GABA more effective, slowing down the speed with which messages are transmitted between neurons. Even though alcohol makes people feel more confident, it is termed a depressant because of this effect on brain activity. It reduces the effectiveness of the inhibitory mechanisms that ensure we behave in a socially acceptable way and also anaesthetises nerve endings at noradrenalin synapses so they become less effective. Noradrenalin synapses trigger the flight-fight mechanism. Alcohol does not just prevent the improvement of the reflexes that these synapses would bring, it also slows the reflexes because of the increased effectiveness of the GABA system. This explains why the ability to respond in an emergency is impaired, even when the amount of alcohol in the body is quite low.

GABA = gamma-aminobutyric acid

Short-term effects

Low to moderate levels of alcohol dilate skin blood vessels; users feel warm and look flushed. Reactions slow down, and at higher levels perception and speech are affected. Alcohol reduces people's inhibitions as it targets the social control areas of the brain. Reduced effectiveness of these inhibitory mechanisms leads initially to relaxed, confident behaviour but can develop into exhibitionism and extreme behaviour at higher levels. The depression of activity in the frontal lobes affects motor skills and co-ordination. Dehydration occurs because the hormone controlling urination is inhibited by alcohol – as blood alcohol levels fall, urination increases as a rebound effect. Dehydration is the main cause of hangovers, at worst causin the brain to lose up to a fifth of its weight.

Tolerance

Alcohol affects behaviour rapidly, and just a small amount produces measurable effects. However, short-term tolerance also develops quickly, so that, as blood alcohol level drops, the individual feels sober before they actually are.

Alcohol consumption stimulates the body to produce an enzyme that breaks alcohol down more quickly – in just a few weeks a drinker will need to consume about 50% more alcohol to achieve the same effect. Behavioural tolerance is largely a result of practice because the individual becomes better at coping with the side effects and appearing less drunk.

Have you ever wondered?

More drivers fail a breathalyser test in the morning rush hour than after the pubs close. Why do you think that might be?

Examiner's tip

When revising tolerance, physiological dependency, psychological dependency and withdrawal, try to ensure you can make four or five separate points about each of these for each drug you learn about.

Physiological and psychological dependencies

Physiological dependency is characterised by a lack of concern for the type of alcohol consumed – in extreme cases alcoholics are known to drink industrial alcohol, which can cause death. They often want to start drinking early in the day as they have withdrawal symptoms such as irritability or shaking. The first drink alleviates these symptoms, so fuelling psychological dependence. The alcoholic cannot restrict their alcohol intake as the physiological need is constant; indeed many are unable to stop on a particular day until they pass out.

Psychological dependency is exhibited by relief at finding a drink, or avoiding 'dry' situations. Getting access to alcohol is put above other activities, including socialising, eating and hygiene. Many consume excessive amounts because of problems in their personal lives and alcoholic oblivion is welcomed as a 'coping' strategy. With increased use the alcoholic becomes psychologically dependent on the alcohol, paradoxically seeing it as a way out of their problems.

Withdrawal

Withdrawal symptoms depend largely on the level of use and addiction. They are influenced by two factors peculiar to alcohol. Firstly, habituation to the level of alcohol is extremely fast both physiologically and psychologically within a drinking bout. Secondly, following a drinking bout the feeling of sobering up occurs much more quickly than the actual physiological process.

Symptoms usually appear 8-12 hours after the last drink, though this can take as long as a week. The individual will become agitated, and may have a range of symptoms including uncontrollable shaking, cramp, nausea, sweating, irregular heartbeat and vivid dreaming. Symptoms can last up to 48 hours.

In people with a heavy addiction the effects of withdrawal are known as delirium tremens (DTs). It is not uncommon for heavy users to experience DTs while still drinking. This is because the **habituation** is happening faster than the intake of alcohol, so the alcoholic experiences withdrawal even while drinking. With DTs, the brain habituates to the effect of the alcohol on GABA receptors, and therefore has a less efficient GABA system. Unless enough alcohol is present to depress brain activity, the flight-fight mechanism starts operating at too high a level, producing symptoms including hallucinations, tremors and delusions, even seizures. Untreated withdrawal is fatal in about a third of cases. Even with early treatment about 5% of patients are likely to die.

Other options

Cocaine affects the uptake of serotonin, dopamine and noradrenalin. It causes the user to feel alert and awake, even euphoric. Repeated use leads to rapid dependency, both physiological and psychological. Long-term abuse can lead to permanent depression and paranoia.

Ecstasy increases energy and positive feelings by increasing the availability of serotonin and dopamine. Dependency is psychological rather than physiological.

Marijuana: The psychoactive substances and mode of action of marijuana have only been known for a few years. There is a lot of disagreement about the effects and possible dangers of long-term marijuana use.

Nicotine

Mode of action

Nicotine stimulates acetylcholine (ACh) synapses that are associated with thinking and learning, so explaining the alertness and ability to react faster reported by smokers. This activates the dopamine reward system. Endorphins are stimulated, producing a feeling of well-being. Nicotine can cross the boundary into the brain's blood supply extremely quickly, typically within 7 seconds of inhalation, making the effect almost instantaneous. It also stimulates the production of glucose and adrenalin. The glucose production raises the blood sugar levels and so inhibits appetite. The influx of adrenalin into the bloodstream further raises the levels of alertness and helps to sustain this feeling for a longer period.

Short-term effects

Smokers feel more relaxed almost immediately upon inhalation. This seems contradictory as nicotine is a stimulant, increasing both physiological and psychological **arousal**. Part of the reason for this paradox is the reduction of stress experienced when nicotine deprivation is relieved. The feeling of pleasure, as the reward system is stimulated, also makes the addict feel more relaxed. These effects happen with every puff, so smoking is intensely rewarding.

The increase in glucose and adrenalin raises energy levels and alertness, so helping to increase performance. Smoking also increases the levels of carbon monoxide in the blood, so the availability of oxygen is reduced. Nicotine restricts the flow of blood to the skin surface – the skin can feel quite cool and clammy. Smokers from pale-skinned racial groups may look quite grey as their usual colour comes from this blood flow. In non-smokers, nicotine induces nausea.

▲ These days, smokers sometimes put up with quite unpleasant situations to get their 'fix'.

Tolerance

The first few cigarettes a person ever smokes will cause several unpleasant effects, notably nausea, dizziness and headaches. However, the body quickly becomes tolerant and these symptoms disappear. In smokers there is a daily cycle,as tolerance develop rapidly during the day, then drops again overnight.

A longer tolerance cycle also develops. Tolerance and dependency owe more to the symptoms of withdrawal than the effect of the drug itself, so more frequent intake is needed as withdrawal gets harder to cope with. A smoker can become habituated to a particular intake cycle, perhaps going all day without a cigarette then smoking a substantial number in the evening. Yet the person who smokes occasionally, but nonetheless feels an irresistible need for a cigarette in certain circumstances, is addicted in the same way as a 40-a-day person. It is merely that the cycle is different. Although nicotine is extremely addictive, the need to increase the intake of the drug is very variable. Some people maintain a relatively light level of smoking for many years, whereas others find their consumption steadily rises and is only restricted by opportunity and cost.

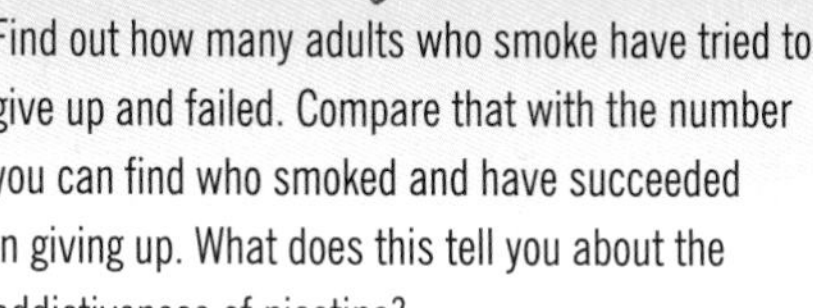

Taking it further

Find out how many adults who smoke have tried to give up and failed. Compare that with the number you can find who smoked and have succeeded in giving up. What does this tell you about the addictiveness of nicotine?

Physiological and psychological dependencies

Physiological dependency develops rapidly. As levels of nicotine in the blood reduce, signs of irritability increase, the addict becomes agitated and ill at ease until they can take in more nicotine. Concentration suffers and responses slow, making the person feel they need to have another cigarette so they can perform normally. The body has adapted to operating with nicotine present and the only way to feel 'normal' is to boost the levels back up. Physiological dependency can also result in headaches and stomach upsets if nicotine levels drop.

Psychological dependency is mainly caused by the need to remove the symptoms produced by physiological withdrawal. Addicts crave nicotine as soon as levels start to lower. The rapid reward gained by puffing on a cigarette means that the behaviour is highly reinforced. However there is also a psychological aspect, in that many smokers find they need to smoke in certain situations more than others. This can make breaking the habit more difficult as the individual feels 'lost' in some situations without a cigarette in their hand.

Taking it further

While some people start smoking at an early age, many current smokers started when introduced to cigarettes in social situations. The prohibition on smoking inside public buildings and the increasing frequency with which people object to smoking inside their home mean smoking is no longer a social habit. How do you think this will affect smoking behaviour over the next decade?

Withdrawal

Initial cravings cause irritability and poor concentration. Anxiety and anger reach a peak over the first few days but stay high for around three weeks. As the body starts to recover ex-smokers may experience headaches, tingling sensations, constipation, insomnia, tiredness, increased appetite and loss of concentration. These symptoms gradually subside over about two months. An addiction to nicotine can bring later sporadic cravings, worst in the first six months but possible even years later. Unless resisted, these cravings can lead the recovered addict straight back into addiction.

Examiner's tip 

When answering a question take one idea and explain it simply in one sentence. Then go on to expand on the idea either with additional information and/or an example showing you understand what you are writing about. Avoid stringing several ideas all together in one sentence as they tend to just get a single mark for a list.

Treating addiction

What you need to know

- Describe and evaluate drug treatment for heroin dependence.
- Describe and evaluate one other treatment or therapy for substance misuse.
- Describe and evaluate one campaign encouraging people not to use recreational drugs.

Taking it further

A major problem for methadone programmes is ensuring addicts do what medical staff want them to do, even when not being supervised. Treatment programmes often suffer from inadequate funding and insufficient staff. The ideal of counselling support for every addict and every dose being supervised is rarely met. Find out about the latest views on methadone treatment programmes. You may find the following link to a report produced for the Scottish government a useful starting point: www.scotland.gov.uk/Publications/2007/06/22094632

Examiner's tip

When learning the evaluation points for a treatment programme it is often useful to organise it so you have a positive and a negative point on a variety of issues. Use the information under strengths and weaknesses to consider how effective the treatment is, whether the treatment can be abused, and whether any abuse could be avoided. Also consider any positives or negatives to the treatment such as ease of use, addiction to the treatment or rates of relapse.

Taking it further

You may find it interesting to look up the current cost to the NHS of a drug treatment programme. Remember that there will be expenditure on the programme that needs to be weighed up against the costs of addiction to the NHS and wider economy. A drug addict who has their habit under control through a treatment programme is more likely to be able to hold down a job, contribute successfully to their family and community and pay taxes.

Treating heroin addiction with methadone

Methadone is a synthetic opiate which replaces heroin at the synapse, allowing the addict to function normally. It avoids withdrawal symptoms and, because it is given orally rather than injected, is less dangerous. It lasts longer – about 24 hours – so one daily dose can avoid the fluctuations experienced with heroin. Methadone also partially blocks the opiate rush, making injecting less desirable.

Addicts are assessed and the level of methadone determined. Initially, an addict must visit a pharmacy to be given the required dose to drink under supervision. Once considered trustworthy, they earn the right to take some advance doses home to self-administer. Once the treatment has stabilised, the process of **detoxification** can begin. In Britain, the NHS recommends that medical checks are undertaken at least once every three months. These include monitoring the level and stability of the addiction, as well as urine tests to check that heroin and other drugs are not being taken. The amount of methadone is slowly decreased, enabling the addict to cope with reduced intake without experiencing withdrawal.

Evaluation

Strengths

- It enables addicts to break links with dealers, so they are no longer pressured into taking heroin and are less likely to be exposed to other drugs.
- Overdosing on methadone is hard, so it is safer than other sources of opiates.
- Because methadone is taken orally, there is no danger of contracting diseases such as hepatitis through dirty or shared needles. Embolisms caused by getting a bubble of air in a vein when injecting are also avoided.
- Some suggest heroin use is seen as glamorous to those tempted by it. Drinking a green liquid over a chemist's counter is definitely not glamorous!

Weaknesses

- Many addicts never try to detox, even though this is supposed to be an important part of the programme. Once stable, they continue to get ready access to methadone for as long as they need it with no conditions attached.
- Methadone withdrawal takes longer than heroin – about a month – so anyone trying to give up has to cope with withdrawal symptoms for much longer.
- It can still be dangerous, as addicts using a cocktail of drugs with the methadone can still overdose.
- Addicts given methadone by a pharmacist have better compliance than those taking doses home for self-administration. Some of this methadone ends up in the illegal drugs market, defeating the object of the programme.

Treating alcohol addiction with aversion therapy

In normal circumstances, when someone consumes alcohol, the alcohol goes through two important changes. Firstly it is metabolised into a compound that is toxic, acetaldehyde. If acetaldehyde builds up in the body it causes the unpleasant symptoms associated with excessive drinking such as nausea and vomiting, dizziness, headaches and palpitations. However, acetaldehyde is normally oxidised very rapidly into acetic acid which is completely harmless.

When disulfiram is administered shortly before consuming alcohol, the oxidising of acetaldehyde is blocked so the individual experiences the unpleasant effects.

This pairing of alcohol with the unpleasant symptoms is used to classically condition in an aversion to alcohol. The association of the taste and smell of alcohol with the unpleasant effects of acetaldehyde creates learning by association and should put the alcoholic off drinking alcohol in the future.

Evaluation

Strengths

- It is very effective in the short term due to the unpleasant side effects.
- It works well if linked to social support, so continued abstinence needs to be positively reinforced.
- It deals effectively with physiological addiction. This allows the psychological reasons for addiction to be addressed separately.

Weaknessess

- Relapse rates are high. When disulfiram is no longer being used the level of nausea experienced relies entirely on the conditioned response, which will gradually become extinguished.
- If nothing is done to resolve the psychological reasons why addiction started, relapse is almost inevitable.
- Only effective if the drinker abstains completely from alcohol in the future. Alcohol consumption without disulfiram would immediately activate the reward system.

Treating nicotine addiction with hypnotherapy

The hypnotic state is a very relaxed state induced by a therapist to increase the suggestibility of the client. Ideas are implanted in the unconscious where they continue to influence behaviour once normal consciousness is restored. Hypnosis does not put people to sleep, rather they become more focused on the hypnotist and can easily exclude peripheral information. It is best understood as an altered state of consciousness or awareness, not a lack.

The principle here is to implant the idea that the person no longer wishes to smoke, indeed the thought of it is unpleasant. Hypnotherapists normally conduct a session lasting between one to two hours.

Evaluation

Strengths

- Hasan et al. (2007) found that patients told they needed to quit smoking were four times more likely not to be smoking after 6 months if they had hypnotherapy alone or in conjunction with nicotine replacement therapy, compared with either nicotine replacement therapy or no treatment.
- If it works, it is very cost-effective compared with other intervention programmes such as behaviour modification, as just one treatment is needed.
- Spiegel et al. (1993) showed that hypnosis was better than unsupported attempts to quit, with 23% of clients still abstaining after two years.
- There are no side effects from a session of hypnotherapy.

Weaknesses

- Although hypnotherapists claim anyone is capable of being hypnotised, there is a great deal of variability in how easy this is to do. If the client cannot relax sufficiently, implantation of the auto-suggestion will be ineffective.
- It only works if the client believes it can change behaviour. People who go for treatment already believe it will work, so the sample is biased.
- A meta-analysis by Green and Lynn (2000) of 59 studies suggests that, while effective, hypnosis works no better than any other therapy.

Disulfiram (available as the medication 'Antabuse') is used in this therapy. An addict being treated with disulfiram will probably undertake the treatment in a clinic under close medical supervision. This is because the nature of the aversive stage of the treatment can be very unpleasant and it is important that the build up of toxins is controlled so they do not reach dangerous levels.

Note that naltrexone, which blocks the dopamine reward system, has been found to be more effective at maintaining low-level drinking.

Have you ever wondered?

Does undertaking treatment for addiction affect life expectancy? Although most people are aware of the likely changes in health and life expectancy when people give up smoking, what about when people kick other drug habits, or when heroin users switch to methadone? Does it have any impact or would it, as some people suggest, be better if heroin addicts were supplied heroin of known strength and purity?

Other options

Cocaine

Currently cocaine addicts are offered social support, counselling and anti-depressants. It has been suggested drugs designed to treat epilepsy may be more valuable. A vaccine that treats addiction by blocking the 'high' may be the way forward.

Ecstasy

There are no specific treatment programmes for ecstasy abuse. Typically if users need help coming off the drug a course of cognitive therapy is recommended.

Marijuana

Cognitive behaviour therapies (CBT) are used to treat marijuana addiction. Restructured thinking aims to delay the first joint of the day for as long as possible. New activities that distract attention away from the prospect of a joint are introduced. Clients are taught to 'de-catastrophise' the situation (I'm not going to die if I don't get a joint) and to develop new strategies for reducing stress.

Anti-drug campaigns

Each year there are many campaigns encouraging people not to take recreational drugs. Advertisements usually take a 'carrot and stick' approach, emphasising the benefits of not taking the drug, but also including information that is designed to scare people who are using the drug to quit, and those not currently using it to avoid starting.

The 2008 anti-smoking campaign 'Scared'

This campaign was launched for Halloween 2008 and capitalised on the traditional Halloween concept of being afraid. The advert starts with a darkened bedroom and a young girl telling us she is not afraid of the dark nor, as the images change, of spiders or clowns. She then explains she is afraid of her mother dying as we see a group of young mothers standing chatting and smoking. One turns towards the camera and smiles, as though to the little girl. The advert finishes by telling viewers that 2000 people a week die as a result of smoking-related diseases and provides a phone number for getting help to quit.

The advert is one of a series under the banner of 'smokefree', aimed at reducing smoking in the wake of the ban on smoking in public buildings in England from the summer of 2007. (Smoking had already been banned in Scotland, Wales and Northern Ireland). Who is it targeting and why?

Aimed at parents of young children

- Having a young family makes people more aware of their responsibility to be there for them as they grow up. Most people reduce their risk-taking once they have a family. By highlighting a child's fears, the advert aims to use this heightened sense of responsibility to encourage parents to quit.
- The fear of the young child is used in a more general way. Adults have an aversion to child distress and share a very strong sense of protection towards children – important to ensure we care for them. By exploiting this, the advert is appealing to adults' desire to be protective towards children in general, as well as their own in particular.
- By linking these two factors together the advert aims to persuade smokers to quit.

Which psychological theories are applicable?

- Viewers are asked to identify with the adult smoker, i.e. it is targeting parents and using Social Identity Theory to do so, so the commentary from the child and the image of the mother in her social group are designed to resonate with the adult smoker who is parent of a young child.
- It is using ideas from social learning theory as it is trying to make the image of smoking aversive (associated with the fear of the child). We know that emotions are affected by learning; this seeks to reverse the conventional pairing and get us to associate the emotion of fear with smoking.
- The advert appeals to our cognition by supplying evidence for us to think about. However, it is interesting to wonder how effective a quote of '2000 people per week' is. Would it work better if it had some context of how many people 2000 is – for example, that it would be like wiping out the entire population of a particular town in so many months?
- The Psychodynamic Approach is also used. The unconscious fear of dying is used to challenge the desire of the id to continue indulging in a behaviour portrayed as irresponsible. In addition, the advertisement appeals to the superego by suggesting that the right thing to do is to quit smoking as that reduces the distress caused to our children.

Taking it further

Any campaign will have strengths and weaknesses. One danger is it may raise the profile of the drug and induce some people to try it who previously had not. Both the Department for Health and the Scottish Government publish the results of health campaigns on their websites, so you can find out how effective the latest campaigns have been (visit www.dh.gov.uk/en/index.htm and www.scotland.gov.uk/Publications).

Examiner's tip

Collect the evidence from a recent campaign. Which drug was the target? Which age group? Who was used in the adverts and what was the message? Look at government resources and newspapers for evidence on its effectiveness. Did it work?

How to describe and evaluate your own choice of campaign

Select a campaign that you have seen. It is ideal if you can find information on how well the campaign has been judged to have worked.

Description

Describe the campaign:

- Be able to give a brief written description of the advert. Ideally this will be about 75-100 words long.

Describe the target audience:

- Decide whether it is aimed mainly at getting users to quit or non-users not to start.
- What age group is being targeted?
- Is the campaign aimed at particular people within the age group, such as young singles (frequent in alcohol campaigns)?
- Does it target males and females equally?

Describe the mechanisms used to get the message across.

- Does it use fear of the health consequences of drug use?
- Does it use fear of social consequences when under the influence of the drug?
- Does it exploit the idea of what is socially acceptable?
- Does it refer to the impact of our actions on others and how does it exploit this?

Evaluation

- The Social Approach may be used by referring to ideas such as conformity or obedience. It may be that the advertisement wants to encourage autonomous behaviour.
- The Cognitive Approach may be used by providing evidence that we are asked to consider. This is likely to exploit our knowledge of past events, such as what happened to a particular person, or our understanding of facts so we can put the information in context.
- The Psychodynamic Approach may be relevant, as adverts may use symbols to remind us of our unconscious fears and hopes. Adverts on drugs are also likely to highlight the conflict between the id and the superego and bolster the ego's attempts to control the id.
- The Biological Approach will be used in some adverts by explaining some of the facts regarding addiction.
- The Learning Approach will be used firstly by the choice of actors and images in the campaign. These will have been selected to increase the chances of the target population identifying with them. There may be a celebrity endorsement, which again exploits the principles of social learning by providing a model we can admire. There may be an example of some type of classical or operant conditioning occurring within the advert, with the consequences of the actions shown. This will provide vicarious reinforcement to the audience.

AS check

See AS page 17 for an explanation of the autonomous state.

Studies

What you need to know

- Describe and evaluate the study by Blättler et al. (2002) in detail.
- Describe and evaluate one other study related to drugs. This study must be about one of: alcohol, cocaine, ecstasy, marijuana, smoking/nicotine.

This study uses quite complex statistical analysis to understand the results collected. Each time a questionnaire was completed the answers were checked for consistency, to test for truthfulness. Results for different categories of drug users were tested as were changes over time for any individual. The researchers also checked that drop-out from the study did not reflect on any particular group more than another.

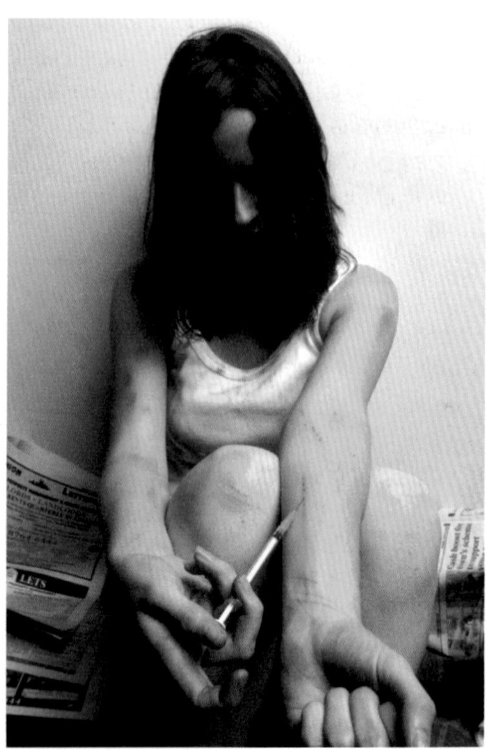

▲ Most of the addicts in the Blättler study were intravenous drug users.

Examiner's tip

Blättler et al. is a named study so you could be asked something quite detailed about it. Make sure you know it in detail so you do not get caught out!

Blättler et al. (2002)

There are many difficulties when working with people whose lives are governed by drug taking. Although nearly 1000 addicts were part of the drug reduction and control programme at the start, there was only sufficient data from just over a quarter of them to form a study sample, due to a combination of drop-out from the programme or insufficient data. The researchers took these factors into account when drawing their conclusions.

Aims

To investigate whether supplying heroin on a medical programme, combined with therapy, would reduce cocaine use among participants, and to investigate what factors were linked to cocaine use in multiple-drug users.

Procedure

Participants were 266 addicts on a drug treatment programme in Switzerland, 97 females and 168 males. All had made at least two previous unsuccessful attempts to give up. Their mean age was 30 years, and they had on average been using heroin for 10 years and cocaine for seven years. All participants gave informed consent.

Information collected at the start indicated a positive relationship between the level of cocaine use and whether participants had gained money from illegal sources over the previous six months. There was a positive association between cocaine use and the amount of contact with the drug scene as well as with the likelihood of working in the sex industry (note that prostitution is legal in Switzerland).

All the participants continued to live and work in their normal environment. The programme prescribed narcotic drugs, provided medical, social and psychiatric support, and therapeutic counselling. Continued prescribing of the drugs was dependent on addicts conforming to an appropriate set of behaviours, such as not selling any of the drugs and not mixing the prescribed heroin with illicit cocaine. Attendance for counselling was compulsory. There was no penalty for using illegal drugs, provided they were not mixed with the prescribed drugs.

Participants were interviewed at the start and then at 6-monthly intervals during the study period of 18 months. All interviews were conducted by trained independent interviewers. The interview consisted of several items from a standardised questionnaire used to identify mental health problems, and questions derived from a standardised questionnaire to assess the severity of addiction. Addicts were asked to respond to questions on how they had felt and behaved over the previous 30 days. The same set of questions was used each time the interview took place.

Drug usage was monitored by unannounced urine tests roughly every two months. The results of these were used purely to monitor which drugs were being taken, as self-report is often inaccurate. Exact dosages, time and method of administration for both the heroin and any other medications (e.g. antidepressants) were recorded.

Results

The difficulty of gaining accurate and consistent data from a sample who, by their lifestyle, tend to be unreliable meant that evidence from the questionnaires, from self-report and medical evidence was cross-referenced throughout to try and improve accuracy. At the beginning of the study, most participants were multiple-drug users, mostly intravenous cocaine, alcohol, cannabis and benzodiazepines. By the end, the number of addicts using cocaine on a daily basis had dropped by more than 80%, while the number of non-users had more than trebled.

Of the 261 individuals for whom the researchers had complete data, 99 had the same pattern of cocaine use at the end of the study as at the start, 15 had started using or increased the amount of cocaine they used, and 147 had reduced their use. Of those who had used cocaine previously, 106 had stopped using it by the end of the study. These changes are significant at $p<0.001$.

Of the participants still using cocaine daily, most were injecting a mixture of cocaine and heroin. There was no relationship between the level of heroin use and the taking of cocaine.

The correlation between self-reported cocaine use and the use level found by urine samples was +0.66 at the start of the study and +0.82 at the end. This shows that the addicts had become more truthful about their use of cocaine.

The factors most associated with continued daily use of cocaine were continued contact with the drug scene ($p<0.001$), prostitution ($p<0.0001$), illegal income ($p<0.0001$), and the use of illicit heroin ($p<0.0001$).

At the start, 84 of the addicts reported they had worked in the commercial sex trade in the previous six months. By the end of the study, this figure had dropped to 7 and none of those who had quit cocaine reported being involved in the sex trade. A similar drop was recorded in illegal sources of income, from 63% to just 10%.

Conclusions

The high correlation between self-report and urine sample evidence for cocaine use suggests self-report, while relatively good, is not completely reliable. Nonetheless this relationship became stronger as the study progressed, suggesting the participants were being more honest. All measures showed that cocaine use fell dramatically over the period of the study. It was the participants continuing to use cocaine who still maintained contact with the drugs scene and were involved in other criminal activities, including illicit heroin use.

Cocaine price during the study period remained stable and low, so other factors must have been responsible for the drop in use. The researchers concluded the heroin maintenance programme meant a higher number of participants kept attending the clinic. This was particularly valuable as it included obligatory counselling/therapy and medical care.

The participants in the study were heavily-dependent addicts who all used several different drugs and suffered from a variety of psychiatric problems. As such they are not representative of the wider population; however the results hold good for this group.

Changes in cocaine use among heroin addicts between the beginning and end of the study period.

	Level of cocaine usage in heroin users		
	Daily	**Occasional**	**Not used**
Start of study	79	143	41
End of study	15	111	138
Change	64 fewer	32 fewer	97 more

Note there are a small number of participants each time for whom data were not available, so the figures do not add up to 266.

AS check

Most of the statistical tests for association conducted by the researchers used the Chi squared test that you used in the Learning Approach (AS pages 132-133, and 150-151) They used this because their data were nominal (see AS page 132).

Although the figures are not significant, it is interesting to note that there were 37 more participants receiving income from a job at the end of the study than at the beginning.

Taking it further

Most of the studies described here are longitudinal, use survey techniques and large samples. Why do you think this is the preferred pattern for this area of research and what are the particular advantages and disadvantages of this methodology?

Taking it further

Though studies are usually investigating something about the impact of the use of one drug on participants, many of the participants are multiple-drug users. Evaluate whether the researchers are taking this into account sufficiently and what strategies they might use to control for the problems caused.

Examiner's tip

Make sure you know enough detail on the aims and procedures for a 5-mark question. Be able to include information about the size and nature of the sample, how data was collected, what form data took and any differences between conditions or groups. The same applies to the results and conclusions, where you should be able to include some detailed figures relating to the results.

Evaluation

Strengths

- Ethical standards were very high. This is important as participants were more vulnerable than average. Participants gave informed consent and the study was approved by the national medical ethics committee.
- The cross-check between urine samples and self-report meant it was possible to assess the reliability of the self-report data. It showed reliability improved over the period of study.
- The provision of heroin made it easier for those wanting to break the link to dealers to do so, facilitating the break with other drug use.
- The study demonstrates that an appropriate programme offering medical, social and psychiatric support can assist even long-term heavy drug users to reduce drug use and the associated undesirable/illegal activities.

Weaknesses

- It is difficult to show any cause–effect relationships in the changes found in drug use and behaviour. However, the changes were sufficiently consistent across the sample to suggest that the programme had an effect.
- Self-report data meant some was not reliable as addicts were not always truthful. The improvement in reliability may have been because they realised they would be found out, or a change brought about by changing drug use.
- Some may have joined the programme merely to obtain easy heroin, with no intention of reducing cocaine use.
- The addicts were unrepresentative of the majority of drug users. They were heavily dependent, used several different drugs and suffered from psychiatric problems, making it difficult to generalise beyond this type of drug user.

Ennett, Bauman and Koch (1994)

Aim

To investigate the role of friendship groups and cliques in the smoking behaviour of adolescents.

Procedure

Participants were students aged 14-15 from five schools in one county of North Carolina, chosen because the social and **demographic mix** is similar to the USA as a whole. Questionnaires were filled in by the teenagers in their own homes.

Participants were asked to identify their three best friends. The data generated was weighted for whether friendships were one-way or two-way, with those identified as two-way (where both sides identified each other as friends) given greater weighting. The researchers then used a computer program that identified friendship groups based on the patterns of friendships given by the participants.

Participants were asked whether they smoked, and this was cross-checked by checking for carbon monoxide in the lungs. Information on gender, race and mothers' education was collected.

Friendships outside school were discarded for practical reasons. Data from those not identified as clique members was also discarded. Seven mixed-sex and eight mixed-race cliques were not analysed as these were untypical cliques. This left usable data from 42% of the original sample of 1092 participants.

Results

A total of 87 cliques comprised of 461 adolescents were available for analysis.

- Average clique size was 5 members, with 81 having between 3 and 10 members. Of the 461 participants in cliques, 414 were non-smokers and 59 cliques were totally non-smoking. Just 2 cliques contained only smokers.

- The smoking rate among clique members at 11.1% was less than the 15.2% found overall in the schools. There was a higher incidence of smoking in those who did not belong to a clique.
- Cliques tended to show greater in-group homogeneity and out-group heterogeneity, i.e. in the majority of cliques there was a high level of similarity in behaviour (homogeneity). In contrast there were bigger differences between different cliques. This was most apparent in all-female compared to all-male cliques; in all-white compared to all-black cliques; and in cliques with lower mother education compared to higher mother education. Therefore, for example, a clique comprised of all white girls with poorly educated mothers was much more likely to have members that either all smoked or all did not smoke than male cliques, black cliques and cliques whose mothers were better educated.
- The researchers tested to see if there was a significant relationship between clique membership and smoking behaviour. In two of the five schools this relationship was significant at $p<0.001$, in a third school the relationship was significant at $p<0.01$ and in a fourth at $p<0.05$. In the fifth school the relationship was not significant.
- The degree of connectedness within a clique bore no relationship to whether everyone in the group had the same smoking behaviour or not.

Conclusions

Adolescents who smoke tend to associate with others who smoke. The lower level of smoking in clique members compared with the total sample suggests clique membership may contribute more to non-smoking than to smoking, and membership of a non-smoking clique may well support maintenance of non-smoking behaviour.

The researchers concluded that understanding the friendship networks is important in understanding the role of peers in determining behaviour. The behaviour of an individual and their friendship clique is likely to coincide, though whether someone joins a clique because of the clique's behaviour, or their behaviour is brought about by clique membership, remains to be investigated.

Evaluation

Strengths

- Participants could name any best friends and 95% of friendship were within-school, suggesting friendships selected were genuinely important.
- One application of these results could be to identify peers as allies rather than enemies in encouraging adolescents not to smoke.
- The research successfully demonstrated the importance of the mutual support of friendship in following a course of action (whatever the age group).

Weaknesses

- Smokers may be members of outside-school cliques which support smoking. Consequently there is a lot of potentially important missing data.
- An alternative explanation for cliques supporting non-smoker status is that adolescents maintain clique membership as long as behaviours coincide. If someone changes their behaviour, e.g. taking up smoking, they tend to leave the clique.
- The higher incidence of smoking in isolated individuals suggests this may be a reason for starting to smoke. The researchers did not investigate whether smokers in primarily non-smoking cliques had weaker connections to the clique than the non-smokers.
- The study uses mother's education to indicate social class. This seems prone to inaccuracy as relative income would have a greater influence on where someone lived or what other opportunities they have.

Examiner's tip

In the exam you might forget the exact number of participants (or a similar fact), even though you learned it. Giving an approximate idea, such as about a thousand, is better than not putting anything and more likely to gain credit than 'a large sample', as that is too vague.

Examiner's tip

It is really important that you clearly identify your studies by using the name(s), date and an indication of what the study is about. Candidates who cannot identify the study have to hope that the examiner recognises it. Give a good impression by providing this detail.

Other options

Stacy et al. (1991)
To investigate whether adolescent sensation seeking and cognitive motivations are predictors of adult drinking problems.

Morgan and Grube (1991)
To investigate the importance of friendships and peer relationships in both initiating and maintaining the use of drugs in teenagers.

Brook et al. (1999)
To investigate the relationship between adolescent marijuana use and the successful assumption of adult roles.

Wareing et al. (2000)
To investigate whether cognitive functioning is affected by the use of ecstasy.

Evidence in practice

What you need to know

- You need to be able to describe a key issue within health psychology and then apply the theories and evidence you have covered in the content to that issue.
- You must also conduct a piece of research relating to health psychology. This must be:
  - either a content analysis of an article concerning the key issue.
  - or a summary of two articles concerning a topic within health psychology.
- You must draw conclusions about the findings, and link to concepts, theories and/or research.

How to prevent drug abuse

Many people consume drugs and, with a widely available drug such as alcohol or tobacco, starting taking the drug may be not only easy but perfectly acceptable. When people start taking a drug, addiction and abuse of the drug are not outcomes they anticipate, yet this may happen. The nature of drugs is such that abuse, addiction and all the attendant problems happen all too easily. A variety of strategies are suggested as helpful in preventing abuse. These are not competing strategies, as most would argue a multi-pronged approach is the best way of dealing with the problem.

Key issues

Two topics are suggested here, but you can select others. The principles are the same:

- Describe clearly why the topic is a key issue.
- Describe the main points relating to the key issue.
- Apply explanations drawing on your knowledge of health psychology.
- Tie in ideas from the approaches you studied at AS.

1. How to prevent drug abuse

The issue: why it is important to prevent drug abuse

- Drug abuse costs societies such as the UK a great deal in money and resources each year. The 2007 bill for methadone treatment alone was £22 million.
- There are days lost from work, and hospital treatment for illnesses contracted through drug abuse, such as lung cancer, liver cirrhosis, AIDS and hepatitis.
- There are ruined lives, broken families and babies born addicted or infected.

Application of theory and research

Social Approach

It is in the interests of dealers to persuade users to increase the variety and quantity of drugs they use. If potential users are not part of the drug scene they will not see it as an in-group, which will reduce its appeal.

Drug taking is seen as an appropriate behaviour in certain groups. In order to prevent abuse it is necessary to either:

- persuade groups to change their behaviour and therefore the norms that new members of the group perceive as appropriate
- make in-groups where the drug-taking behaviour is seen as desirable, less attractive to join (and vice versa).

Cognitive Approach

Successive health campaigns have used scare tactics to get across the dangers of drug abuse. One problem is that we prefer to remember pleasant images rather than unpleasant ones, so information that scares may not be remembered as readily.

Graphic images of what happens when drugs are abused can lose impact because of cognitive dissonance – a mismatch between our behaviour and the knowledge we have about that behaviour. This is uncomfortable so we either have to change our behaviour – stop smoking, for example – or our cognitions. No one today denies the dangers of smoking, so strategies include attitudes such as 'I object to being told what I should do by a nanny state that gets the tax off my cigarettes'. In people who have not already tried a drug, graphic images of the consequences are likely to be more effective at preventing them starting.

Psychodynamic Approach
Many drug users use defence mechanisms to justify continued abuse. Arguments such as knowing a heavy smoker who lived to a grand old age, employ denial. Such mechanisms can be countered by factual information but are very hard to shift. Drug abuse can be seen as the dominance of the pleasure-seeking id, therefore according to the Psychodynamic Approach, bolstering the ego and superego to counter the id should assist in preventing abuse.

Biological Approach
It appears that some people are more able to break an addictive habit than others. However there is no systematic scientific evidence for this. The mechanisms of addiction are very powerful. When this is combined with the importance of keeping the balance of neurotransmitters in the brain within certain limits for healthy brain functioning, it is easy to see how abuse can begin and ceasing abuse is difficult – the addict will be faced with unpleasant symptoms if the drug level falls low enough to affect neurotransmitter functioning. However, drugs such as naltrexone are now available that prevent a drug affecting synapses.

Learning Approach
As well as helping explain addiction, classical conditioning can be harnessed to prevent abuse. People can learn to associate drug taking with negative stimuli. Awareness of unpleasant aspects can help, but direct experience such as with aversion therapy is more effective.

Operant conditioning can be used to prevent drug abuse. Drugs produce rewards in the brain which are very hard to resist. However, humans are capable of understanding and choosing between different reward mechanisms. Often drugs are promoted as having the reward of improved social life. If the rewards of abstaining, or using a legal drug in moderation, can be promoted in a way that counters the lure of excessive drug taking, operant conditioning becomes effective.

Social learning theory principles should be applicable. Although the role of celebrities shown 'enjoying' a drug-fuelled lifestyle is now viewed as only a minor cause of experimenting with drugs, it can have a disproportionate effect on impressionable young people. Celebrity endorsement has yet to be used in a campaign against drug abuse. Other potential role models such as parents and admired peers are also important if abuse is to be avoided.

◆ Conclusion

Preventing abuse is not easy. Campaigns such as those run under the 'Ask Frank' heading show the negative side, so exploiting the Learning Approach. This campaign also draws on other approaches as it includes information relating to the biological aspects of drug use and tackles the social pressure of conforming to drug use found in some groups.

See http://www.talktofrank.com/ for information about 'Ask Frank'.

2. How drug abuse can be treated

◆ The issue: treating drug abuse

- Drug abuse can be treated by helping the addict to manage their abuse. This may mean supplying the drug or a substitute such as methadone. It can enable the addict to break the link with suppliers and manage their addiction without breaking the law.
- If the person is coming off drugs they are likely to need support or medication to help with withdrawal symptoms.
- Successful treatment may need to look for the underlying reasons why abuse started in the first place and deal with these.

How drug abuse can be treated
Addicts who want to break with drug use have to wean themselves away from physical dependence and psychological dependence and cope with withdrawal, most likely all at the same time. Strategies that deal with the different elements of addiction separately may be the most effective. It is important to realise that ending drug abuse may not involve giving up the drug.

- Support from counselling or other sources of social support is also necessary.

Application of theory and research

Social Approach

Social support is essential to successful treatment. Many addicts may have alienated friends and family because of their behaviour. Former addicts can be useful in providing social support, as someone an addict can relate to and who will listen without prejudice. Policies that assist the addict to identify themselves with an in-group of recovered or recovering addicts are therefore beneficial.

Cognitive Approach

Often addicts develop a set of cognitions that suggest that taking more of the drug will help because it alleviates withdrawal symptoms. They also ignore the knowledge that the more they use the drug the worse these symptoms become. Context dependency can also mean that what is remembered is how much better they feel having taken a fix and not the unpleasantness as the effect wears off or produces unpleasant symptoms as it takes hold.

Addicts approaching treatment may believe the habit is too difficult to break. However, with counselling, such faulty cognitions can be challenged and changed.

Psychodynamic Approach

If a treatment programme is to be successful, the causes underlying the addiction need to be discovered and addressed.

Biological Approach

All treatments involve tackling dependence on an artificial boost to certain neurotransmitters. In the case of heroin, methadone treatment may be used, yet it is often not successful and some addicts may even continue using heroin at the same time. Some clinics prefer to manage a period of withdrawal lasting up to a week, assisting the addict with pain relief, and a strong social support and counselling structure that will continue for a considerable time afterwards.

Learning Approach

Aversion therapy uses classical conditioning to treat alcoholism and has been tried with other drugs, though with limited success. One problem is that, although it can be effective in the short term, its long-term effectiveness is less clear. Treatment is likely to be more successful if linked to addressing the causes of addiction. Using an understanding of the classically conditioned development of abuse can also help in treatment. Pairing the consumption of alcohol with having a good time with friends quickly assists in the alcohol being perceived as the source of the enjoyment. Learning a new set of associations is one possibility.

Operant conditioning can be used to treat addiction by blocking the ability of drugs to stimulate the dopamine reward system so that taking the drugs is no longer positively reinforced. It is also used to make breaking the habit more rewarding than continuing to take the drug.

Social learning theory exposes the addict to appropriate role models. People who have succeeded in kicking the habit are probably the most effective role models as the addict will be able to relate to them more easily. This is used by Alcoholics Anonymous when they pair alcoholics with a buddy.

Operant conditioning in practice

Some smokers wisihing to give up save up the money that would have been spent on cigarettes each day to buy something worthwhile. £70 a week is not an uncommon amount for a smoker to spend on cigarettes. An extra £3500 a year can buy a lot and can be a powerful incentive.

Examiner's tip

Never try and memorise large chunks of pre-prepared material for the key issue. Learn a series of headings which prompt you to raise particular issues. Remember, it could be an essay question, so you need enough different ideas to gain all the marks.

Conclusion

One reason a treatment programme can fail is because it does not address all aspects of the addiction. For example, a major criticism of the current methadone programme is that the prescription and administration of the methadone is not sufficiently policed by health workers because of staff shortages. Another problem is that attendance at counselling sessions is patchy, not compulsory and therefore unlikely to be effective in the majority of cases.

Other options

There are clearly different norms about drug taking in different cultures, whether that is different countries, or different cultures within a society. Often the reasons for particular choices are historical, for example:

Native South American Indians chewed coca leaves for hundreds of years to sustain themselves on treks in the High Andes. It was not until Europeans developed the techniques of extracting and refining the psychoactive ingredient that cocaine became a problem.

Alcohol has been the most widely used drug in European culture for over 6000 years. Most Europeans can cope with moderate amounts of alcohol without any difficulty, but when it has been introduced to other racial groups it can be a very different story.

Examiner's tip

Do remember to include some theory as part of your evaluation. This might include competing theories about why people become addicted, or competing theories about the most effective way of treating misuse.

Article summaries

There are many articles about drugs, their use, dangers and treatment, and one useful strategy is to take two articles that have very different views. An example might be one article suggesting that legalising many drugs would in fact reduce the use of these drugs and a contrasting article which advocates even stricter legislation to try and prevent access to drugs. If you have studied either alcohol or nicotine as your second drug you may be interested to choose articles that demonstrate the way views on the use of these two legal drugs is changing.

Here is a summary of an article where the original was 1000 words.

This section focuses on summarising magazine or newspaper articles. Remember that you may instead choose to undertake a content analysis of a newspaper or magazine article (web-based or TV material is permissible). You must do one of each for the content of Unit 3.

See also page 48 for advice on summarising. The articles, and pages 93-95 for help with content analysis.

"Heroin is hard work" by Martin Samuel (Times Online September 2008)

Can someone really start taking heroin simply because of their admiration for a celebrity? That is just what the family of an 18-year-old boy who died from an overdose believe. They claim it was the first time he had taken Class A drugs and that the example set by celebrities was the reason for him being led astray.

The article explains the complex requirements for taking heroin – the equipment and preparations as well as the process of injecting – and points out that these are not actions someone would normally undertake just because they consider a particular celebrity is cool. It takes a great deal of effort and preparation to inject heroin. Samuel argues no one becomes a casual heroin user because it is too much like hard work and the notion that teenage deaths from heroin are unlucky novices led there by wayward celebrity icons is wrong. Samuel argues that boredom and curiosity are the real reasons why teenagers try drugs. Drugs are available. The teenagers are bored and drugs are portrayed as boredom busters. So teenagers try drugs.

◆ Evaluating the summarised articles

Now apply what you have learned to the articles. Looking at the article above, each of the following can provide at least one evaluation point.

- Is it true that someone is unlikely to overdose the first time they take heroin?
- How might someone have got into heroin? Does this article recognise this issue?
- The article considers then rejects the celebrity model idea. Is a rejection of social learning justified?
- The article claims boredom as the reason. What type of explanation is this? Is it justified?
- The article makes no mention of the biological aspects of starting drug taking or addiction. Why might this be? Are there issues it therefore ignores?
- The article emphasises how complex injecting heroin is and suggests users are determined to take the drug. Knowing that – but also how addictive drugs can be – is the article correct or does it ignore some factors?

The original article can be found at www.timesonline.co.uk/tol/comment/columnists/martin_samuel/article4827014.ece

Over to you

- Choose two suitable articles.
- Summarise each article, remembering to avoid copying. Keep it short but informative.
- Evaluate each article in its own right. Go through a section at a time and apply your knowledge to it. You don't have to agree with the opinion in it.
- Comparing the articles would make a really good evaluation.

Summary

Health psychology considers the reasons for behaviour that is detrimental to health, such as substance misuse. The emphasis then is on how to promote healthy living.

Look back at the list of key terms for health psychology on page 51 and check you can define and use them all effectively.

Methodology

- Describe and evaluate the use of animals in laboratory studies when researching into drugs.
- Describe and evaluate two research methods using humans to study the effects of drugs.
- Evaluate, including practical and ethical strengths and weaknesses, research methods using animals.
- Evaluate, including issues of reliability and validity, research methods using humans.

Content

- Explanations of substance misuse:
  - Describe and evaluate one explanation from the Biological Approach.
  - Describe and evaluate one explanation from the Learning Approach.
- Describe and compare the relative strengths and weaknesses of the Biological and Learning Approaches as explanations for substance misuse.
- For heroin and one other drug (alcohol, cocaine, ecstasy, marijuana, or nicotine), describe:
  - mode of action
  - effects
  - tolerance (or absence of tolerance)
  - physical dependency
  - psychological dependency
  - withdrawal.
- Treatments for substance misuse:
  - Describe and evaluate drug treatments in heroin dependence.
  - Describe and evaluate one other treatment or therapy for substance misuse.
- Describe and evaluate one campaign encouraging people not to use recreational drugs.

Studies

- Describe and evaluate Blättler et al. (2002) study on decreasing intravenous use of cocaine in opiate users.
- Describe and evaluate one other study which must be related to the use of one of the following drugs: alcohol, cocaine, ecstasy, marijuana, smoking/nicotine.

Evidence in practice

- Describe one key issue related to the content of this chapter.
- Conduct a content analysis of articles or produce a summary of two magazine articles related to this topic.
- Draw conclusions about your findings.
- Make links to concepts and theories.

Examzone

*1 Describe the mode of action at the synapses of one drug other than heroin. (4 marks)

*2 Outline two reasons why researchers may sometimes prefer to use animals rather than humans for studies into the effects of drugs. (4 marks)

3 Assess the effectiveness of one method used to treat substance misuse. (5 marks)

4 Evaluate the study by Blättler et al. (2002) into decreasing intravenous cocaine use in opiate users. (4 marks)

5 Describe one key issue in health psychology. (4 marks)

6 In October 2008 the Department of Health launched a television anti-smoking campaign aimed at families. A series of images was voiced over by a little girl telling the viewers she wasn't scared of the dark, spiders or clowns, but she was scared her mum might die because she smoked. Explain the strategy behind campaigns such as the one described above and how successful they are likely to be. (8 marks)

7 Describe and evaluate one or more explanations for substance misuse. (12 marks)

*8 Evaluate the reliability and validity of one method using human participants that researchers use to investigate the effects of drugs. (6 marks)

4. Sport psychology

What you will learn about in this chapter

- The ways in which psychologists study sport.
- Factors affecting participation and performance.
- Ways of improving performance.

Key terms

- participation
- excellence
- intrinsic motivation
- extrinsic motivation
- arousal
- anxiety
- audience effect
- qualitative data
- quantitative data

What is sport psychology?

Sport psychology aims to study the behaviour of people in sport. This includes why people choose to participate in sport, which sports they pursue and their progress within the sport. It looks at how mental state can influence performance as well as how sport can influence mental state. Sport psychologists apply understanding of these factors to help people in sport gain the greatest benefit from what they do.

Who participates in sport?

Sport can be defined as: 'an activity governed by a set of rules that participants must abide by and where the individual is required to use physical skills they possess, or can learn'.

Children learn many skills through sport. Adults, too, enjoy the challenge and satisfaction of acquiring and improving skills. It is rare to find someone who has never participated in sport, but participation in organised sport does decline as we grow up. Children almost always participate in sport. However, during adolescence, participation does drop, particularly among females. So, although participation in sport does continue throughout adulthood, it is at a reduced level. There is evidence that someone is more likely to maintain an active participation in sport if their parents or carers have also participated in sport, or actively supported them during childhood.

What determines the sport you choose?

- Opportunity: If facilities are limited, through either cost or location, this will influence choice.
- Personality: People who are happiest in company are more likely to choose a team sport, whereas a shy person may prefer a more solitary sport.
- Gender: Some sports are taken up much more by one gender than another.
- Encouragement: Children may be encouraged or discouraged to take up a particular sport by family or friends.
- Ability: Being good at a sport brings positive reinforcement.

▲ Personality is often a significant factor in determining whether someone prefers team or individual sports.

How well will you do?

Many factors can influence how well you do in sport. Of particular importance are:

- Ability: Particular skills can mean you are better at one sport than another.
- Effort: Top sportspeople spend many hours practising skills and maintaining peak fitness. Many talented people do not put in this effort, so never reach the top.
- Personality: Some sportspeople show tremendous potential but 'bottle it' in competition, when the stress and tension affect their performance. Unless they are taught ways to control their stress levels, they will always underperform in competition.
- Coaching: An outstanding coach can raise performance significantly.

Methodology

What you need to know

- The way both questionnaires and correlations are used in sport psychology research.
- The strengths and weaknesses of questionnaires and correlations as research methods.
- The reliability and validity of questionnaires and correlations.
- Ethical issues relating to research in sport psychology.
- What is meant by qualitative and quantitative data.
- Strengths and weaknesses of qualitative and quantitative data.

AS check

You learned about questionnaires in the Social Approach (AS page 9). You also planned and carried out a questionnaire as Evidence of Practice (AS pages 30-35).

Research methods in sport psychology

Sport psychology has become very important in helping improve the performance of athletes in a wide variety of sports in recent years. However, sport psychology can only help improve performance if psychologists understand the nature of performance and what can affect it. Psychologists researching sport psychology use a variety of techniques, two of the most common being questionnaires and correlations. Both these techniques may allow researchers to draw out general principles by using large samples. This means that the findings are more likely to be generalisable to the wider population.

Questionnaires

Psychologists often use questionnaires to collect information. Questionnaires collect data directly from participants by asking a series of questions, usually gaining information about attitudes and opinions. The participants for a questionnaire are called respondents.

Questions posed take two basic forms – closed questions and open questions. Closed questions limit the respondent, as answers are selected from a limited range of options, or a simple yes or no. Imagine a series of questions asking footballers whether they agree or disagree with statements such as 'I always give 100% effort in training sessions'. By asking the same set of questions of a large numbers of players it may be possible to discover a difference in attitude towards training between the most successful teams and others. Closed questions are useful to gain an overall impression from a large number of people.

If researchers want to tap into a much richer type of information, where they look in detail at exactly how participants in their study view the issues being investigated, they will use open-ended questions. For example, an athlete may be asked what makes them feel a training session has been worthwhile and is expected to answer in their own words.

AS check

Correlations as a research method are covered in the Psychodynamic Approach (AS pages 75-78). You also undertook a piece of correlational research as part of the Evidence of Practice section (AS pages 92-95).

Correlations

Correlations are looking for a systematic relationship between two variables. Within sport psychology the most likely types of variables are for one of the features to be a characteristic of the person, such as their personality, temperament or a physical attribute. This is then correlated with some aspect of performance or choice within sport. For example, it may be that when looking at middle-distance runners the taller an athlete is the faster they are able to run, or that the more shy someone is the fewer people they work with in their chosen sport.

If the two factors increase in relation to one another they are said to be positively correlated. If as one factor increases the other decreases, they are said to be negatively correlated. A perfect correlation means there is complete predictability from one factor to the other, which is represented by a figure of either +1 or −1, depending on whether the correlation is positive or negative. If there is no correlation between the two factors the figure will be 0. In real life, correlations as high as 1 are extremely unlikely to occur; however, the closer to 1 the correlation is, the more closely related the factors are.

The diagram shows how, as the amount of training increases, so does the standard of performance. It is important to remember that, while it may well be the case that the amount of training may be the cause of the standards achieved, it is not possible to be certain that it is indeed the cause.

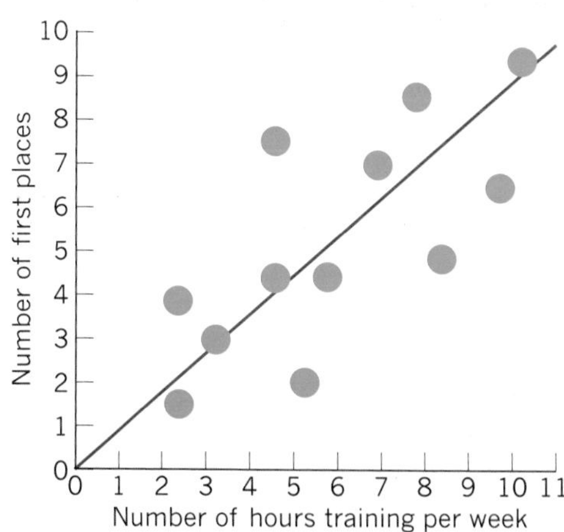

▲ This shows a positive correlation between the number of hours training athletes put in each week and their level of success, as measured by the number of first places they achieve.

Evaluating research methods

Strengths and weaknesses of questionnaires

Strengths

- They allow researchers to access information that is difficult to obtain by other means, as they measure people's perceptions of their situation.
- Printed questionnaires enable data to be collected from a very large number of people, using mail shots.
- With large samples it is possible to see trends that are difficult to spot in any other way.
- Open-ended questions avoid the problem of inappropriate choices as the respondent uses their own words to answer the question.
- Open-ended questions can produce information that adds depth to what the researcher knows.

Weaknesses

- A question may be interpreted differently by different respondents, creating inaccuracy in the data.
- The number of returns from mail shots can be very low, which creates bias as not all groups of people will be equally likely to reply.
- Closed questions can frustrate respondents as no given option fits exactly how they feel.
- Different people will use different words in open question responses, so they may not be directly comparable.
- The presence of a researcher may cause people to alter their answers to ones they believe are more socially acceptable.

Strengths and weaknesses of correlations

Strengths

- They allow researchers to identify a relationship which is not measurable in other ways.
- They can suggest an experiment where one factor is manipulated to see if it causes the other to change.
- They can use data that already exists, e.g. money spent on transfers by football clubs correlated with their finishing place in the league tables.
- They can use data from the past to show effects.
- A strong correlation allows a prediction to be made from one factor to the other. If there is not a correlation, any apparent relationship between the two factors must be due to chance factors.

Taking it further

Deciding on suitable measures for correlations is tricky. For your chosen sport decide on something other than ability that could be measured and that may be able to predict differences in level of success in sportspeople of similar ability. Try devising a way to measure this feature and see if you can get it to work.

Taking it further

Ask family and friends how many postal questionnaires (on any topic) they have completed and returned, recycled or forgotten recently. Is there any pattern in the type of people who are most, or least, likely to submit data?

AS check

The issues of reliability and validity of research findings are covered in the Cognitive Approach (AS pages 44–45) and the Social Approach (AS page 11).

Examiner's tip

Make sure you don't confuse reliability and validity. Remember that reliability means you can re-do the measurement and get the same results. Validity is whether something measures what it claims to measure correctly.

Taking it further

One area where questionnaires are used in sports research is in studying how personality may be related to sports participation. Devise two closed questions and two open-ended questions to measure sport participation, then try out the questions on some friends and compare the results they produce.

Weaknesses

- They do not manipulate variables so cannot show a cause–effect relationship.
- It is impossible to know if one factor is causing the other to vary, or if something else is causing both.
- The researcher may not have all the information that is relevant if past information is used.

Reliability and validity

Questionnaires

Closed questions are reliable, as the format of the questions and the way they are presented will be consistent. In contrast, open-ended questions are potentially less reliable, as the words used by respondents may be interpreted incorrectly. However, closed questions are restricted in the answers gained, whereas open questions have the potential to produce more varied and more truthful answers. This will increase validity, as the questions are focused on what the researchers are interested in.

Both the reliability and the validity of questionnaires depend on the quality of the questions being asked. Researchers pilot questions extensively to ensure they are appropriate. This means that a small number of people are asked to complete the questions and their results are studied in detail to check that everyone understood the questions (adding reliability) and that the answers differentiate between people successfully (adding validity).

Questionnaires often include questions to check the truthfulness of respondents. Sometimes a lie scale is used, so questions are included that might tempt people to give unrealistic answers in order to show off, or appear a nicer person. Alternatively, the same question may be asked more than once, in slightly different words, to check for consistency. If respondents are not being truthful but their data is used, this would have an adverse effect on both reliability and validity.

Correlations

Many correlations are conducted using publicly available information. This can be a very reliable means of gaining data, but only as long as the source of the information can be trusted. Correlations themselves are used to test the reliability of many tests and questionnaires, as they are a very good way of checking for consistency both over time and within a test.

One factor believed to be important within sport is the sportsperson's personality and, as a result, personality is often assessed by researchers and sport psychologists. A test for personality needs to be reliable if it is to be of any value.

To test for reliability over time, **test-retest reliability**, participants complete the same test twice with a time gap in between. Each person will therefore have two scores for the same test, one taken at time A and one at time B. Because personality is believed to be a stable characteristic (that is, it does not change over time), when the results are correlated, a high positive correlation shows that the test is consistent over time.

To test for internal reliability, a test is split into half and the scores for the two halves correlated. This is known as **split-half reliability**. A high positive correlation indicates good internal consistency. Internal consistency is important because it demonstrates that the questions are all measuring the same phenomenon.

Ethical issues

Researchers in sport psychology are bound by ethical guidelines in the same way as any other researchers. A great deal of research is carried out using sports clubs and often the participants are children. Clearly the issue of informed consent is important here, as children will not be in a position to understand all the issues. In these circumstances researchers should always obtain parental consent. However, they should also ask the children for consent, as the children do have a right to decide not to take part, even if their parents are happy for them to do so.

Researchers using a sports club should avoid the participants feeling under pressure to participate because of their club membership.

Another major ethical issue for sports researchers is ensuring their research does not adversely affect performance in competition. It may be that responsible researchers should limit their research to training situations or friendlies. This is a particular problem when studying the way people feel in the run-up to a competitive event. Researchers may want to interview or get questionnaire information as close as possible to the start of the event; however; most athletes feel a need to focus exclusively on the upcoming competition and may be put off by the intrusion of a researcher's questions.

▲ Ethical guidelines must be followed by all researchers when working with any participants. If the participants are children, the need for parental consent is an added issue.

Types of data

Quantitative data

Quantitative data is numerical and is potentially very reliable. Counting the number of personal bests, hours of training or the frequency with which an athlete agrees with positive statements about their attitude towards competition, are all reliable as they are repeatable time and time again. However, being reliable may not mean the data collected is useful. If it does not provide information on what is of interest, it is not valid.

AS check

You learned about both qualitative and quantitative data produced by surveys in the Social Approach (AS page 8).

Qualitative data

The nature of qualitative data means it is likely to involve a great deal of interpretation by both researchers and participants. The data gathered is usually in the form of words. This may be the words a participant has selected to express what they think in response to a series of questions, or an impression by an observer of how much effort an athlete is putting into a training session. It is thought to have very good validity as complex ideas and feelings are not reduced to numbers. However, it is also considered to be less reliable because it is more open to interpretation by both researchers and participants.

Examiner's tip

Remembering which is which between qualitative and quantitative data can be tricky. Use some feature of the words to help you, e.g. quaNtitative is for Number and quaLitative is like Literature.

Comparing qualitative and quantitative data

One advantage of quantitative data is that it allows statistical tests to be conducted on results. This means the likelihood of any effects being real or due to chance can be estimated quite accurately. Qualitative data, on the other hand, cannot be analysed in this way, so lacks the objective, scientific rigour that some researchers prefer.

Qualitative data enables researchers to investigate subtle differences in the way participants think or feel that would be overlooked if using quantitative data. It therefore has a richness and detail that is impossible to achieve with quantitative data.

There is a role for both types of data. Both have their strengths and weaknesses and it is only by having both types of data available that a complete picture can be drawn.

Taking it further

Researchers collecting data using questionnaires are likely to hand these out at sport training sessions. It would not be surprising if some people fill them in together, even if they are asked not to! Assess what impact this might have on the data collected and therefore on the results of the research.

Content

What you need to know

- The personality trait explanation for participation and performance in sport and one other explanation chosen from reinforcement, socialisation or attribution.
- Achievement motivation theory and one other theory of motivation.
- The inverted U hypothesis and one other theory relating to arousal.
- Two psychological techniques for improving performance in sport.

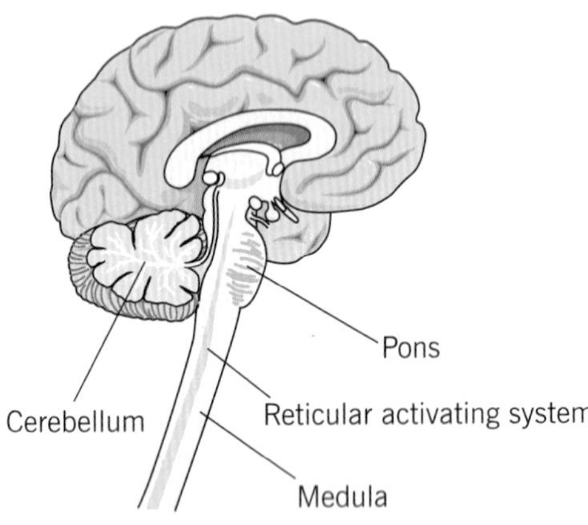

▲ According to Eysenck's theory, the level of sensitivity of the RAS alters the level of stimulation in the cortex.

▲ Phillips Odowu is a typically extravert sportsman. He will raise his arousal level by encouraging his audience to clap and chant as he prepares for a jump.

Individual differences in participation and performance

People differ physically and psychologically. Individual differences can be used to explain which sports you choose to pursue and how well you do at them.

Personality traits (Biological Approach)

Eysenck's trait theory of personality argues there are biological reasons for being an extravert or an introvert. Extraverts are excitable and enjoy lots of company. Introverts prefer to do things on their own and dislike situations which set the heart racing. Eysenck believed that how much of an extravert or introvert you are is determined by biology. Part of the brain called the reticular activating system (RAS), linked to feelings of motivation and arousal, varies in its level of sensitivity. A very sensitive RAS will allow more stimulation of the cortex and a higher level of **arousal**. In contrast, if the RAS is not sensitive the cortical arousal level will be low. The brain has an optimal operating level and humans seek to maintain this optimal level of arousal by the way they behave. If you have a very sensitive RAS and cortical activity is already high, you look for situations that allow you to lower the activity. This means you seek out quiet, calm activities, so you are introverted. In contrast, if your RAS is not sufficiently sensitive to maintain the optimal level of cortical arousal, you feel a need to raise it and do this by seeking out situations that will stimulate it, so you are an extravert.

According to this explanation of individual differences, sport choice is influenced by biology. Introverts avoid sports that stimulate the RAS, while extraverts do the opposite.

Biological differences in personality can also affect performance. Introverts become over-aroused very quickly and so are more likely to suffer an early deterioration in performance due to stress.

Strengths and weaknesses

Strengths

- There is some evidence from EEG measurements that extraverts do have a higher level of arousal than introverts (e.g. Gale 1983).
- Eysenck and Eysenck (1985) showed introverts need more drugs to achieve sedation and less to achieve arousal because of higher levels of brain activity.
- **Galvanic skin response**, pupil size and self-report all support the differential levels of arousal in introverts and extraverts.
- Evidence shows extraverts and introverts work better in training if the training regime is designed for their different arousal levels (Czajkowski 1996).

Weaknesses

- It is difficult to measure arousal accurately as low arousal situations may bore extraverts who then try to raise their arousal levels.
- It is possible that other areas of the brain may be less aroused, so it is the pattern rather than the level of arousal that is critical (Geen 1997).
- It may be that being extravert causes arousal levels to be higher, rather than arousal level causing someone to be an extravert.
- Over half the children asked why they tried a sport gave school or friends as main reason, so personality is not a significant factor (Scully and Clarke 1997).

AS check

The principles of operant conditioning were covered in the Learning Approach (AS pages136-137).

Reinforcement (Learning Approach)

There are several ways in which reinforcement can explain how you learn skills and why you persevere with a sport.

When you start a sport, the coach will shape your behaviour through reinforcement. At first, a reasonable try will be reinforced. However, over time the standard needed to gain reinforcement is raised, so that eventually the standard is very high. This uses the principles of reinforcement and is common to most learning of sport skills.

Praise is a very powerful reinforcer, particularly when children are praised by adults. Praise may be given for effort or for excellence; in either case it is likely to reinforce the performance and increase the likelihood of the individual trying to repeat the performance. Excellent performance may win trophies, achieve a personal best or other rewards. These are also reinforcers.

All the reinforcers just described come from outside the person and provide **extrinsic motivation**. It can be shown that people will develop and maintain a behaviour for extrinsic motivation.

People also find personal satisfaction in acquiring, improving and possibly even perfecting a new skill. They may also feel a sense of achievement in completing a programme like 'swimming the Channel' by clocking up lengths in the swimming pool over a set period. This is an internal reinforcer and is known as **intrinsic motivation**.

Coaches use both extrinsic and intrinsic reinforcement to motivate athletes. There is some evidence that extrinsic motivation can, in some circumstances, undermine intrinsic motivation. However, reinforcement, whether from personal satisfaction or by recognition of achievements, can reinforce behaviour and so encourages athletes to maintain their efforts.

Reinforcement can also explain participation in sports at which a person does not excel. Training sessions can be reinforcing because of the opportunity to meet friends there – so attending training is reinforced not by praise for improving but by social interactions.

Other option

Socialisation (Social Approach)

This explains how others influence your decisions about sport. As you grow up you internalise attitudes and values from parents and influential others. These will influence your choice of sport, your level of effort and your commitment.

Children who see parents enjoying sport are likely to imitate parental behaviour. Even choice of sport is influenced. In some communities certain sports may be seen as inappropriate because of gender, culture or social class.

The high number of children who follow parents into the same sport, and the high drop-out rate of girls, especially in certain groups, supports this view. However, it could simply be a matter of opportunity rather than being socialised. Also, there are sporty children in non-sporty families and vice versa.

Strengths and weaknesses

Strengths

- Both real-life situations and experiments demonstrate that reinforcement is a powerful tool in creating and maintaining behaviour.
- Many coaches do use positive reinforcements to encourage their athletes.
- Athletes don't win every time, so they don't get reinforced every time. This increases the persistence of behaviour. Research shows that behaviour which is not reinforced every time is more likely to continue during a period when no reinforcement occurs than a behaviour that had previously been reinforced every time.

Examiner's tip

When explaining a strength or a weakness of a theory or study, be sure to say clearly why it is a strength or weakness. For example, in the first strength point looking at reinforcement, explain one of the techniques.

Other option

Attribution (Cognitive Approach)

What you believe about your participation and performance in sport has a big effect on your effort level, or even whether you continue. Ideas and beliefs are used to explain why you did well or badly. This is called attribution. If you attribute success to your own hard work and effort you are likely to want to continue to try hard. However, if you believe your success is just luck you will see no point in working harder.

Research suggests differences in attribution can explain gender differences in attitudes and attributional retraining has been shown to improve performance. However, it is necessary for the athlete to be able to understand and have insight into thoughts for retraining to be effective.

▲ Kelly Holmes was able to fight back to win double Olympic Gold, after many setbacks, because of high achievement motivation.

Weaknesses

- Not all behaviour can be explained through reinforcement. Alternative explanations such as social learning theory are also necessary.
- Reinforcement ignores the role of ability in performance, as effort will not always bring improvement.
- Uptake of a sport probably has more to do with social factors and opportunities than with reinforcement.

Theories of motivation

There are different theories to explain a person's motivation to pursue a sport.

◆ Achievement motivation

McClelland and Atkinson's achievement motivation theory suggests that a person may work hard at a task because they want to do well. Winning a trophy, recording a personal best or achieving a particular goal can all be motivating factors. This is called need for achievement (nAch). Someone with strong achievement motivation prefers situations where they control the situation and can take and have responsibility for the things they do.

High achievement motivation also means a person prefers tasks and situations that are challenging. This is because they find doing well at a demanding task more satisfying than doing well at something easy. A person with high achievement motivation pushes themselves hard even if they sometimes fail to achieve their goal. They will cope with setbacks, whereas someone with low achievement motivation will avoid such risks through fear of failure.

◆ Strengths and weaknesses

Strengths

- Gill (1986) showed support for the presence of achievement needs in successful athletes.
- It is good at explaining why some people desire success more than others, and why certain individuals desire success in all areas of their lives.
- Balance and level of achievement motivation factors are different in elite athletes from that found in ordinary athletes (van Rossum, 2005).

Weaknesses

- Gill and Deeter showed that two factors – competitiveness and win orientation – are both necessary for athletes to persist and succeed, and may be components of achievement motivation.
- The link between competitiveness and win orientation is quite low in most studies, suggesting they are not necessarily linked.
- Many studies have shown that competitiveness is a good predictor of later outstanding success (e.g. Smoll and Smith, 2001).

◆ Cognitive evaluation theory

This theory (Deci and Ryan, 1985) explains how extrinsic motivators can influence intrinsic motivation. Some extrinsic motivators are obvious, such as prize money or trophies, but others are less obvious, like a promise that more effort in training will lead to a place in the first team. Motivators can control behaviour, and it is how this is done that this theory explains.

If extrinsic motivators make someone feel they have no control over their situation, they undermine intrinsic motivation. In contrast, if extrinsic motivators encourage feelings of autonomy, they boost intrinsic motivation. This is because people need to believe they are making the decisions and are not being manipulated by others. This makes them feel more competent, which in turn further increases intrinsic motivation.

According to this theory you evaluate your sporting experiences in two ways. Firstly, you assess how much information the experience has given you. Sometimes, for example, performance in a race may be very informative – it was a tough race, you came a close second, but the winner was someone you have never come near before. This tells you a lot about the quality of your performance, so is high in information. Experiences that have high information value increase levels of competence and raise intrinsic motivation. Secondly, you assess the situation for how much control you feel you had over it. You may feel that you were unable to perform in a way that suited you, perhaps because rival team tactics blocked your moves or instructions from your coach meant you had to support another athlete's efforts rather than going all out for yourself. In these situations, if control (by other people) is high, it reduces intrinsic motivation.

Strengths and weaknesses

Strengths

- It enables predictions to be made about how motivating a situation is likely to be.
- Studies such as Deci and Ryan show that solving puzzles for pleasure produces more effort than when the same puzzles are solved for a reward.
- Verbal praise increases motivation. This has to be intrinsic and cognitive as there is no other reason why it would work (Deci et al. 1999).

Weaknesses

- It sees lower intrinsic motivation as inevitably leading to poorer performance, yet this may not be true for all people in all situations.
- It predicts that competition where the motive is to beat other people reduces intrinsic motivation, as it is controlling. Yet high-level competition is almost always about beating others.
- Cameron and Pierce (1999) in a meta-analysis of 96 experiments found no reduction in intrinsic motivation when rewards were given, which contradicts the theory's predictions.

Other option

Another theory that considers motivation is Bandura's theory of self-efficacy. This is belief in one's own ability, which in itself makes success more likely. Furthermore, any lack of success is seen as being due to factors that can be changed, such as amount of effort or training, insufficient information or a skills deficit.

The effects of arousal, anxiety and audiences on performance

Arousal is a physical change experienced in certain situations. In competition, extra effort is required and the body responds by becoming aroused. Adrenalin is produced, causing both heart rate and the blood flow to limbs to increase. Hearing and vision become more acute and extra energy is produced. These changes prepare the body for action. However, in some circumstances, although the body is ready for action, performance is well below the standard expected, and anxiety is one explanation for this. Anxiety is a mental state and is perhaps best described as a feeling of dread. Audiences can also affect performance because they increase arousal level.

There are a number of theories to explain these effects.

Some definitions

Arousal is a biological state where the body is prepared for action. Heart rate increases, extra blood flows to the limbs, the body starts to produce extra energy and the senses are heightened. The blood flow to the gut slows right down (one of the reasons that pre-match nerves can cause you to vomit).

Anxiety is a cognitive state. It is the feelings we have when we are worried or concerned things may not go well. It is associated with apprehension about future events as we are unsure what will happen.

Audiences are people who observe our actions and pass judgement on the quality of our performance.

Inverted U hypothesis

This explanation was first introduced by Yerkes and Dodson (1908). As arousal increases so does the level of performance, but only up to an optimal point. If arousal increases above the optimal point, performance will decline. The optimal level of arousal depends on several factors:

The nature of the task – fine motor skills, such as are involved in archery, are better with lower levels of arousal, whereas large motor skills, such as are involved in rugby, are better with higher levels of arousal.

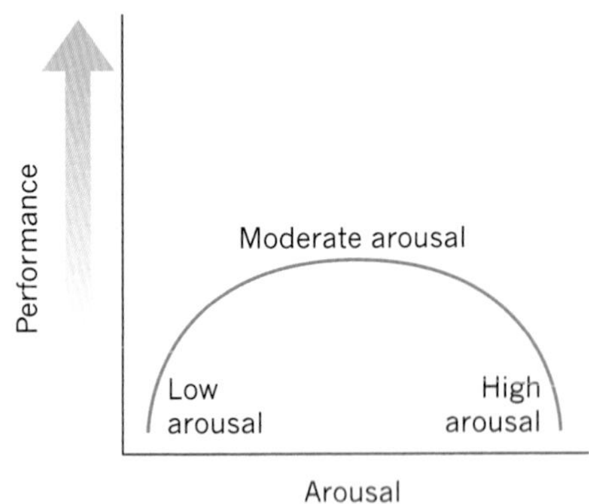

▲ The inverted U hypothesis.

The level of expertise – for tasks that are 'over-learned' (you feel you could do them in your sleep), optimal arousal level is high, whereas for less well-practised tasks, optimal arousal level is lower.

Tasks needing stamina and persistence are better with high levels of arousal, whereas complex tasks requiring concentration are better with lower arousal levels.

Thus it can be seen that arousal level will influence the quality of the performance, but the level of arousal that is best for you will depend on the nature of the task and how experienced you are at it. It is a useful theory to explain why someone who has been doing really well during the heats of an event sees their performance deteriorate in the final as the pressure starts to build.

Strengths and weaknesses

Strengths

- Landers (2003) found performance of students using exercise bikes followed the inverted U curve exactly.
- Mahoney and Avener (1977) supported the U-shaped nature of performance when studying elite gymnasts.
- It is good at addressing the arousal component of performance, because clearly performance improves as arousal increases.

Weaknesses

- Hardy and Fazey (1987) argued for a more dramatic decline in performance once above optimal level (catastrophe theory – see opposite).
- It doesn't address the idea that there are separate cognitive and somatic components to arousal (Martens, 1990).
- It is less good at addressing the anxiety part of performance, as evidence from other research suggests fall-off in performance is not always gradual.

Examiner's tip

While having a diagram to explain theories such as the inverted U is useful, never rely on them to explain your answer in an examination. If you use a diagram you still need to explain in words to get the marks.

Evaluation apprehension

Cottrell (1972) suggested that poor performance may be the result of **evaluation apprehension**. This theory suggests that the origins of performance quality are in childhood, when your performances are evaluated, with praise for doing well and criticism for doing poorly. Repeated evaluation gradually builds a level of anxiety. The anxiety felt for fear of a negative evaluation from an audience causes arousal levels to rise. If a task is well learned and simple to undertake, the arousal caused by the presence of an evaluating audience will improve performance, as it is raising arousal higher and nearer to the optimal level. However, if the task is complex or not so well learned, performance is likely to deteriorate as arousal increases. This is because the additional arousal caused by the presence of an audience pushes the arousal level above the optimum. Therefore, an audience is important in determining how well you perform, but the effect it has depends on your starting level of arousal.

Strengths and weaknesses

Strengths

- It explains both the positive and negative effects of audiences on performance, unlike the inverted U hypothesis, which does not consider the effect of an audience.
- It can explain why home teams (e.g. in football) sometimes do badly, because of critical home audiences.
- There is support from several studies, e.g. Michaels et al. (1982) on pool players, where practised players improved with an audience while novices did worse.

Weaknesses

- The mere presence of an audience is sufficient to affect performance, as long as they are detected by the performer (Schmitt et al., 1986).

- Evaluation apprehension doesn't work as well if the audience is perceived as members of an out-group (Social Identity Theory).
- It doesn't account for supportive audiences who will help the person to do better.

Catastrophe theory

Hardy and Fazey (1987) developed catastrophe theory to explain the sudden drop in performance often seen in competition. It is based on the inverted U hypothesis but with an additional cognitive component. They argued that the inverted U hypothesis, while explaining the increase in performance up to the optimal level, fails to explain what happens past that point. Very frequently an athlete will be performing well as they go through the heats of an event, with performance fairly steady or slowly improving, then in the final stages there is a dramatic deterioration.

Catastrophe theory argues that, when arousal goes past the optimal level, the competitor starts worrying about their deterioration in performance. They experience cognitive anxiety. When their physiological arousal and cognitive anxiety, which are both increasing, are combined they reach a critical level or 'cusp', where performance changes rapidly and dramatically. Once the cusp is reached they need to suppress some of the cognitive and physiological resources in order to lower the high levels of stress. This results in a catastrophic drop in performance.

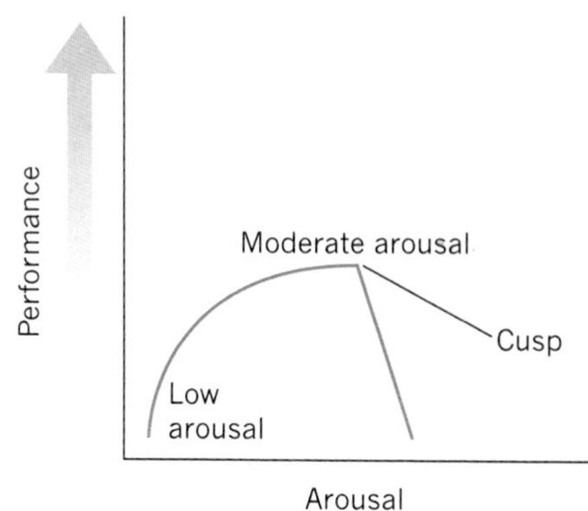

▲ Cusp point and drop in performance predicted by catastrophe theory.

Strengths and weaknesses

Strengths

- It is particularly useful in explaining the sudden inability to perform.
- It explains individual differences between athletes as well as inconsistency in an individual athlete's performances.
- Evidence supports an interaction between physiological and psychological states in predicting performance.
- It explains why recovery after a catastrophe is difficult and slow.

Weaknesses

- It ignores the role of somatic arousal (how aware one is of physiological state).
- It does not distinguish between cognitive anxiety and excitement.
- It ignores self-efficacy as a way of improving performance.
- It fails to include factors such as self-confidence as a factor in performance.

Examiner's tip 

Remember that one of the most effective ways of evaluating a theory is to compare it with a different theory and comment on which one is better at explaining a particular situation.

Psychological techniques for improving performance

Goal setting

Goal-setting theory was developed by Edwin Locke (1968) and has been used to explain the way that performance can be improved by the use of psychological principles. It is based on ideas derived from nAch, self-efficacy and reinforcement.

Firstly, it recognises that difficult goals can lead to higher achievement and that targets that are reached too easily are not likely to motivate further effort. So, to ensure high levels of effort, goals should be challenging but achievable. A second component of the theory is that specific goals work better than general goals. Many coaches will follow this when devising a programme for their athletes. A coach might give you a specific target, for example of achieving a qualifying time by a certain date.

A final component of goal setting is feedback. Feedback is a very effective way of shaping and improving performance. Effective performance is more likely to be repeated, and errors avoided. Goal-setting theory argues that feedback is essential to achieve a difficult goal, as otherwise progress cannot be monitored.

Other options

These are two further theories sometimes used to explain the effects of arousal, anxiety and audiences on sports performance:

Optimal level of arousal theory suggests there is an optimal level of arousal at which one performs best. If arousal level is below optimal the athlete seeks activities to raise the level; however, if arousal is too high the athlete aims to lower it by the way they behave.

Drive theory states that, as arousal increases, so does performance. However, it does not address the issue of performance deteriorating.

It is widely agreed that goal setting is an effective technique for improving motivation in athletes. Targets set must be specific to the individual athlete, be sufficiently short term that progress is easily monitored and be demanding but not impossible.

Evidence shows that, for goals to have any value, you need to accept the goals set. One of the most effective ways of doing this is to be involved in the goal-setting process – you will then be more willing to accept the challenges than if goals are imposed by a coach. Commitment to the goals is essential if you are to be motivated to achieve them.

It seems that one of the reasons why goal setting works is because it encourages athletes to plan how they are going to reach the goal. Better planning, and thinking through strategies of how to achieve the goal, means less time is wasted on activities that are not goal-orientated.

Feedback comes in two distinct forms, internal and external. Internal feedback is within yourself. It may be the completion of a task so that you are ready to go on to the next step or the personal satisfaction of achieving a personal best. It is important to note that, because self-monitoring is difficult to do accurately, internal feedback is often not sufficiently clear to be helpful. However, at its best this internal feedback can be very sustaining as it allows you to keep working hard at something even when no-one else is aware of the effort you are putting in. Feedback from self-monitoring is a form of **intrinsic motivation**.

Feedback from an external source is also valuable, whether it is confirmation you are performing well or guidance on how to work more effectively to achieve the goal. External feedback can range from a simple 'well done' through to trophies and medals. It is a form of **extrinsic motivation**.

Examiner's tip

Always make sure you are using psychological explanations, not just common sense in your answers. Examiners want to see that you have learned some psychology. If your answer is one that anyone interested in sport could produce, it is unlikely to get any marks.

Strengths and weaknesses

Strengths

- Goal setting is effective, especially if goals are agreed rather than imposed.
- It works best if tasks are broken down into manageable-sized chunks that can be mastered before moving on.
- Effectiveness can be explained using concepts such as self-efficacy and achievement motivation so goal setting theory links well with other theories.

Weaknesses

- It can be difficult to self-monitor performance, so feedback from external sources is needed.
- It is not always easy to break down skills into components. Also, putting together items learned separately can be hard.
- It will not work if goals are too vague or too difficult.

Imagery

Mental preparation can be as important as physical preparation in improving performance.

Sportspeople use imagery to help with mental preparation, in training and competition. There are two main types of imaging, cognitive and motivational.

Motivational imaging can be used in specific and in general ways. One specific way is to visualise a specific goal or target; this is believed to help you then work towards achieving that goal. General motivational imaging can be used to assist with mastery; this means that imaging success in completing a task or skill will build confidence and allow you to focus on the eventual outcome. General motivational imaging can also be used to raise arousal levels, to 'psych' yourself up.

Cognitive imaging is where you focus more on the performance itself. Specific cognitive imaging is used to mentally practise skills to, for example, assist you in mastering a new technique, whereas general cognitive imagery is what is used to rehearse a game or race plan. There is a growing amount of evidence that general cognitive imaging can be of great assistance to athletes.

To be effective, imagery must be as vivid, positive, detailed, close to 'real' time and involve all the senses. While kinaesthetic and visual imaging are the most widely used, other senses such as olfactory and auditory are also important. You may rehearse your race strategy and focus on likely key points and how to deal with them. This means you are mentally prepared for what might happen and can solve anticipated problems in advance. You may image from your own viewpoint, but it is also useful to image from an external viewpoint. This allows you to see yourself as others see you and toidentify specific or areas that need working on.

▲ In the moments before the start, cyclists once more use imagery to focus on the race to the exclusion of everything else. The ability to image successfully varies but everyone can improve with practice.

Strengths and weaknesses

Strengths

- Many athletes report that imagery helps them focus on specific aspects of an event or competition so that they have more targeted strategies.
- Olympic gold medallists report using the technique to in race preparation.
- It creates a positive mind set, known to improve the chances of success.
- It is effective at keeping complex skills practised during lay-offs due to injury.
- If an athlete is focused on the process involved in a race they are unlikely to have time to feel nervous.

Weaknesses

- Most research is on imaging in practice, and its widespread use in competition has little data collected on it to test its effectiveness.
- It does not guarantee success, as the losers of events also use imagery.
- Creating effective imagery is a demanding skill requiring time and effort.
- Imagery alone cannot improve fitness levels or develop co-ordination skills.

Attribution retraining

Attributions are the reasons athletes give for success or failure. If they think success is due to luck, or failure due to lack of ability, they will feel powerless to repeat the success or prevent failure. Attribution retraining teaches them to attribute success and failure to hard work, or the lack of it – bringing it within their control. It is based on three models, one of which is **self-efficacy**. It ensures an athlete feels more in control of their performance, which helps to boost confidence.

A second theory that relates to attribution retraining is the opposite of self-efficacy, and that is **learned helplessness**. It describes the mental state where, because of repeated negative experiences, you believe you can never succeed. The task is to change learned helplessness into self-efficacy.

The third theory related to attribution retraining is Weiner's theory of attribution. Weiner suggests that the ideal attributions are for success to be attributed to effort and ability, and failure to lack of effort and bad luck. If you are successful you will maintain effort, whereas if you fail you will continue trying. Weiner argued that attributions could be retrained to bring improved performance.

Modelling and information techniques are used to retrain attributions. Information demonstrating that more effort will reap rewards can be provided by looking at the performance of others. Similarly, the mastery of a skill and its impact can be readily seen. Sometimes it may be more difficult to demonstrate ability and bad luck as factors by informational processes. At club level, models can often be found among the senior members for the younger members to look up to. Feedback is also important as part of the retraining, so that athletes understand what impact the extra effort has had on their performance.

Studies in detail

What you need to know

- Describe and evaluate Boyd and Munroe's (2003) study of the use of imagery in climbing, plus one other study.

Boyd and Munroe, 2003

Aims

To discover how frequently and in what ways imagery was used by climbers and whether there was any variation between beginner and advanced climbers.

Procedure

A random sample of 48 climbers (indoor and outdoor), of whom 18 were beginners, was used. Results were compared with a random sample of 38 track and field athletes (athletes). Both groups included males and females and were of similar mean ages. Participants completed questionnaires asking how frequently they used imagery, when competing for the athletes or when attempting a climb for the climbers. Participants rated their use of imagery on a 7-point scale ranging from rarely used (1) to very often used (7). Athletes completed the questionnaires as a group before a training session. Climbers completed their questionnaires independently during a session on an indoor practice wall, either during rests or at the end of the session. Climbers were categorised as beginners or experienced depending on the rating of the toughest climb they had attempted.

Results

The researchers found no difference between climbers and athletes in their use of specific cognitive imaging (CS), used to imagine perfectly-executed skills, or general cognitive imagery (CG), used to imagine strategies to be employed.

The questionnaire measured three types of motivational imagery – mastery (MGM), anxiety (MGA) and specific (MS). Climbers used all types of motivational imagery significantly less than athletes, and used MS at a much lower level than other types of imagery. As MS imagery involves imagining winning and gaining trophies, it is not surprising this is rarely used by climbers.

There was no difference between beginner climbers and advanced climbers.

Mean score on questionnaire (min 1 max 7)

Imagery	Climbers	Athletes	
CS	4.54	4.69	n/s
CG	4.68	4.77	n/s
MGM	4.63	5.54	$p<0.05$
MGA	4.26	4.86	$p<0.05$
MS	2.95	4.53	$p<0.05$

▲ Table of results adapted from Boyd and Munroe (2003).

Conclusions

The researchers concluded that one reason for the difference in the use of specific imagery between climbers and athletes is that climbers have very strong intrinsic motivation, whereas athletes frequently use extrinsic motivation. The lower than expected MGA score in the climber group may be because those who climb have lower trait anxiety to start with. The lack of difference in the use of MGA in the two groups of climbers may be because experienced climbers tackle harder climbs, so fear of falling is similar in both groups.

Evaluation

- The small sample sizes compared with similar studies into the use of imagery may mean that small but real trends were not apparent in the data.
- All the athletes were experienced, which may account for the high use of imagery found. Prior research suggests experienced athletes use imagery more often.

- There was no distinction made between individual or team athletes, meaning the group may have been very varied, whereas climbers are more similar as they always climb in small, interdependent teams.
- The mastery scale scores relate to self-confidence and show only a moderate mean score for the climbers, in contrast with previous research by Robinson (1985) whose climbers had high self-confidence levels.

▲ Rock climbers often find themselves in tricky situations. Keeping control of anxiety is important if they are to succeed.

Cottrell, 1968

Aim

To test whether audiences enhance the dominant response in a performance.

Procedure

Two studies were carried out. In Study 1, 132 male students learned word pairs and were tested by having to supply the other word of a pair when one word was shown on a screen. All participants did five practice lists under identical conditions before the experiment. They were randomly allocated to one of four groups. The two competitive groups had to achieve two consecutive trials with no mistakes; the non-competitive groups had no such pressure on them. One competitive and one non-competitive group completed the experiment alone; the other two groups had an audience of two students who observed quietly and attentively. The experimenter was screened from view. Practice list results were used to sub-divide the participants into fast, medium and slow learners.

In Study 2, 45 participants were divided into three groups and given a recognition task. Participants were either alone, in the presence of two attentive students, or in the presence of two blindfolded students, as the 'mere presence' condition. As before, the experimenter was screened from view.

Results

Performance was affected by whether the recall was competitive or not as well as whether the initial learning standard had been fast, medium or slow. The non-competitive groups had low error rates whether there was an audience or not and irrespective of their speed of learning. In the competitive condition, both medium and slow learners with an audience made significantly more errors than their counterparts without an audience ($p < .025$). The competitive fast learners with an audience made slightly fewer errors than their counterparts without an audience, though the difference was not significant.

Study 2 produced almost identical results for the alone and mere presence condition. However, in the audience condition there was a significant increase in the dominant response ($p < .025$).

Conclusions

Audience presence has a positive effect on the performance of participants who are not proficient, provided the situation does not cause arousal. However, if this type of participant is already aroused an audience causes performance to be worse. In contrast, the proficient performers do better when an audience is present. This effect is only likely to occur when the audience is in a position to judge the performance – the mere presence of others is not enough change to performance.

This supports Zajonc's theory that arousal enhances the **dominant response**. However, it shows the mere presence of others does not increase arousal.

Robert Zajonc (pronounced like 'science' with a Z) (1923-2008) was a Polish-born American who worked on the effect of an audience on performance. According to Zajonc, presence of an audience increases arousal and makes the dominant response more likely to occur. For an expert performer, the dominant response is the correct one and this will be the most likely response when aroused. However, for the novice, the dominant response is likely to be incorrect and this will dominate when arousal is raised.

Evaluation

The biased nature of the samples means generalisation needs to be viewed with

Examiner's tip

Remember to learn enough detail so that you can answer a question asking just about the procedure, or the results and conclusions, as well as general description and evaluation questions.

caution, particularly as some research, e.g. Schmitt et al. 1986, found mere presence sufficient to affect performance in some cases. There was an element of deception involved in the studies, though it cannot be considered particularly distressing for participants. The experimental tasks were very artificial and unlike behaviours that are normally observed by an audience. It is therefore questionable how applicable the findings can be to sportspeople competing.

Koivula, 1995

Aim

To investigate links between views on the gender appropriateness of sports and the scores participants received on the Bem Sex Role Inventory (BSRI).

Bem Sex Role Inventory

Respondents rate 60 words on a 1-7 scale for how true the terms are of them. The list is equally split between masculine, feminine and neutral words. The average rating for the three categories is calculated. Those who score high on male and low on female are judged as masculine, while the reverse trend is feminine. Those who score high on both masculine and feminine scales are androgynous and those who score low on both are undifferentiated.

Procedure

Questionnaires were completed by 104 women and 103 men. Of the respondents, 79% were students (mostly of psychology). The remainder were military recruits. Respondents completed the BSRI and were categorised according to their scores as sex-typed, (those with a higher rating for the scale that matched their gender), cross-sex-typed (those with a higher rating for the scale different from their gender), androgynous (high scores for both masculinity and femininity) or undifferentiated (low scores on both scales).

Respondents rated the gender appropriateness of 60 sports, using a 7-point scale where 1 was a masculine sport unsuitable for women, and 7 was the reverse. Scores were used to classify sports as neutral, masculine or feminine.

Results

Nearly half the male respondents were classified as sex-typed and over 40% of the female respondents were classed as sex-typed.

Men gave sports stereotyped as masculine or feminine more extreme scores than did women ($p<0.02$ for masculine sports, $p<0.04$ for feminine sports). There was no difference for neutral sports. Amongst the male groups the sex-typed and cross-sex-typed men were the most likely to select strongly stereotypical scores; indeed, these two groups classified surfing and tennis, generally viewed as neutral, as masculine. In contrast the androgynous, cross-sexed and undifferentiated female groups classified a higher number of sports as gender neutral.

Conclusions

The relatively low level of gender stereotyping by respondents classed as androgynous or undifferentiated could be because such people use gender-based schematic information processing less than sex-typed people. Whether this difference is because they do not feel bound by the stereotypes or because they choose to stand up for change is unclear. Some differences in responses could be caused by society's tendency to value masculine activities more highly than feminine ones. The results suggest participation in sport is still strongly based on gender and men hold this view more strongly than women.

Evaluation

The use of a sex role inventory immediately before the sports inventory may have increased awareness of gender issues and so increased the level of stereotyping in the answers. Respondents were asked to use their own judgements about sports, however it is possible demand characteristics of what were perceived as appropriate responses, caused bias.

Having used respondents' rankings to classify sports as masculine, feminine or neutral, Koivula then tested to see whether the mean rankings differed across the classifications. Not surprisingly they did, as she was testing divisions she had just created using exactly the same data.

AS check

See AS page 44 for an explanation of demand characteristics.

Craft et al., 2003

This study is a meta-analysis of studies using the Competitive State Anxiety Inventory-2 (CSAI-2).

Aim

To investigate the nature of the relationship between each of the sub-scales of the CSAI-2, and between those sub-scales and performance. There are three sub-scales: cognitive anxiety, somatic anxiety and self-confidence.

Procedure

The researchers looked at the evidence from 29 studies on the relationship between state anxiety and performance. They also looked at differences in findings to see if these could be explained by sample size, recruitment, gender, sport, type of event or how long before competition data collection occurred.

Results

Initial analyses correlated each sub-scale with performance. Results showed no relationship between either cognitive or somatic anxiety and performance ($r = +0.01$, $r = -0.03$). There was a weak positive correlation between self-confidence and performance ($r = +0.25$). Studies on individual sports showed a stronger relationship between self-confidence and performance than did studies on team sports.

In top athletes, higher levels of cognitive and somatic anxiety were associated with higher standards of performance, whereas in lower-level athletes no such relationship was apparent.

Sports with a constantly changing environment showed stronger relationships between anxiety and performance.

Conclusions

- The researchers concluded a lack of relationship between somatic anxiety and performance could be because it is testing for a linear relationship. If somatic anxiety is inverted U, a linear correlation will give a result of near zero.
- The weak correlation between self-confidence and performance may be due to the general nature of the questions. Self-efficacy scales may be more useful.
- Questionnaires administered less than 30 minutes before competition give poor accuracy compared with those given earlier.
- The CSAI-2 is not an accurate tool for measuring the relationship between anxiety and performance.

Evaluation

- A distinction between cognitive and somatic anxiety may be invalid, as results show the scales are not as independent as claimed.
- The researchers suggested that the lack of correlation with somatic anxiety could be because of the inverted U pattern of performance, yet failed to test this by using a suitable statistic.
- Some sports have both team and individual elements, and the sports included were very varied; however, the researchers only stated that they coded the studies and did not explain what rationale they used to classify sports.
- The elite American athletes group was very diverse so generalisations were difficult. It included anyone from athletes who represented a local club up to full internationals.

Taking it further

The Craft et al. study concluded that data collected less than 30 minutes before the competitive event was likely to be unreliable. Discuss why this might be and, from your own experience, what the optimal time might be.

Evidence in practice

What you need to know

- You need to apply the content you have studied in sport psychology to one key issue.
- You must conduct a piece of research relating to sport psychology. This must be:
  - Either: a content analysis of an article concerning the key issue.
  - Or: a summary of two articles concerning a topic within sport psychology.
- You must draw conclusions about the findings, and link to concepts, theories and/or research.

▲ Some of Britain's successful Olympic team in 2008. Ability, motivation, hard work and a bit of luck – part of the recipe for becoming a winner!

Key issues

What makes a winner?

You might know someone who is very talented in their sport but never seems to achieve to their potential in tough competition. You may also know someone who fails to achieve good performances in training but then excels at the big events. Sport is full of examples of such competitors. What can explain the difference between these two types of people?

- People with high achievement motivation will be prepared to go to great lengths in terms of effort and commitment to win. High nAch individuals may not always win, but they don't quit, they work hard to win next time (see achievement motivation on page 82).
- The saying that success breeds success fits well with winners using cognitive evaluation. Winning increases feelings of confidence and, provided the attributions a sportsperson makes are tied in with effort and hard work, this will motivate more effort and hard work, so increasing the chances of success in the future.
- A person's level of self-efficacy will affect their approach to competition, as belief in one's own ability to succeed means setbacks are seen as merely temporary.
- During competition, levels of arousal will increase dramatically. If this raises the level of arousal too much the competitor may 'choke'. One explanation for arousal being too high is personality. Extraverts are comfortable with high arousal levels whereas introverts are not.
- Evaluation apprehension theory can explain why, under the duress of competition, a sportsperson makes an unforced error. For example, the tennis player who double-faults may be a victim of arousal causing the dominant response to re-emerge.
- Once a minor error has crept in, arousal and anxiety rise even further, possibly resulting in a catastrophic drop in performance as described by Hardy and Fazey (see page 85).

What makes a good coach?

Top coaches are often tempted with large salaries to move to train a particular team or sportsperson. The reasons are clear. The right coach can make the difference between winning and losing. Anyone who has experienced coaching from the receiving end is aware there are some who are good and some who are, at best, mediocre.

In the first few weeks of the 2008 season, Tottenham Hotspur gained just two points from eight games. The recruitment of Harry Redknapp as manager saw a change of fortunes, with the next eight matches producing 16 points and Spurs moving steadily up the table from the bottom position they held when Redknapp took over.

Coaches are involved in the development and practice of relevant skills, ensuring a programme of practice and exercise to develop and maintain fitness is in place and helping to create and maintain the right mindset. It is this last skill that is probably what makes the biggest difference between coaches.

- Coaches use a blend of extrinsic and intrinsic motivation. A good balance means extrinsic motivators help to increase intrinsic motivation. If extrinsic motivators become too strong they may undermine intrinsic motivation.
- Need for achievement can be nurtured by a coach helping a sportsperson to judge which events to enter, so that they are able to achieve, but not too easily.
- This ties in with the use of appropriate goal-setting targets as it is important the sportsperson feels they are improving and developing in their sport.
- The feedback given by a coach during training can affect levels of self-efficacy. This will have a major impact on how well the sportsperson is likely to believe they can do in competition.
- Sportspeople who attribute their success or failure to luck are unlikely to be motivated to try harder. Coaches need to train them to believe hard work, effort and the development and application of skills are the most important factors.
- The high level of arousal experienced by sportspeople at a major event can enhance performance if the coach has ensured the correct response is the dominant one and that the sportsperson is able to harness the arousal to improve performance rather than to cause anxiety.

Taking it further

Watch a few pairs of interviews with top sportspeople, one when they have won and one where they did not. Try to identify attributions for performances, comments on self-efficacy and evidence of achievement motivation.

Other option

Gender differences

There are large differences between both the numbers of males and females that participate in sport, the types of sports they tend to pursue and whether childhood interests will continue into adulthood.

- Cultural norms mean that in some societies opportunities for female sport are severely constrained. In these cases girls may be unable to pursue a sport, even if they wish to.
- The dominance of male sport in the media means male sport is perceived as acceptable and to be admired, whereas female sport gets no such positive publicity.
- Girls who take up sport seriously may receive negative comments about their appearance or behaviour. This may act as a punishment and lead to a learned response of less involvement in sport.
- Evidence from research suggests females are more likely to attribute success to luck, whereas males are more likely to attribute success to ability. This means females are less likely to sustain effort in the belief they can win again.

Content analysis of articles

Content analysis: What makes a winner?

Articles that relate to what makes a winner tend to have two or three dominant themes. If you use articles that cover more than one type of sport it will give you a broader range of themes and therefore more to write about.

The first and most consistent theme you may find is motivation. Look for:

- Comments that relate to achievement motivation and aspects of behaviour and attitudes that reflect a need to achieve. Many of these comments also link to self-efficacy.
- Comments that give you evidence for coping with setbacks and failures, showing how individuals with high nAch push themselves to the limits of their ability but do not always succeed.
- Comments about ways that self-efficacy and the need to achieve allow sportspeople to cope with a setback and come through to win again.
- Comments about failure – there will not be many.

A second major theme is **goal setting**. Look for evidence of:

- Stepped goals in those facing a comeback after injury.
- Strategies used to turn round a losing streak.

Another theme you may find is **reinforcement**. Look for points about:

- The effect of reinforcement and how winners feel about their victories, remembering that not all winners gain financial rewards for their ultimate prize. For example, there is no direct financial reward to go with winning the Formula 1 drivers' championship, despite the wealth within the sport, though of course promotional work may be significant.

Interviews by sportspeople after an event often include attributions about the outcome, though these are rarely found in articles written by journalists unless they are quoting from the sportsperson. However, they may well comment on attribution retraining if the article is at least partially retrospective.

There are sometimes articles about a sportsperson who underachieves because they 'choke' at the crucial time in major events. This person may then take on a new coach or sports psychologist who helps them to overcome this and they start winning. Such articles usually show how the attribution retraining has turned someone back into a winner.

Over to you

Choose two or three sources for your content analysis that give you a range of issues to discuss. Aim for between two and four themes, as more gets unwieldy. You may find it easiest to have a mix of sports in your articles, as different sports raise different issues.

Remember to keep the articles as well as the work you do on them, so that when you come to revise you can remind yourself of the context of your analysis.

Content analysis: What makes a good coach?

While few newspaper articles analyse what makes a good coach in any depth, there are thousands of websites that aim to tell future coaches what qualities they must have or develop in order to be a good coach. If you are using such sites, do be aware that the content is often more to do with what a school or local authority might perceive as important rather than what will get the best out of the people being coached.

The main themes you are likely to find in this area are to do with developing skills, with improving performance, with maintaining motivation and with arousal. Often these issues will overlap.

Look out for:

- What types of reinforcement a coach uses.
- When reinforcement is used, for example to enforce discipline, develop skills, or work on fitness levels.
- Evidence of the type of reinforcement and link to intrinsic/extrinsic motivation.
- Evidence that a coach is trying to ensure skills are so practised that in competition the extra arousal produced does not create too high a level of arousal leading to anxiety and deterioration in performance.
- Strategies being employed to reduce negative effects of arousal.

Content analysis: Gender differences in sport

An interesting content analysis strategy is to start by looking at the amount of coverage for male and female sports in the media. If you analyse the content for themes it is useful to look at the language used and level of detail given. Female sport rarely gets the same level of coverage as male sport. There are a few sports where there is more equality, notably athletics, though even here the differential coverage for male and female relay teams at major events is very marked.

This then feeds back into the issue of gender difference and socialisation, as one argument for the lower level of coverage for female sport is that there is not as much, so to report more would be biased in favour of female sport. Similarly, female sport is often seen as less skilled, spectacular or demanding.

Other option

Instead of a content analysis you may choose to summarise two magazine or newspaper articles (TV or web-based material is permissible) concerning a topic covered in the sports section of the specification. In addition to the summaries, you must also draw conclusions about the findings, link the ideas to concepts, theories and/or research from the sports section.

For example, if you took an article written about the hope that children will be socialised into taking up more sports as a result of the 2008 Olympic successes, the 2012 London Olympics and 2014 Glasgow Commonwealth Games, and another article on the type of person who takes up a particular sport, there would be an opportunity to draw some interesting comparisons as to what motivates people to participate in sport and whether any effect will be enduring.

Summary

Look back at the list of key terms for sport psychology on page 75 and check you can define and use them all effectively.

Methodology

- Describe and evaluate the use of questionnaires in sport psychology.
- Be able to describe and evaluate the use of correlations in sport psychology.
- Consider issues of reliability, validity and ethics in the use of questionnaires and correlations.
- Compare qualitative and quantitative data in terms of strengths and weaknesses.

Content

- Explanations of sports participation and performance:
  - Describe and evaluate personality traits.
  - Describe and evaluate one other theory chosen from reinforcement, socialisation or attribution.
- Describe and evaluate achievement motivation theory.
- Describe and evaluate one other theory of motivation (e.g. cognitive evaluation or self-efficacy).
- Explanations of the effects of arousal, anxiety and audiences:
  - Describe and evaluate the inverted U hypothesis.
  - Describe and evaluate one other theory (e.g. evaluation apprehension, catastrophe, optimal level of arousal, drive).
- Psychological techniques used to improve performance:
  - Describe and evaluate two techniques, e.g. goal setting, imagery, attribution retraining.

Studies

- Describe and evaluate Boyd and Munroe's (2003) study on imagery in climbing.
- Describe and evaluate one study from:
  - Cottrell et al. (1968)
  - Craft et al. (2003)
  - Koivula (1995)

Evidence in practice

- Describe one key issue related to content of this chapter.
- Conduct a content analysis of articles or produce a summary of two magazine articles related to this topic.
- Draw conclusions about your findings.
- Make links to concepts and theories.

Examzone

1. Explain the terms intrinsic motivation and extrinsic motivation as used in sport psychology. (4 marks)

*2. Questionnaires are sometimes given to sportspeople to discover how they feel when competing. Outline one weakness of this means of collecting evidence. (3 marks)

3. Assess the effectiveness of one explanation for individual differences in sport participation. (5 marks)

*4. Evaluate one study in detail from sport psychology. (4 marks)

*5. Describe one key issue in sport psychology. (4 marks)

6. Using evidence from both your content analysis/article summaries and psychological theories, explain conclusions that can be drawn about one key issue in sport psychology. (8 marks)

7. Describe and evaluate psychological techniques used by coaches to improve performance. (12 marks)

8. Evaluate psychological explanations for differences in how good a sportsperson someone may be. (8 marks)

5. Clinical psychology

What you will learn about in this chapter

- What is meant by the terms primary and secondary data.
- Two research methods used in the study of schizophrenia and one study for each method.
- How abnormality is defined and how it is diagnosed.
- The symptoms, causes and two treatments for schizophrenia and one other disorder.
- One treatment or therapy from the five approaches studied in Units 1 and 2.
- Three studies on clinical psychology, including Rosenhan and two others.

Key terms

- statistical definition of abnormality
- social norm definition of abnormality
- schizophrenia
- reliability
- validity
- primary and secondary data

Clinical psychology is concerned with abnormal behaviour. It seeks to define what makes a behaviour abnormal, and then to diagnose what the problem is so that it can be treated. Psychiatrists take a note of the symptoms their patient is suffering from and how long they have had them, plus information about their general health, and any social or psychological problems they may have. From this they can decide what disorder the person is suffering from and give them appropriate treatment.

Even amongst psychologists there is disagreement about the causes of abnormal behaviour. Depending on what approach the psychologist comes from, he or she will have a different view of the causes of the mental disorder, the reasons why that person has that disorder, and so what the correct treatment is.

AS check

Think back to your AS work and the five approaches that you studied:

- Social Approach
- Cognitive Approach
- Psychodynamic Approach
- Biological Approach
- Learning Approach.

They all offer different explanations and treatments or therapies for people with mental disorders.

◆ Defining abnormality

Two ways of defining abnormality are considered here. The statistical definition of abnormality uses the curve of normal distribution and assumes that any normal characteristic occurs in 95% of the population. Therefore any abnormal characteristic occurs in 5% of the population. The social norm definition of abnormality is based on what society sees as desirable behaviour. Anyone who deviates from such behaviour is classed as abnormal.

◆ Schizophrenia

Schizophrenia is a **psychotic** disorder that affects about 1% of the population. It can cause disturbances in a person's thoughts, emotions and behaviours that can lead to the person withdrawing from social life.

◆ Diagnosis

Psychiatrists use a classification system to measure mental disorders such as schizophrenia. The system must be both reliable and valid:

- Can it diagnose a disorder based on symptoms that will be different from the symptoms of any other disorder?
- Can it successfully predict how the disorder will progress?
- Can it successfully predict how someone with that disorder will respond to a specific treatment?

◆ Data collection for research

Primary data is data that you collect yourself using methods such as experiments, questionnaires and observations. **Secondary data** is data that was collected by someone else and not the person currently using it. It may even be being used for a different purpose. A **meta-analysis** is a way of accessing a large number of participants, especially if what is being studied is not common.

Examiner's tip

There are a lot of new terms to learn. Rather than leave it all until it is time for revision, write each key word on a piece of card and underneath it write two or three words that will help you remember the definition of the term. On the back of the card write the full definition in your own words. Look at the front of the card at regular intervals and say or write out the full definition on another piece of paper. Use the back of the card to check that you have got it right.

Methodology

What you need to know

- Describe what is meant by primary and secondary data in doing research.
- Evaluate the use of primary and secondary data in doing research.
- Explain how issues of validity and reliability arise in clinical psychology.
- Describe and evaluate two research methods used in the study of schizophrenia, including one study for each of the two research methods.

▶ Observing gender differences in aggression at a playground like this would involve primary data.

Research which is carried out first-hand gains credibility and respect from others. This is because it is founded on authentic evidence, empirical data, original documents and so on, rather than on interpretations, explanations and opinions. In order fully to trust a study, psychologists will usually want to see the original evidence or specific data upon which it is based. Interpretations, explanations and opinions, however, are also important in the analysis of a topic.

Data can be classified as either primary or secondary.

Primary data

Primary data means original data that has been collected by those who witnessed an event first-hand or who collected data themselves for a specific purpose. It may present original thinking or new information.

Examples of primary data include results from a questionnaire or experiment, which can be qualitative or quantitative. Data can be sets of statistics that you then input to a computer program to construct frequency distributions or other descriptive statistics. Primary data can come from an observation you have carried out where you may have raw data – for example a tally chart of aggressive behaviours between boys and girls in a playground.

◆ Evaluation

Strengths

- In general, primary data is a reliable source because the researcher can replicate the procedures to check results, as they know the procedures and how the data was collected and analysed.

- The chances are that it will also be more up-to-date. Data gathered years previously is less likely to provide reliable answers to the questions your data needs to address.
- Since primary data is taken directly from the population in question, it is one of the best types of data to collect for research methods like the survey.

Weaknesses

- Researchers may be subjective in what kinds of data they look for, in particular data that 'fits' the hypotheses they are trying to test.
- The data has to be gathered from scratch, which involves finding a large enough population (to make the sample credible and generalisable) and in turn glean a large volume of data. This usually makes it more costly and time-consuming (because of the direct and personal intervention) than collecting secondary data.

Taking it further

Think about all the data you collected for your practicals at AS. Was this primary or secondary data? Make a list of the following criteria and evaluate your data. Was it: reliable; subjective; generalisable; time-consuming to collect; valid and accurate? Do you have more strengths or weaknesses in your list?

Secondary data

Secondary data is second-hand analysis of pre-existing (primary) data. It may be analysed in a different way or used to answer a different question from that addressed in the original research. Secondary data analysis uses data that was collected by someone else, in order to further a study that you are interested in completing.

Secondary data usually interprets, analyses, evaluates, explains or comments on a primary source or event. After statistical operations have been performed on primary data, the results become known as secondary data.

In some cases, secondary data is gathered before primary data in order to find out what is already known about a subject before embarking on the new investigation.

The Internet is a great source of secondary data. Many published statistics and figures are available on the Internet either free or for a fee.

Using the example opposite of gender differences in the playground, secondary data might be used to try and explain why more boys were more aggressive than girls, etc.

◆ Evaluation

Strengths

- It saves time and expense that would otherwise be spent collecting data.
- It can provide a larger database (e.g. a university library) than an individual researcher could hope to collect.
- In some cases, for example historical documents, secondary data is often the only resource and thus the only way to examine large-scale trends of the past.

Weaknesses

However, secondary data has limitations and should be carefully evaluated to determine the appropriateness for the task at hand:

- The researcher cannot personally check the data so its reliability may be questioned.
- The researcher may have no knowledge of how the data was collected, and has no control over it. Therefore, they do not know anything about its accuracy or its bounds of error.
- The data may be out-of-date and therefore not suitable for current research.

Examiner's tip

When describing either primary or secondary data, try and give actual psychological examples of research rather than anecdotal ones. For example, it's useful to say the findings of Gottesman's (1991) research are an example of secondary data as it shows the examiner you know what secondary data is.

Reliability and validity

In clinical psychology the goal of diagnosis can only be achieved if it is both consistent (i.e. clinicians must agree) and it reflects an actual disorder (and cause/possible treatment).

◆ Reliability

A diagnosis is considered reliable if more than one psychologist gives the same diagnosis to the same individual. In other words, clinicians' diagnosis of disorders must be consistent with each other.

It follows that issues of reliability arise when clinicians disagree over diagnosis. Beck et al. (1961) found that the agreement among clinicians was at about the level of chance. They gave two psychiatrists 153 patients to diagnose, but the two only agreed 54% of the time, suggesting that diagnosis can be highly unreliable. Similarly, Zeigler and Phillips (1961) found between 54% and 84% agreement amongst clinicians. Although this upper figure might seem quite high, it still leaves at least 16% disagreement, which has implications for the patient in terms of their diagnosis and treatment.

In some cases the issue may come from the patient rather than the clinician. Patients may vary in the detail, emphasis and type of information they give, which can affect the diagnosis. For example, an individual may go to their GP reporting symptoms of depression such as lack of motivation. Once referred to a psychiatrist, the patient may then emphasise other symptoms such as an irrational fear. This could result in a different and therefore unreliable diagnosis.

There can also be disagreements over different classification systems and different cultures. Cooper et al. (1972) showed American and British psychiatrists the same video-taped interview and asked them to make a diagnosis. New York psychiatrists said it was schizophrenia twice as often, whereas the London psychiatrists said it was depression twice as often. As both are Western cultures with similar lifestyles, one would normally expect more agreement.

◆ Validity

This refers to the extent to which a diagnosis reflects an actual disorder (and possible cause) and therefore enables a suitable treatment to be identified. For example, if individuals with the same diagnosis show different symptoms, the diagnosis has low validity. Similarly, if individuals with the same diagnosis do not respond to the same treatment, the diagnosis also has low validity. The problem is that, because few causes of psychological disorders are actually known, it makes any type of valid diagnosis difficult. Most disorders are rarely due to one identifiable cause. Instead, they are more usually a combination of biological, social and cultural factors.

The importance of diagnosis is to enable a suitable treatment to be given. This is known as **predictive validity**, whereby effective treatment means the diagnosis was valid. However, in 1000 cases studied by Banister et al. (1964), there was no clear-cut relationship between diagnosis and treatment, giving low predictive validity. Moreover, research suggests that there is only a 50% chance of correctly predicting the treatment a patient will receive on the basis of diagnosis (Heather, 1976). It is argued that one reason for such low validity may be that factors other than diagnosis are equally important in deciding a particular treatment; for example, patients may vary in the detail, emphasis and type of information they give.

AS check

You were introduced to the concepts of reliability and validity in both the Social Approach (AS page 11) and Cognitive Approach (AS pages 44-45). These concepts are concerned with the consistency of data and the genuineness of the results.

You may find it helpful to look at the section on the Diagnostic Statistic Manual (used for diagnosing mental disorders) on page 105 while you consider issues of reliability and validity.

Taking it further

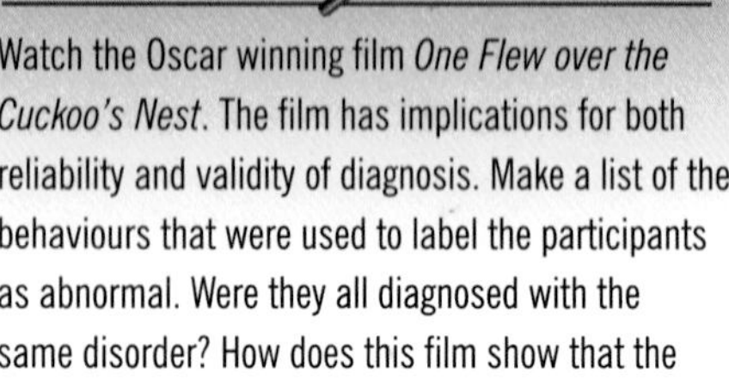

Watch the Oscar winning film *One Flew over the Cuckoo's Nest*. The film has implications for both reliability and validity of diagnosis. Make a list of the behaviours that were used to label the participants as abnormal. Were they all diagnosed with the same disorder? How does this film show that the diagnosis was neither reliable nor valid?

Examiner's tip

- When looking at reliability in research, ask yourself whether the same diagnosis has been given by others. The more consistency of diagnosis there is with the same symptoms, the more reliable the diagnosis.
- When looking at validity in research, ask yourself whether the diagnosis led to suitable treatment that works. Are the symptoms shared by others with the same disorder? If the answers are yes, then it is valid.

Research methods in clinical psychology

Three popular and successful research methods used in clinical psychology are twin studies, case studies and animal experiments. These are commonly used when researching explanations and treatments of mental illness such as schizophrenia. From these methods we can try and establish whether an illness has a genetic or biochemical component, which may then influence possible treatments. Twin studies and animal experiments in particular feature control over most variables, meaning they can be repeated and their findings tested for reliability.

◆ Animal experiments

There is a long tradition of using animals in psychological research. Knowledge gained from this research has played a significant role in the development of many psychological theories and applications. Despite this, the popularity of animal research has diminished, particularly within the UK over the last 15 years, largely as a result of the Animals Act of 1986. Research is dependent on obtaining Home Office licences before any particular project is carried out, so that it can be closely monitored. The role of the Home Office is to check whether the end justifies the means, i.e. does the certainty of any medical benefit outweigh any suffering? The answer must be 'yes' before any individual licences can be approved.

In the majority of cases, psychologists use two main types of research to study animals:

- **Ethological methods** – this is where the animals are studied in their natural environment, often through naturalistic observation, or by experimentation, where some aspect of the animal's environment is manipulated.
- **Laboratory studies** – this is where the animals are studied in an artificial environment that allows precise control and measurement of variables. Whereas ethological methods are primarily designed to provide insight about animals, laboratory studies are often intended to allow generalisations from animals to humans.

The following are some of the main ethical considerations that must be taken into account under the terms of the Animal Act (1986):

- If animals are to be constrained, harmed or stressed in any way, assessment must be carried out to ensure the knowledge gained justifies the procedure. Procedures that cause pain or distress to animals are illegal in the UK.
- Researchers should have knowledge of a species' natural history as well as its special needs. Endangered species should not be collected in the wild except as a serious attempt at conservation.
- Caging conditions must take into account the social behaviour of the species.

Schizophrenia study using animals

Schizophrenia is one of the key mental disorders you need to study. It has been described as a psychotic disorder which involves loss of contact with reality, typically involving hallucinations and/or delusions. The idea is that if schizophrenia can be transmitted genetically, then bio-chemical abnormalities should be detectable in the brains of those diagnosed with schizophrenia. Subsequently, research suggests that one of the main causes of schizophrenia is thought to be due to chemical imbalances in the brain, specifically the overproduction of the neurotransmitter dopamine. The dopamine hypothesis is described in more detail on page 109.

AS check

You were introduced to animal experiments (see AS page 102) and how they are used by psychologists in experimental research. This brought up many ethical and practical issues to go alongside the usual methodological issues.

▲ Research has looked at the effect of a range of drugs, including amphetamines, which increase dopamine activity. These are known as dopamine agonists, i.e. they increase dopamine levels in the brain.

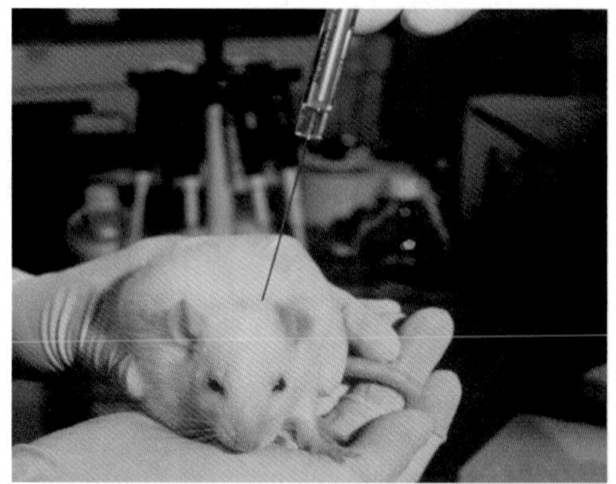

▲ Randrup and Munkvad (1966) demonstrated that injecting rats with amphetamines could induce schizophrenia-like symptoms.

▲ The argument of evolutionary continuity means we can apply findings from animal experiments to humans, as we are basically the same.

Have you ever wondered?

How many and what kinds of animals are used in laboratory research in particular? Follow the link below to an article on the BBC website which discusses how experiments on animals year on year is starting to grow again. http://news.bbc.co.uk/1/hi/sci/tech/7517022.stm

Examiner's tip

Make a list of psychological studies using animals that you have studied at AS and A2. Do these break ethical guidelines regarding the use of animals in any way? If so, say how.

Taking it further

Make a list of arguments for and against using animals in research. You may find this link useful to help you research:
http://www.bbc.co.uk/ethics/animals/

Randrup and Munkvad (1966) aimed to see whether schizophrenia-like symptoms could be induced in non-human animals by giving them amphetamines. Amphetamines worsen schizophrenic-like symptoms by releasing dopamine at the central synapses. The procedure involved injecting rats with doses of 1-20mg/kg of amphetamines. In their findings, all the known symptoms of schizophrenia were reported, including stereotypical activity. They concluded that experiments with a number of different animals – including chickens, pigeons, cats, dogs and squirrels – show that stereotypical schizophrenic activity can be produced by amphetamines. This supports the theory that dopamine contributes to schizophrenia.

◆ Evaluation

Strengths

- Using animals as opposed to humans is more convenient and practical. Animals reproduce more rapidly than humans and we can therefore study them across their lifespan more quickly. Animals are also easier to control than humans, which means it is easier to conduct experiments on them because experiments require the control of variables.
- Some theories believe that humans and animals do share a number of characteristics, for example humans and monkeys have lots of genetic similarities. From this, some psychologists have put forward the argument of evolutionary continuity. If we accept that argument, studying animals can offer an insight into, and possible explanations of, human behaviour. Human suffering can therefore be alleviated through knowledge gained from animal experimentation.
- Animals can be used for experimentation where ethical considerations would prevent the use of human participants.

Weaknesses

- Some (often for religious reasons) reject the argument of evolutionary continuity. Instead, they believe that humans and animals are separate creations, i.e. that there is evolutionary discontinuity between humans and animals. If we accept this, the study of animals can reveal little about humans.
- Animal studies are often criticised for being **anthropomorphic**. This is the tendency to believe that an animal's behaviour is due to the same type of thinking and reasoning as a human's, even though there is no real evidence to support it. Critics argue that animals are totally different from humans and therefore can tell us nothing about human behaviour. The wide diversity and variation in animal species make extrapolation to humans invalid.
- The single biggest argument against using animals in experiments is that we cannot assess their suffering. It is morally wrong to inflict pain and distress on animals. They are as important as humans and have rights.
- Animals may be more practical to use and bringing them into a laboratory environment will of course mean variables are controlled. However, this type of experimentation lacks ecological validity as it involves taking the animal out of its natural surroundings. It is therefore of little use.
- Regan and Singer (1976) saw animal experiments as a form of discrimination and called it specieism: 'We don't need larger, cleaner cages but empty cages…'. However, some scientists such as Gray (1989) point out that opposition to animal research is contradictory in a society which has a heavy reliance on intensive farming methods. Gray goes on to suggest that, rather than having to justify the use of animals in research, scientists have a responsibility to use animals whenever their use could make a significant contribution to the relief of human suffering.

Twin studies

In order to investigate the influence of genes – and in particular to see whether there is a genetic predisposition to schizophrenia – researchers focus on the study of identical twins (monozygotic or MZ twins) because they share 100% of their genes. The results are then compared with findings from pairs who are less genetically alike, i.e. fraternal or non-identical twins (dizygotic or DZ twins). DZ twins share 50% of their genes. A **concordance** rate is given, which states the rate of agreement between the two variables. Other topics which have been investigated in this way include IQ, personality, depression, dyslexia and bulimia.

For example, with regards to schizophrenia, if we look at a pair of MZ twins who have been reared apart (adopted, for example) and they both develop schizophrenia, then we can reasonably assume that there is probably a genetic basis. However, we may find that the concordance rate is only 70% not 100%.

Gottesman (1991) argued for a genetic cause of schizophrenia. He found that, when one MZ twin is schizophrenic, the other one has about a 50% chance of being schizophrenic or having other disturbances. With DZ twins, however, there is only around a 15% concordance rate. The evidence is, therefore, quite strong that schizophrenia has a large genetic component.

Gottesman's (1991) research is discussed further on page 109, under the biological explanation of schizophrenia.

◆ Evaluation

Strengths

- Studies using twins can help identify **trends** in families. Once such trends have been identified, researchers are then able to carry out DNA testing to try and isolate the genes involved.
- Findings from twin studies regarding the genetic basis of behaviour provide controlled evidence for the nature side of the nature/nurture debate. They demonstrate that much of our behaviour is inherited and not merely due to environmental influences.

Weaknesses

- Twin studies do have problems with their designs. For example, a 50% concordance rate in schizophrenic MZ twins may mask other possible causes.
- Twin studies can also be criticised for not showing cause and effect. For example, a 50% concordance rate suggests that schizophrenia runs in families. However, this does not mean that the cause is necessarily passed on through genes. Families share similar environments and experiences, so any concordance may be to do with a shared environment.
- In many cases, it is difficult to find a large sample of identical twins who possess the variable we are looking for (e.g. schizophrenia) and it is even harder to find such twins who are reared apart.
- It can be argued that twin studies operate on the assumption that both twins have an identical environment and this may not be the case. Rosenthal (1963), for example, reports the case of the Genain quadruplets who were four identical quad sisters born in the 1930s. They all developed schizophrenia in the course of their life, but each did so in a different form and at a different age. So, whilst all of them inherited an identical predisposition to the disorder, they had sufficiently different experiences within the family to alter the onset and the outcome of the disorder.

AS check

You were introduced to twin studies (see AS page 100) and how they are used to see if behaviours are shared by those who are genetically similar. They are particularly useful if the twins are reared apart, so sharing a close genetic link but not the same environment. This isolates genetic causes from environmental ones. See if you can recall what concordance rate means in this context.

Other options

Case studies represent another way of researching schizophrenia. You were introduced to them in the Psychodynamic Approach at AS. Case studies involve an in-depth look at one person over a long period of time to see the causes of their particular behaviour. Use the link below to watch the case study of Gerald S. He is grossly delusional and thought-disordered, and exhibits most of the symptoms of schizophrenia. You can also access the case study by going onto You Tube and searching for schizophrenia.
http://uk.youtube.com/watch?v=gGnl8dqEoPQ

Content

What you need to know

- Describe and evaluate the statistical definition and the social norms definition of abnormality.
- Describe and evaluate the reliability, validity and cultural issues regarding the diagnosis of disorders using the findings of studies.
- Describe the symptoms, and describe and evaluate two explanations and two treatments for schizophrenia and one other disorder.
- Describe and evaluate one treatment from each approach studied in Units 1 and 2.

Taking it further

Other definitions of abnormal behaviour include maladaptive or dangerous behaviour, personal distress and unexpectedness. Use the Internet and abnormal psychology textbooks to look up these definitions.

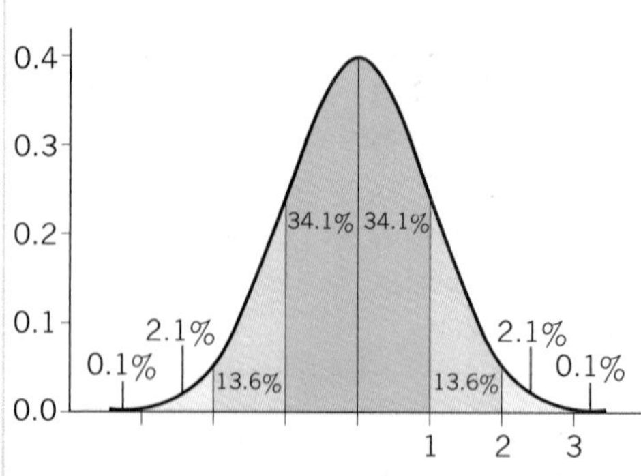

▲ A curve of normal distribution.

AS check

Standard deviation is a measure of dispersion. It allows us to see how spread out the scores are from the mean.

Definitions of abnormality

When defining abnormality it is best to look at all the possible definitions together rather than focusing it on just one definition. (Note: in the exam you will be expected to focus on two separate definitions.)

◆ Statistical definition

The assumption is that any human characteristic is spread in a normal way across the general population. When the incidence of that characteristic is plotted on a graph, the graph will form a curve of normal distribution. The majority of people will fall in the middle of the graph, with a minority being at either extreme of the graph.

The same is true of normal and abnormal behaviour. If someone's behaviour falls in the bottom or top 2.5% – i.e. more than two standard deviations away from the mean in the centre – then it is considered to be abnormal. For example, 65% of the population have an IQ between 85 and 115 and the average IQ is 100. The majority (95%) of the population have an IQ of between 70 and 130. Therefore those with an IQ of below 70 fall into the bottom 2.5% of the population and so could be considered abnormal. Indeed, it is one of the criteria for diagnosing mental retardation.

◆ Evaluation

- This definition does not tell us the difference between desirable behaviour that is statistically infrequent and undesirable behaviour that is infrequent. No one would argue that having an IQ of over 130 makes someone abnormal but, using this definition, they would be classed as abnormal.
- A person may be one score above what is classed as abnormal according to this definition, e.g. an IQ of 71, and so be classed as normal but they still may need help.
- Some behaviours that would be classed as within the normal range because so many people have them, such as anxiety, are seen as abnormal in a clinical sense.
- However, it does give us a definite cut-off point, and one which is objective, therefore taking away the subjectivity of some of the other definitions of abnormality.

◆ Social norms definition

In every society there is a set of unwritten rules about the behaviour we expect in others and the behaviour that we don't expect. This sets our social norms, which decide what behaviour is seen as normal, or moral.

If someone behaves in a way that does not conform to our social norms we may feel anxious or threatened by them. For example, we don't expect to see people talking to themselves and may try to avoid them. However, if we see that they have a mobile phone then this behaviour becomes acceptable, as it is a social norm to talk on mobile phones in public. Some roles in society also come with what is considered to be normal behaviour, such as that doctors are expected to be caring towards their patients.

▲ How would you feel if a teacher came to work dressed like this?

◆ Evaluation

- This definition of abnormality can lead to an abuse of a person's rights based on what society sees as normal. In the past, for example, slaves who had an 'irrational' desire to run away from their masters were said to be suffering from drapetomania. This would be an example of social control (see Chapter 6).
- It is also culturally biased, as what may be seen as unacceptable in one society may be seen as acceptable in another society.
- Norms change over time, so what one generation sees as abnormal the next generation may see as normal. It wasn't so long ago that single females who became pregnant could be placed in mental asylums.
- However, the definition does allow us to take several behaviours into account which altogether may make us feel uncomfortable, but which on their own would not be classed as abnormal.

Diagnosing mental disorders

Once someone has been defined as abnormal they need to know what specific disorder they have, which can then lead to the appropriate treatment. The diagnostic system that we need to look at is the Diagnostic Statistic Manual (DSM), though there are others. The British classification system is called the International Classification of Diseases (ICD) and is published by the World Health Organisation. The two classification systems have developed alongside each other, being revised and updated a number of times and including more disorders.

◆ The Diagnostic Statistic Manual

DSM is the American system used to diagnose and classify mental disorders. The major categories are shown on the right. It is based on five axes. Axis 1 and 2 are both concerned with the diagnosis of mental disorders. Axis 1 looks at all disorders apart from personality disorders and mental retardation, which are in Axis 2.

The other three axes do not look at mental disorders, but look at factors that may affect the mental disorder or its treatment:

- Axis 3 looks at general medical conditions, as the symptoms of some medical disorders are similar to mental disorders. For example, hypothyroidism (an underactive thyroid) has the same symptoms as depression, so needs to be ruled out on the way to a diagnosis of depression.
- Axis 4 looks at psychosocial and environmental problems, which may have an effect on the disorder. This includes problems such as family problems, problems with employment and social problems, all of which may contribute to the disorder.
- Axis 5 is called the Global Assessment of Functioning (GAF) scale, which ranges from 100 to 0. The psychiatrist has to assess how able the patient is to cope with everyday life, and so how urgent their need for treatment is. Someone with a score of 100 has perfect functioning, whilst someone with a score of 40 can have serious problems in several areas, such as family relationships, ability to hold down a job and ability to think rationally.

Clinical syndromes

1. Disorders usually first diagnosed in infancy, childhood, or adolescence
2. Delirium, dementia amnestic and other cognitive disorders
3. Substance-related disorders
4. Schizophrenia and other psychotic disorders
5. Mood disorders
6. Anxiety disorders
7. Somatoform disorders
8. Factitious disorders
9. Dissociative disorders
10. Sexual and gender identity disorders
11. Eating disorders
12. Sleep disorders
13. Impulse control disorders not elsewhere classified
14. Adjustment disorders

Example of a diagnosis from Davidson and Neale (1994)

Alex was assessed after having been arrested for sexually assaulting a woman when he was drunk. He had been almost continually drunk for the past four years, since his daughter was killed in an accident. He now has liver damage. It was also found that he had a history of gang violence and domestic violence. He showed no remorse about any of his actions.

Axis 1: alcohol dependence
Axis 2: anti-social personality disorder
Axis 3: liver damage
Axis 4: arrest, death of his child
Axis 5: 42.

There are several ways reliability can be tested, for example:

- **Inter-rater reliability** is the extent to which two or more observers agree, or in this case two or more psychiatrists agree on the diagnosis.
- **Test-retest reliability** is assessed by testing the same person twice, with a time gap of weeks or months between the two tests. If the test is reliable, the patient should have the same diagnosis both times.

Reliability and the diagnosis of mental disorders

Any classification system that is used to diagnose mental disorders must be reliable, so that different psychiatrists studying the same patient or symptoms should come to the same diagnosis and therefore offer the same (correct) treatment.

Several studies have looked at the inter-rater reliability of DSM, with varying results:

- Brown et al. (1996) found that there was a 67% agreement rate for major depression, which is classed as good reliability.
- Zigler and Phillips (1961) found a 54% to 84% agreement rate when looking at broad categories for disorders, and reliability has increased since then so, depending on the disorder, the reliability is fair to good.
- Davison and Neale (1994) also found a variable reliability rate for different disorders, with 92% for psychosexual disorders, but only 54% for somatoform disorders.
- However, Kendal (1975) looked at specific disorders and the reliability rate fell to 32%–57%.
- Willemse, Van Ypreen and Rispens (2003) tested the reliability of ICD 10 for children's disorders and they found that unless the category was objective the reliability was poor, especially when the diagnosis was based on observations of the children.
- Nicholls et al. (2000) compared the reliability of DSM IV, ICD 10 and Great Ormond Street's classification system for children with eating disorders. ICD had a reliability rate of 36%, DSM of 64%, but only because 50% of the raters agreed they couldn't make a diagnosis. The Great Ormond Street system had 88% agreement.

However, some have argued that the reliability of classification systems is as good as the reliability for medical disorders. This was shown by Falek and Moser (1975), who found a 66% agreement rate between what doctors indicated was the cause of death without the aid of any tests, and post-mortem findings.

Summary of reliability studies

Name of study	Results	Reliability
Brown et al., 1996	67% for major depression.	Good
Zigler & Phillips, 1961	54% to 84% for broad categories	Fair to good
Davison & Neale, 1994	92% for psychosexual disorders, 54 % for somatoform disorders	Good and fair
Kendal, 1975	32% to 57% for specific disorders	Poor to fair
Willemse, Van Ypreen and Rispens, 2003	An unobjective category of children's disorders	Poor
Nicholls et al., 2000	ICD 36%, DSM 64%, Great Ormond Street 88%, for children's eating disorders ICD poor, DSM	Fair, Great Ormond Street Good

Validity and the diagnosis of mental disorders

A classification system also needs to be valid, so that it can correctly diagnose the mental disorder the person is suffering from, and accurate predictions can be made about how the disorder will develop and how effective certain treatments will be. Whether a disorder is medical or mental, a valid diagnosis is essential to the patient.

A diagnosis can have three types of validity:

- If it has **etiological validity**, a group of people who have been diagnosed with the same disorder will have the same factors causing it; so, if schizophrenia is caused by too much of the neurotransmitter dopamine, then to have etiological validity, people diagnosed as schizophrenic should all have an excess of dopamine in their brain.
- For a diagnosis to have **concurrent validity**, symptoms that form part of the disorder but are not part of the actual diagnosis, should be found in those diagnosed. For example, schizophrenics often have problems with personal relationships, but this is not a characteristic that is looked at when diagnosing them according to the classification system.

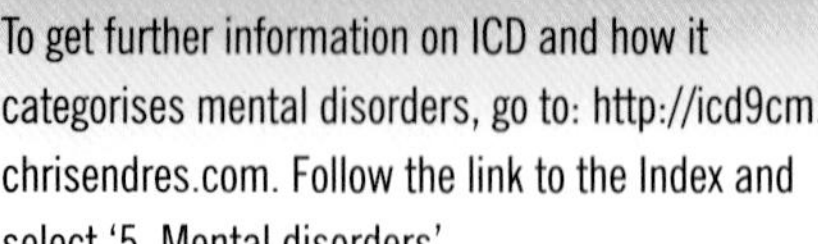

Taking it further

To get further information on ICD and how it categorises mental disorders, go to: http://icd9cm.chrisendres.com. Follow the link to the Index and select '5. Mental disorders'.

- **Predictive validity** is present if diagnosis can lead to a prediction of future behaviours caused by the disorder. If a diagnosis has predictive validity we should be able to say whether a person is likely to recover or whether the symptoms will continue. It should also be possible to predict how someone with a specific disorder will respond to specific treatments. For example, the drug lithium carbonate is effective for bipolar disorder, but not for other mental disorders. If a classification system has good predictive validity and diagnoses someone with bipolar disorder, they should respond to lithium carbonate.

A famous study on validity was carried out by Rosenhan (1973) (see page 124). Rosenhan concluded DSM III wasn't valid, as it couldn't tell those who did have mental disorders from those who did not. In a second study he said he would send pseudo-patients to psychiatric hospitals over three months, when in fact he didn't send any. About 10% of the patients who did go to the psychiatric hospitals involved were thought to be pseudo-patients by a psychiatrist and another member of staff, again showing that DSM is not valid, according to Rosenhan.

Several other people have looked at the validity of DSM by comparing it with other classification systems. The validity of one system can be checked by comparing it with another system already known to be valid. If they both agree then the system being checked is also valid. This is known as **criterion validity**.

Andrews et al. (1999) looked at how much DSM IV agreed with ICD 10. They found good agreement on disorders such as depression, general anxiety disorders and substance abuse, moderate agreement on other anxiety disorders and poor agreement on post-traumatic stress disorder. So validity appears to depend on the disorder. Cleusa et al. (1990) compared DSM IV and the Portuguese classification system for dependence disorders and found good agreement for measuring the severity of dependence on cocaine, cannabis and alcohol. However, a problem with both these studies is that they assume the alternative classification systems (ICD or the Portuguese version) are valid, when they might not be.

Lahey et al. (2006) found there was good predictive validity in relation to their social and academic functioning over a six-year period for children diagnosed with ADHD.

Cultural issues

Culture can affect the diagnosis and treatment of mental disorders, as different cultures have different attitudes to mental disorders. In Morocco, for example, it is thought you can catch a mental illness by accidentally encountering some sorcery, such as stepping on it. They believe mental disorder comes from sorcery and evil things. This affects treatment and how the mentally-ill person is seen – they are often feared as there is a possibility the evil could spread.

Culture can also affect how much information a patient is likely to disclose. This can affect diagnosis, as not all symptoms may have been mentioned. Casas (1995) found that a lot of African Americans do not like to share their personal information with people of a different race, for example. Sue and Sue (1992) found that many Asian Americans don't like to talk about their emotions and so are less likely to admit they have a problem – and when they have admitted it are less likely to talk about it with their therapist.

Examiner's tip

Criticisms of studies can be used when evaluating the validity or reliability of classification systems. If there are problems with how the studies were carried out, then there are problems with their conclusions about the classification system.

The number of patients thought to be pseudo-patients in Rosenhan's (1973) study

No. patients seen	193
No. patients thought to be a pseudo-patient by at least one member of staff	41
No. patients suspected by a psychiatrist	23
No. patients suspected by a psychiatrist and another member of staff	19

Taking it further

Several criticisms have been made of Rosenhan's original study. Go to http://www.holah.karoo.net/rosenhanstudy.htm to review some of these criticisms.

Taking it further

To see a variety of mental disorders that are specific to certain cultures, go to http://anthro.palomar.edu/medical/med_4.htm.

Culture can also affect your expectations of the diagnostic process. Cinnerella and Loewenthal (1999) compared cultural influences on mental disorders between white Catholics, black Christians, Muslim Pakistanis, Orthodox Jews and Indian Hindus. They found that all the groups thought depression was caused by life events, and all the groups except the white Catholics had a fear of health professionals misunderstanding them. The black Christian and the Muslim Pakistani groups both felt that there was a social stigma associated with depression, and both believed that prayer could be used to help alleviate the symptoms. This has the effect of possibly making these two groups less likely to seek medical help if they have depression.

Banyard (1996) found that, in Britain, 25% of the patients on psychiatric wards were black, whilst they only made up 5% of the total British population. Once in a psychiatric hospital, black patients were more likely to be seen by a junior doctor, whilst white patients were more likely to be seen by a senior doctor (Littlewood and Lipsedge, 1989).

Examiner's tip

There are a lot of studies and terms to remember in this section. It may help you to remember them if you create a spider diagram each for reliability, validity and cultural issues with the key points on and the name and results of the studies. A simple cross or tick can indicate whether the study shows classification systems to be reliable or valid.

Schizophrenia

In the 1890s schizophrenia was called *dementia praecox*, which means 'senility of youth'. This is because it was thought be a type of mental deterioration that started in adolescence. It has been called schizophrenia since 1908, when it was found that it wasn't necessarily the start of mental deterioration, nor does it have to start in adolescence. In men it often begins in the mid-20s and in women in the early 30s. Some schizophrenics can completely recover from the disorder, however many need ongoing treatment with drugs to allow them to live independently. Fifteen percent will need help and support for the rest of their lives and 15% don't respond to treatment.

Signs and symptoms of schizophrenia

1. At least two of the following symptoms for at least one month:
   - delusions
   - hallucinations
   - disorganised speech
   - grossly disorganised or catatonic behaviour
   - negative symptoms.

   If the delusions are bizarre or the hallucination is a voice that keeps up a running commentary on the person's behaviour or thoughts, or two or more voices are conversing with each other, then this on its own is enough for a diagnosis.
2. Social/occupational functioning is below levels prior to onset.
3. Continuing signs of disturbance for at least six months.
4. No major changes in mood (depression or elation).
5. No evidence of organic factors (e.g. drugs) or medical conditions.
6. If there is a history of developmental disorder, prominent delusions or hallucinations must be present for a month.

◆ Symptoms of schizophrenia

The condition refers to psychotic disorders that are characterised by major disturbances in thought, emotion and behaviour. It affects about 1% of the population and is equally common amongst men and women. Schizophrenics can have positive or negative symptoms. Positive symptoms refer to excesses in behaviour that are present in the patient, whilst negative symptoms refer to behaviour that is missing.

Positive symptoms include:

- hallucinations, where the patient hears or sees things that do not exist, such as voices commenting on their behaviour
- delusions, such as delusions of control, where the patient thinks their actions are being controlled by outside forces
- thought insertion, where the patient thinks that the thoughts in their head are put there by someone else
- thought withdrawal – the belief that outside forces are taking thoughts from the mind
- thought broadcasting, where the patient believes their thoughts are being broadcast to others.

Negative symptoms include:

- poverty of speech, where the patient uses as few words as possible
- social withdrawal, where the patient no longer interacts with family and friends
- the flattening affect, where the patient has a lack of expression in their voice and does not show emotions on their face.

There are five different types of schizophrenia: catatonic, paranoid, disorganised, residual and undifferentiated. Different symptoms are present in the different types of schizophrenia.

Taking it further

To see the effects of schizophrenia and why schizophrenics find it hard to recognise they have a disorder, as well as problems with being treated by drugs, watch *A Beautiful Mind*, starring Russell Crowe.

Biological explanation of schizophrenia

The Biological Approach sees the causes of schizophrenia as physiological. These include genetic factors and biochemical factors (the effect of neurotransmitters).

◆ Genetic factors

Schizophrenia does seem to run in families and to have a genetic link. The common view now is that schizophrenia is caused by a number of genes rather than one specific gene. Both family studies and twin studies have been used to study the genetic influence on schizophrenia.

◆ Evaluation

- Gottesman (1991) pooled data from 41 different European studies to see if there was a genetic link with schizophrenia, using the relevant diagnostic criteria. He found that 1% of the general population had schizophrenia, but that the percentage chance of having it increased the closer you were genetically to someone who had it, increasing to 48% if the sibling is an identical twin. Whilst this shows a genetic factor in schizophrenia, it also shows that the environment plays a part. If schizophrenia was totally genetically-caused then the risk of an MZ twin having schizophrenia if their other twin already had it, would be 100%.
- Heston (1966) compared adopted children whose natural mother had schizophrenia and adopted children whose natural mothers didn't have a mental disorder. Of the children with schizophrenic mothers, 10% went on to develop it, whilst none of the other group did, suggesting it is passed down from parent to child.
- Recent research has focused on trying to identify the gene responsible for schizophrenia. Hong et al. (2001) found that a variation of the TPH gene was more common in Chinese schizophrenics than in the general population.
- A study by the International Schizophrenia Consortium (2008) found that schizophrenics are more likely to have structural changes to their genes. The abnormalities were found in chromosome 22, chromosome 1 and chromosome 15, all of which had missing DNA when compared to non-schizophrenics.

◆ Biochemical factors

The **dopamine hypothesis** looks at the role of the neurotransmitter dopamine as a cause of schizophrenia. The drugs that are used to treat schizophrenia cause symptoms similar to Parkinson's Disease, which is known to be caused by low levels of dopamine. It is therefore assumed that the drugs reduced levels of dopamine by blocking dopamine receptors and, as they successfully treat schizophrenia, an excess of dopamine must be the cause of schizophrenia.

◆ Evaluation

Strengths

- Several studies have looked at the dopamine hypothesis. Lindstroem et al. (1999) used a PET scan to investigate the uptake of IDOPA (used to make dopamine) in 10 schizophrenics who weren't being treated and 10 normal people. They found the IDOPA was used more quickly in the schizophrenics, suggesting that they make more dopamine.

AS check

Remind yourself about neurotransmitters and genes on AS pages 104–105.

AS check

Look at AS page 100 to remind yourself of twin studies.

The risk of developing schizophrenia, from Gottesman (1991)

Relationship to schizophrenic person	% risk
General population	1%
Spouse	2%
Uncle or aunt	2%
Nephew or niece	4%
Grandchild	5%
Half-sibling	6%
Parent	6%
Sibling	9%
DZ twin	17%
Two schizophrenic parents	46%
MZ twin	48%

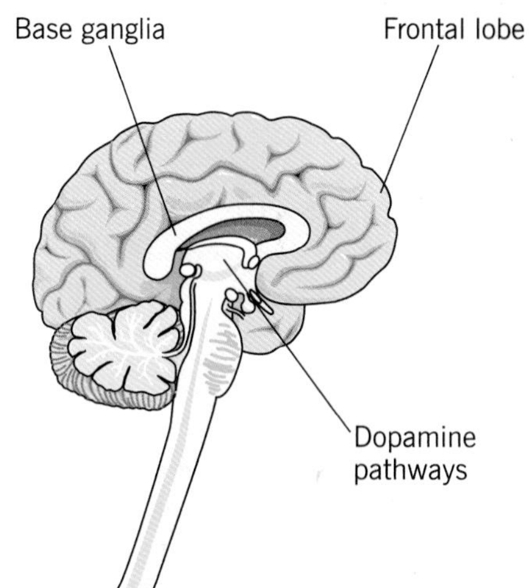

▲ Dopamine nerve pathways in the brain.

AS check

To recap what a PET scan and an MRI scan are, look at AS page 102.

- Donnelly et al. (1996) looked at homovanillic acid, which is a waste product of dopamine that is passed out of the body. They found that schizophrenics have more homovanillic acid than non-schizophrenics, again suggesting that they produce more dopamine.
- Figee et al. (2008) looked at the results of 13 studies using MRI scans to see the effect of antipsychotic drugs on the brain. Most of the studies showed that there was enhanced activity in the prefrontal region of the brain of schizophrenics, confirming that the prefrontal cortex is important in causing schizophrenia.

Weaknesses

- However, Depatie and Lal (2001) found that apomorphine, a drug that increases the effect of dopamine, did not create schizophrenic symptoms in their participants.
- It is hard to know if excess dopamine causes schizophrenia or if schizophrenia causes excess dopamine.

Look again at the symptoms of schizophrenia on page 108. Not all schizophrenics have all the symptoms; some have hallucinations, some have delusions, some have neither.

Cognitive explanation of schizophrenia

The Cognitive Approach sees the cause of schizophrenia as a problem with processing information. It is thought that schizophrenics have distorted beliefs and that these beliefs influence their behaviour. For example, they may believe that what was in fact a neutral message from someone was actually directed negatively. They also have an inability to reflect on their own thoughts and behaviour. This means they have problems recognising that their behaviour and thoughts are actually carried out by themselves; instead, they think they are from an outside agency.

◆ Evaluation

- Bentall et al (1991) asked participants either to think of category items for themselves, such as types of cars, or to read the category items they were given, such as a list of cars. He wanted to see if there was a difference in performance between schizophrenics who had hallucinations, schizophrenics who did not have hallucinations, and non-schizophrenics. A week later they were given a revised list of words, from which they had to pick out words they had thought of themselves, words they were given originally, and new words. Schizophrenics with hallucinations did the worst, schizophrenics without hallucinations did better, and non-schizophrenics the best.
- Frith and Done (1989) asked participants to follow a target on a video game with a joystick. Both schizophrenics and non-schizophrenics could do this when they could see the errors they made on the screen, but when the errors were not visible, schizophrenics with delusions did a lot worse than the control group. Both these studies suggest that schizophrenics have difficulty monitoring their own actions.

Negative symptoms are thought to be caused by an inability by schizophrenics to use the cognitive processes that are responsible for initiating their own actions – for example, social withdrawal is due to not initiating contact with family and friends.

Frith and Done carried out studies focusing on the negative symptoms of schizophrenia to see if cognitive functioning differed for non-schizophrenics:

- Frith and Done (1983) gave schizophrenics and non-schizophrenics a design fluency task and found that those with negative symptoms had more difficulty in creating their own responses. This implied that their cognitions were different – they had more trouble thinking of their own words.

Examiner's tip

As well as using studies to evaluate the causes of a mental disorder, you can use other approaches/explanations. Briefly compare the two approaches, and say if the alternative approach looks at factors which the approach you are talking about does not consider. The Biological Approach ignores cognitive factors, for example, but these are looked at by the Cognitive Approach.

- Frith and Done (1986) found that, when asked to give as many responses as possible to a verbal prompt, schizophrenics with negative symptoms produced fewer words than non-schizophrenics. They often repeated words they had already said, gave irrelevant words or said nothing, again implying that they have more difficulty thinking of relevant words, and more difficulty monitoring what they are saying and whether it is relevant to the task.

A problem with all these studies is that they focus on the symptoms of schizophrenia – they do not study what causes the problems with processing information in the first place.

Other options

There are other explanations about the causes of schizophrenia, including psychodynamic and social explanations. The Psychodynamic Approach looks at the effect of family interactions, whilst the Social Approach looks at factors in the environment.

Have you ever wondered?

Schizophrenia can be a very distressing disorder, especially if you believe your behaviour and thoughts are beyond your control. Why is it that, once they realise they have a disorder, schizophrenics don't take the chance to get rid of their symptoms by taking antipsychotic drugs? Some of the side effects on the next page may explain why.

Treatments for schizophrenia

Just as different approaches suggest different causes of schizophrenia, they also suggest different treatments. The treatment focuses on what that approach feels is the cause. So, a biological treatment will focus on changing the neurotransmitters and getting them back in balance, whilst a cognitive treatment will focus on changing our thinking patterns as cognitive psychologists feel that is the cause of mental disorders.

◆ Drug therapy: a biological treatment

Antipsychotic drugs, also known as neuroleptics, were first developed in the 1950s. They helped sedate the person and also reduced the intensity and frequency of hallucinations and delusions, amongst other psychotic behaviours. Further antipsychotic drugs have since been developed. These fit into the dopamine receptors in the brain, blocking the dopamine and stopping it being picked up, so minimising its effects. They are more effective when given at the onset of schizophrenia. Clozapine, which was developed in the 1970s, also appears to reduce the negative symptoms, though some debate remains as the evidence is inconclusive. Some studies have found it to be effective, whilst others have not.

◆ Evaluation

Strengths

- Drugs allow the patient to live in society, so avoiding being institutionalised by a long-term stay in hospital. It also allows them to access other therapies, which may help cure them.
- Pickar et al. (1992) compared the effectiveness of clozapine with other neuroleptics and a placebo drug. He found that clozapine was the most effective in treating the symptoms, even in patients who did not respond to previous drugs, and the placebo was the least effective.
- Emsley (2008) studied the effect of injecting the antipsychotic drug risperidone. He found that those who had the injection early in the course of their disorder had high remission rates and low relapse rates. In 84% of the patients there was at least a 50% reduction in positive and negative symptoms, and over the two years of the study, 64% of the patients went into remission.

Side effects of antipsychotic drugs:
- tightening of the muscles, especially neck and jaw
- decrease of spontaneous movements
- decrease in emotional spontaneity and motivation
- motor restlessness and fidgeting
- sedation
- dry mouth
- constipation and weight gain
- neuroleptic malignant syndrome (can be fatal).

Examiner's tip

When evaluating a drug therapy, do not just concentrate on the negative side effects, as marks for these will probably be limited.

Weaknesses
- One problem with all drugs is that there are side effects (see left). These side effects may be enough to put people off taking the drug.
- Non-compliance or partial compliance when it comes to taking the drugs is a major barrier to the treatment schizophrenia, and can lead to relapses and readmittance to hospital. After several relapses, patients are at increased risk of never getting back to the functional level they were at before developing the disorder. Rosa et al. found that only around 50% of patients comply with their drug therapy. Even if patients do comply and take their drugs, it has been found that 50% of them still have distressing symptoms.
- Drug treatment cannot be seen as a cure, as patients have to be kept on maintenance doses of the drug to maintain the therapeutic effect.

Cognitive Behavioural Therapy (CBT): a cognitive therapy

This therapy combines the cognitive and the behavioural approaches. The cognitive assumption behind it is that our beliefs about the world affect how we see the world and ourselves; the behavioural part aims to change our behaviour.

CBT focuses on present behaviour and thoughts instead of focusing on how those thoughts developed. The therapist has to accept the patient's perception of reality and then use this misperception to help the patient manage. It aims to allow the patient to use information from the world to make adaptive rather than maladaptive decisions. It does not aim to cure schizophrenia but to allow the patient to function relatively normally.

An agenda is set so that both therapist and patient know what they aim to get out of the sessions. The therapist helps the patient identify their faulty interpretations of the world and correct them. This is done by questioning and challenging maladaptive thoughts so that the patient realises they are incorrect and can change them to more realistic thoughts. Patients are also taught how to ignore the voices they hear, if that is one of their symptoms.

◆ Evaluation

Strengths
- Until recently it was thought that CBT would not be effective for schizophrenics as their whole perception of reality is different. This makes it difficult to get them to challenge their beliefs, which to them are rational. However, Chadwick (2000) studied 22 schizophrenics who heard voices. They each had eight hours of CBT, and all had reduced negative beliefs about how powerful the voices were, and how much the voice controlled them, thus allowing them to live with the voices better.
- Gould et al. (2001) carried out a meta-analysis of studies that looked at the effectiveness of CBT in conjunction with taking antipsychotics. He found that there was a large reduction in positive symptoms in most cases, with drop-out rates of about 12%, considerably lower than amongst those who stop taking antipsychotics without CBT.
- Pfammatter (2006) also carried out a meta-analysis on CBT and found that it was highly effective in reducing severe positive symptoms.
- Tarrier carried out a review of studies and found that, as well as reducing positive symptoms, CBT also helped to moderately improve the rate at which patients recovered, and helped reduce relapse rates.

- Beck and Rector found that CBT used alongside antipsychotics was more beneficial than just receiving routine care, though this only studied the patients in the short term and it is not known if these benefits lasted in the long term.
- Other studies have found that, as well as being useful for patients on antipsychotics drugs, CBT is effective on patients who do not respond to the drugs and has the added benefit of not producing any side effects.

Other options

There are alternative therapies from the other approaches, including the Psychodynamic Approach and the Social Approach.

Examiner's tip

When evaluating a treatment or therapy you can use alternative therapies to comment on an area that the treatment you are looking at does not consider. For example, the Psychodynamic Approach would argue that CBT will not be effective because it does not look at the actual problem causing the disorder, which is in the unconscious.

Anorexia nervosa

Anorexia nervosa means 'nervous loss of appetite' (though this is something of a misnomer, as there is no loss of appetite in many cases). Although by no means a modern disorder, it is in the last 20 or 30 years that the disorder has attracted interest and been publicised in the media.

Symptoms	Prevalence	Course and outcomes
• Refusal to eat and maintain a minimum average expected body weight • Fear of gaining weight or becoming fat • Distorted perception of body weight and shape • Amenorrhea (absence of at least three consecutive menstrual cycles) • Weight less than 85% of expected	• 90% of cases are in females between 13 and 18yrs • Rarely begins before puberty • DSM-IV states it occurs in 0.5-1% of females in adolescence and early adulthood	• Variable – **20%** have one episode and recover completely, while **60%** follow an episodic pattern of weight gain and relapse over a number of years. • Remaining **20%** continue to be affected and often require hospitalisation. • Mortality rate of those admitted to hospital is over **10%** due to starvation or suicide

Explanations of anorexia nervosa

◆ Learning Approach (behavioural)

Learning theorists suspect that anorexia nervosa has developed due to rewards from the environment. It is thought that the physical changes that come with adolescence could be a cause. A commonly held philosophy in today's society is 'slim is in'. Individuals are therefore rewarded for not eating, and the abnormal behaviour is reinforced. In today's Western society, in which advertising models and pop stars are mostly very slim, concerns about weight are common among young people in particular.

Individuals may want to lose a little weight at first due to social pressures and, if successful, they get an intrinsic reward (feel better). They may then become fearful of regaining the weight they have lost. Thus the fear of gaining weight is paired with eating and a classically-conditioned anxiety response develops. Next time the individual has food they will feel anxious and believe that in order to reduce the anxiety they must avoid eating. This explanation uses classical conditioning principles.

AS check

The key issue in the Learning Approach (AS page 146) focused on whether role models encourage eating disorders such as anorexia. It tried to explain this using social learning theory, which argues that these teenagers imitate role models whom they see as important.

AS check

The Learning Approach introduced you to classical and operant conditioning and social learning (AS page 127). These three theories of learning believe maladaptive behaviour such as anorexia is learned through association, consequences of actions and imitation of role models, respectively (AS pages 134–139).

Another idea is that avoidance of food is associated with anxiety on the part of parents and others, so that when an individual avoids food they get attention. As a result, the individual has learned that not eating brings attention and their fasting behaviour is reinforced. This explanation uses operant conditioning principles.

Social learning theory can also provide explanations, in terms of the way that thin models give expectations and help shape an adolescent's body image. It is thought that magazines play a huge part in shaping perceptions of desirable figures. Also that classmates can be role models, providing aspirations to others on a daily basis.

- **Classical conditioning** – slimming becomes a 'habit' like any other, through Stimulus-Response mechanisms. The individual learns to associate being thin (stimulus) with admiration and feeling good about themselves (response).
- **Operant conditioning** – the attention (reinforcement) from parents for not eating acts as a reward for the individual and the satisfaction (reward) of punishing the parents.
- **SLT** – the influence of media and culture, identifying with role (super!) models through attention, retention, motor reproduction and motivation.

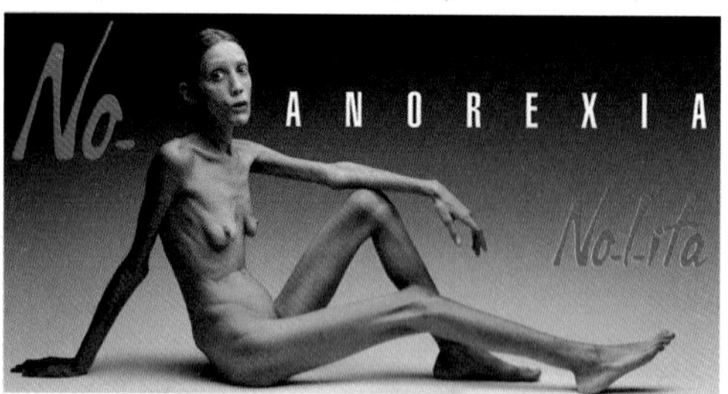

Have you ever wondered?

Why are anorexia sufferers mostly female? If learning theory is correct then there should be at least as many males influenced, as both genders are prone to the same advertising from the media. What do you think it is about males that makes them less prone to these media influences (or makes females more prone)?

- Make a list of your own role models. Which gender comes out on top?
- Now make a list of the most popular male and female role models. Is there a difference between your two lists?

Examiner's tip

Make sure you don't get carried away talking about the lives of celebrities in exams when answering questions on SLT and media influences on the public. One clear example using ARMM (attention; retention; motor reproduction; motivation) is all you need to highlight how we imitate role models.

◆ Evaluation

Strengths

- SLT is useful in explaining the acquisition of behaviours, such as anorexia, through observation. It has helped provide an understanding of the disorder and has been invaluable in informing the debate over media influences. It recognises that there is a short cut to learning, in that rather than having to learn through trial and error/experience, we can learn through observation.
- Its appeal lies in the fact it is based around observable behaviours. Gender differences can be explained in that females are more prone to anorexia due to the social pressures and stereotypes expected from them.

Weaknesses

- It is difficult to show that anorexia is acquired through either classical or operant conditioning. Because the person has not been studied from birth, it is impossible to identify the specific causes or consequences which may have led to the behaviour.
- Like all learning theories, SLT ignores the role of genetic or innate factors in behaviour. It is more likely that innate factors interact with our experiences to produce learning. For example, we would need an innate device to enable us to model and imitate in the first place.
- It does not explain excess dieting or individual differences. Most people in the West are exposed to thin models, but only a small percentage develop anorexia. Similarly, many people are influenced by social pressures into dieting, but don't take it to extremes and become anorexic. It is clear that different individuals respond differently to the same stimulus. Therefore, other factors must be involved in learning, such as cognition and innate factors.

◆ Biological Approach

The Biological Approach assumes that our behaviour is controlled by the activity in the central nervous system, specifically the brain. The brain itself is organised into regions which have different roles, so a malfunction in one region may cause a behavioural problem in the individual.

Malfunctioning of the hypothalamus has been suggested as a possible cause of anorexia, as the **hypothalamus** plays an important role in the regulation of eating. Animal experiments which involve lesions in a particular part of the hypothalamus have led to either over-eating or starvation in the animals.

It is believed that noradrenaline acts on part of the hypothalamus, which leads to eating; in contrast, it was found that serotonin suppresses appetite in non-human animals.

This biochemical imbalance has been used as an explanation for anorexia in humans. The **lateral hypothalamus** (LH) produces hunger and the **ventromedial hypothalamus (VMH)** depresses hunger. A malfunction here may be the cause of loss of appetite in some, and over-eating in others. For anorexics, it is as if their VMH is jammed in the on position.

Another type of biological explanation is that anorexia may run in families, so inheritance and genetics could play a part. Research involves comparing the resemblance of monozygotic (identical) twins with dizygotic (non-identical) twins. Resemblance is defined in terms of the strength of the correlation (concordance rate).

Both studies in this table demonstrate that genes seem to play an important role in anorexia, as both percentages are higher for MZ twins.

Researchers	MZ	DZ
Holland et al. (1984)	56%	5%
Kortegaard et al. (2001)	25%	13%

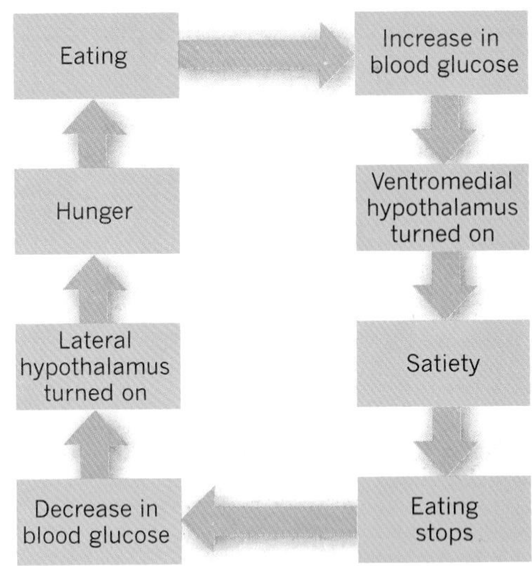

▲ This flowchart shows at what points in our eating cycle the VMH and LH are activated, and the resulting decrease or increase in hunger.

◆ Evaluation

Strengths

- The anorexic is not held to be responsible for their behaviour and is more likely to be seen as a victim of a disorder over which they have little or no control. This takes away issues of blame and labelling the person, and places the emphasis firmly on the disorder.
- Current research has shown that anorexia does have at least a degree of biological basis. Genetic and neurochemical abnormalities have been found using scientific methods, which can then be tested for reliability – unlike other non-scientific explanations.

Weaknesses

- The problem with this type of research is that it is difficult to differentiate between the cause and the effect, since the behavioural symptoms of anorexia have a direct and significant adverse effect on the person's physiology, which, in turn, may affect their biochemistry. It is therefore difficult to establish whether a biochemical imbalance in the hypothalamus causes anorexia, or whether anorexia causes a biochemical imbalance.
- It can be argued that twin studies operate on the assumption that both twins have an identical environment, and this may not be the case.
- The fact that MZ twins can be discordant for anorexia, suggests that the environment plays a significant role in the expression of the disorder.
- These explanations are of little help for anorexics as they are not useful in offering possibilities for treatment. Clinicians are then left having to seek out other possible causes, which may in turn have issues for reliability and validity of diagnosis and treatment.

It has been suggested that neither biological factors nor environmental factors cause anorexia in isolation, but that a mixture of both may provided an answer. This classic **diathesis–stress model** suggests that some individuals have a genetic predisposition to certain disorders, but that these lay dormant until some environmental event may trigger them. This could mean that anorexia is the result of a dormant gene being activated by stressful life experiences, including pressure from the media and peers to be thin. These presures may also come from within the family itself. A combination of these risk factors could increase the likelihood of the disorder in some.

Taking it further

This biological explanation has implications for other kinds of eating disorders such as obesity. A number of animal experiments have been carried out where lesions have been given to rats in particular. The lesions have caused over-eating or starvation depending on whether the LH or VMH was cut. Find out more about these experiments and decide whether the results can be applied to humans.

Examiner's tip

You must be able to explain and understand the concept of concordance and disconcordance when looking at twin studies. The fact that no one study has a 100% concordance rate suggests the environment plays a part in any type of disorder.

AS check

The Biological Approach introduced the concept of concordance rates (AS page 100). This is the likelihood that, if one twin has a certain trait, the other twin will also have it.

AS check

The Cognitive Approach uses information processing (AS page 39) to explain how we receive, interpret and respond to information. It describes this flow of information using the terms **input**, **process** and **output**.

Two therapies

This section will consider two different therapies for treating anorexia, Rational Emotive Therapy and free association.

◆ Rational Emotive Therapy (Cognitive Approach)

Ellis (1991) devised the ABC model to illustrate how irrational, self-defeating thoughts can lead to maladaptive behaviour. This can be applied to anorexics as in the following example:

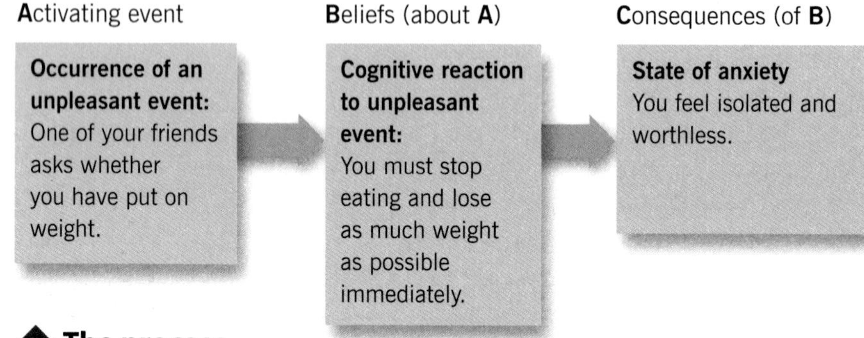

◆ The process

The aim of **Rational Emotive Therapy (RET)** is to help the client identify their negative, irrational thoughts and to replace these with more positive rational ways of thinking. A therapy session involves both cognitive and behavioural elements, with homework between sessions. The client is asked about the activating event to try and make them aware of the (negative) beliefs which are affecting their psychological well-being, for example:

– Tell me why your friend thought you had put on weight?
– Why is it important what your friend says about you?

◆ Behavioural elements

The therapist and client decide how to reality-test these hypotheses through experimentation. They devise experiments which can be carried out either during the session as role-plays or as homework tasks later. The aim is that, by actively testing out possibilities, clients will come to recognise the consequences of their faulty cognitions.

Together, the client and therapist decide on new goals which will enable more realistic and rational beliefs to be incorporated into the client's thinking. These are usually graded in stages of difficulty so that clients can build upon their own success.

Clients are then taught to replace their faulty and irrational beliefs with more realistic ones, in other words, to develop a dispute-belief system (D), for example:

– Your friend may be jealous of the way you look or is actually displacing fears she has about her own weight on to you.

In this way clients are encouraged to take a more realistic and rational view of life, in which failures are normal but unfortunate, rather than disasters that reveal the individual's lack of worth.

Taking it further

Think about an activating event and how you dealt with it using the ABC model. What was the thought process in your mind? How might RET explain other disorders such as depression or phobias?

◆ Evaluation

Strengths

- Brandsma et al. (1978) reported that RET is effective in producing behaviour change amongst those who are self-demanding and who feel guilty for not living up to their own high standards.

- RET is seen to be more effective than psychoanalytic therapies as it aims to help people get better rather than feel better during the session, and to accept reality, however bad it is. In this respect the therapy is not interested in Freudian 'long-winded' expensive dialogues, which are seen as indulgent.

Weaknesses

- The argumentative nature of the therapy has been questioned, particularly by those who stress the importance of empathy in therapy.
- Fancher (1995) argues that cognitive therapists may not be capable of identifying faulty thinking. What is foolish and illogical to the therapist may not be foolish and illogical in terms of the individual's own experiences.

AS check

Freud used a number of techniques to access the unconscious, including a combination of free association, slip of the tongue (Freudian slip) and dream analysis.

◆ Free association (Psychodynamic Approach)

The aim of the therapy is to enable the anorexic to cope better with internal conflicts that are causing disturbance. By uncovering these unconscious conflicts, the anorexic can work through them at a more conscious level. The job of the therapist is to uncover, explain and then help the patient come to terms with this conflict. The patient lies on a couch in a position where they can't see the therapist (to avoid any demand characteristics and allow open honest feelings to flow through).

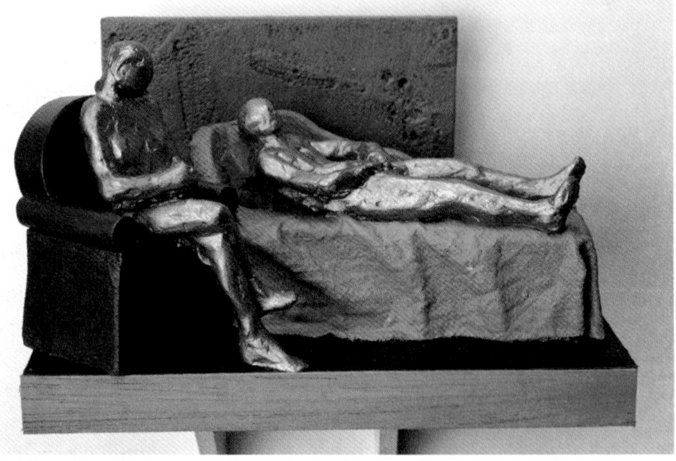

▲ The client is in a comfortable position and cannot see the therapist. This is to enable them to talk and answer questions freely, without the added pressure of seeing the therapist's reaction.

During therapy Freud often asked his patients to talk freely about their earliest memories and how they felt about the people in their lives. If they seemed to run out of things to say Freud would give them key words, such as 'happiness', 'love' or 'fear'. When Freud asked them a direct question their replies were often fairly predictable, but when they were just talking freely they occasionally said things that were more revealing. Freud thought they seemed to give some clues about what was going on in their unconscious. Several patients mentioned being very frightened of some things. It was as though they were off their guard when talking freely, and able to say things which they may not have said otherwise.

Taking it further

Try out free association on a friend. Prepare some key words in advance and tell them you will say a word and they have to say the first thing that comes into their head. These responses should come from the unconscious mind; as soon as your friend pauses to think, it means their response to your cue word is from their conscious. It is a sort of quick-fire question and answer session.

◆ Evaluation

Strengths

- Free association is in depth and includes all aspects of functioning from early childhood onwards, so takes all experiences in to account.
- It is a unique method as is needed to uncover the unmeasurable unconscious.
- Analysis of what the client says during free association may provide a useful tool in psychotherapy. It appears to provide access to the unconscious, allowing subsequent interpretation. For example, anorexia is often seen as a manifestation of underlying unconscious conflicts between the id and superego.

Weaknesses

- Free association may actually be inappropriate for people with certain disorders. Encouraging the client to talk at length about the issues on their mind, may reinforce thoughts that are already obsessive.
- Interpretation of what the client says is clearly subjective and may therefore be considered unscientific. Any interpretation is possible, making the theory unfalsifiable. Therefore, it is not possible to validate the interpretation of free association.

Treatments and therapies from each approach

What you need to know

You need to be able to describe and evaluate one treatment/therapy from each of the following approaches:
- Social Approach: family therapy or care in the community programmes.
- Cognitive Approach: Cognitive Behavioural Therapy or Rational Emotive Therapy.
- Psychodynamic Approach: free association or dream analysis.
- Biological Approach: use of drugs (chemotherapy) or electro-convulsive therapy (ECT).
- Learning Approach: Token economy programme or systematic desensitisation.

AS check

The Psychodynamic Approach introduced you to free association and dream analysis (AS page 72) and the debate about whether dreams have meaning formed the key issue (AS page 90). The Learning Approach included discussion of both the token economy programme and systematic desensitisation (AS page 139). The Biological Approach introduced you to brain scans that allow us to see the living brain and its relationship with our behaviour (page 99).

AS check

The Biological Approach introduced you to how surgery is used to disable parts of the brain to see how this affects behaviour (AS page 99). It assumes that our behaviour is controlled by the activity in the central nervous system, specifically the brain.

◆ Electro-convulsive therapy (Biological Approach)

If it is assumed that psychological problems originate on the biological level, then it follows that the treatment of psychological problems should also be biological in nature. This is the rationale behind the biological (medical) approach to therapy.

ECT involves inducing a convulsive seizure. It was introduced by Cerletti during 1935/6 and was originally based on the (incorrect) premise that schizophrenia and epilepsy do not occur in the same person and hence that, if one can induce an epileptic fit in a schizophrenic patient, that patient should be cured of his/her condition.

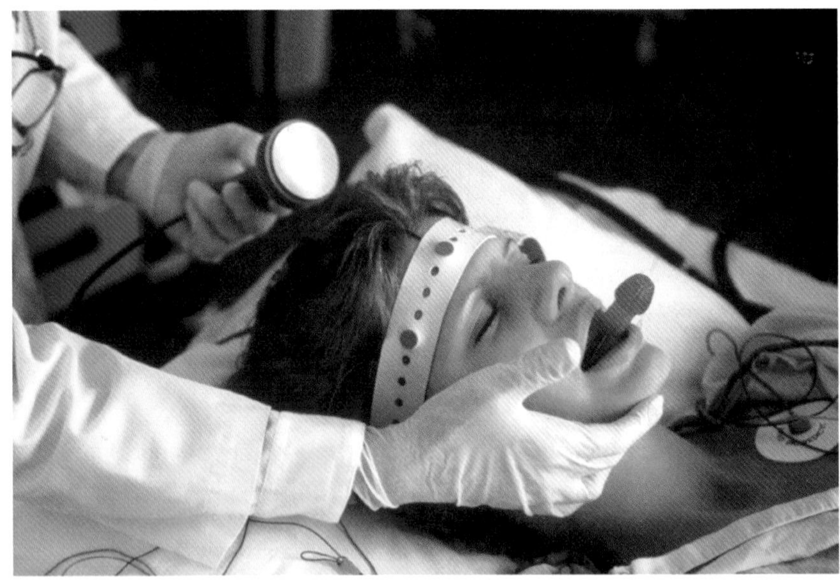

▶ The patient is strapped down and has a rubber spoon inserted in their mouth to prevent them choking or biting their tongue.

◆ Process

1 Preparation

A medical examination is carried out and the patient is allowed no food for six hours. The patient is put to sleep with barbiturates, muscle relaxant to minimise the danger of physical injury and oxygen to guard against brain damage.

2 Administration

Two electrodes are attached to the patient's head. Electrical current from 65 to 140V is passed though the brain for up to half a second. This shock can be passed through both temples simultaneously (bilateral ECT) or only one temple (unilateral ECT). Current causes a convulsion which lasts from 25 seconds to a few minutes. For severely depressed patients bilateral ECT is often preferred by psychiatrists, since it acts more quickly and fewer treatments are required.

However, unilateral ECT has fewer side-effects, particularly with regard to memory disruption, and consequently is used whenever possible.

3 Recovery

The patient awakens approximately 10 minutes after the current was applied. Typically, a person with depression will receive 6-9 treatments over a 2-4 week period.

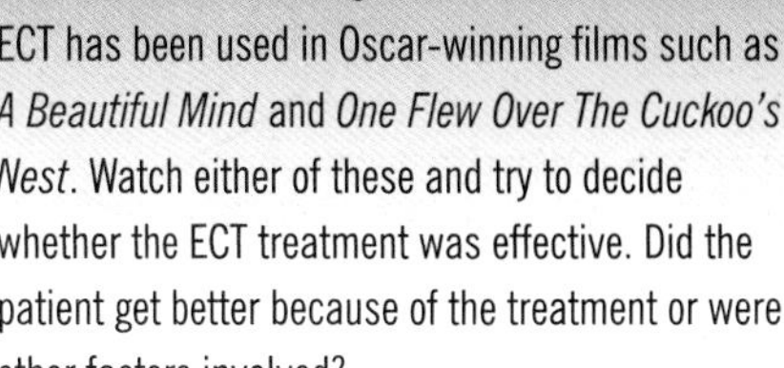

Taking it further

ECT has been used in Oscar-winning films such as *A Beautiful Mind* and *One Flew Over The Cuckoo's Nest*. Watch either of these and try to decide whether the ECT treatment was effective. Did the patient get better because of the treatment or were other factors involved?

◆ Evaluation

- Opponents, including MIND (The National Association for Mental Health) and PROMPT (Protect the Rights of Mental Patients in Therapy) make a number of ethical objections – notably that since we do not know how, or indeed if, ECT works it should not be used, as it is a procedure often used on patients unable to give informed consent as a result of their condition.
- Clare (1980) cautions against the overuse of ECT, maintaining that, as with valium, ECT is much abused and over-used because it is relatively quick and easy to administer.
- ECT can cause memory disruptions ranging from minor short-term memory loss to more severe retrograde amnesia and an impaired ability to acquire new memories.
- Compared with depressive patients who have received psychotherapy alone, those who have received ECT treatment are much less likely to commit suicide. Without ECT treatment 11% of depressives commit suicide within a five-year period. Thus, ECT is low risk.
- Compared with other treatments (e.g. psychotherapy, drugs), ECT has a 60% to 90% success rate for psychotic-depressive and manic patients.
- ECT can often be effective when anti-depressant drugs have failed.

◆ Systematic desensitisation (Learning Approach)

The Learning Approach to psychological therapies is based on the assumption that psychological disorders are behaviours that are learned from the environment by classical and operant conditioning and social learning.

Treatments focus on changing the abnormal behaviour rather than considering thought processes or underlying causes. If we assume that psychological disorders are learned behaviours, then treatment aims to help the person unlearn the maladaptive behaviour and substitute a more adaptive response in its place.

Systematic desensitisation is based on the principle of incompatible responses, i.e. the idea that you cannot be both anxious and relaxed at the same time. As this is the Learning Approach, phobias, for example, are thought to be learned anxiety responses to particular stimuli. Therefore, the treatment assumes that the phobia can be removed by teaching someone to relax when in contact with the phobic object.

systematic = gradually facing up to the phobic object throughout a hierarchy of exposure (least fearful to most fearful).
desensitisation = brought about through relaxation techniques taught before facing up to the phobic object.

The process is explained overleaf, with an example given of one of the key stages in the process.

Hold the spider

Walk towards the spider

Be in the same room as a spider

Look at the picture of a spider in a book

Imagine a spider on your hand

▲ A typical anxiety hierarchy from the least fearful to the most fearful situation.

Process

Treatment takes place over a number of sessions depending on the strength of the phobia and the client's ability to relax. Therapist and client jointly agree what the therapeutic goal should be and the therapy is deemed successful once this goal has been reached. The process can either be *in vivo* (exposure to the real object) or *in vitro* (imaginary exposure to the object).

There are four stages:

1 **Functional analysis** – careful questioning to discover the nature of the anxiety and possible triggers.

2 **Construction of an anxiety hierarchy** – client and therapist derive a hierarchy of anxiety-provoking situations from the least to the most fearful (see left).

3 **Relaxation training** – the client is taught to relax using the methods which suit them best, e.g. listening to their favourite music.

4 **Gradual exposure** – the phobic object is slowly introduced.

Effectiveness

- It is very effective with simple phobias such as those of a particular species like spiders. McGrath et al. (1990) found that 75% of patients with specific phobias showed clinically significant improvement following the treatment.
- The treatment is considered to be more ethical than others based on classical conditioning, such as aversion therapy. This is because the patient is given more control in the procedure and will only move on when they feel ready to.
- Because the goals are clearly specified, the therapeutic outcomes are easy to measure. This means that data on the effectiveness of the treatment is easily compiled, providing what is seen as good scientific justification for the use of this therapy.
- However, complex and social phobias such as agoraphobia (a general fear of being in open spaces) do not respond so well and relapse rates are high.
- Craske and Barlow (1993) found that between 60% and 80% of **agoraphobics** show some improvement after treatment, but it was only slight and clients often relapse completely after six months.
- The treatment only focuses on observable symptoms rather than any deeper underlying issues and as such makes little or no attempt to address these other possible causes.
- Some therapists argue that neither hierarchies nor relaxation training is required, and that systematic exposure is, in itself, enough to be effective.

Examiner's tip

Make sure you can make the links between systematic desensitisation and the principles of classical conditioning from the Learning Approach. You will need to be able to describe and evaluate the treatment. A good way of evaluating any therapy/treatment is by seeing how appropriate and effective it is and how it compares to others. For example, which disorders and types of client respond best to which treatment? Does the treatment have any evidence that it actually does work? Is the treatment only effective in the short term, meaning the client might relapse?

Examiner's tip

You might want to make a grid with a list of each possible treatment from each approach along the top, and down the side the following categories: rationale; process (how the treatment works); role of the therapist; what disorders they work on and effectiveness. You can then fill in the boxes along each row to provide a useful summary.

Care in the community (Social Approach)

According to the Social Approach, mental disorders can be triggered by factors in the environment (social factors) in conjunction with other causes. Followers of the approach see long-term stays in psychiatric hospitals as leading to institutionalisation. Patients become so used to having everything done for them, and not being able to make their own decisions, that it is hard to adjust to living outside.

In the 1970s and 80s there was a move towards caring for patients with mental disorders in the community, to avoid this institutionalisation. This led to the closure of a number of psychiatric hospitals and wards, with community-based care programmes being set up instead. These programmes rely on a number of different agencies providing a variety of services, with the aim of rehabilitating the patient and ensuring they can function as normally as possible in society. These services can include sheltered accommodation, with 24-hour care available for those who cannot cope by themselves and have nowhere else to live.

Care staff are available to provide help and support when it is needed, and oversee the day-to-day living if needed, though residents are encouraged to make their own decisions and be as independent as possible. It can also include the chance to work in co-operative businesses or sheltered social firms. Specialist mental health teams provide the care and support needed in the long term. Those who do need to be hospitalised are admitted to psychiatric wards, but this is usually on a short-term basis, with the aim of getting them back into the community as soon as possible.

◆ Evaluation

Strengths

- When properly funded, community care does seem to be better than hospital. Trauer et al. (2001) studied patients for a year after their release from hospital and found that, whilst their symptoms didn't really change, their quality of life did improve.
- Leff (1997) found that schizophrenics in long-term sheltered accommodation had less severe symptoms than those still in hospital.
- Others have found that those patients who receive care in the community prefer it to being in hospital.

Weaknesses

- There may be a lack of co-ordination between the different services involved, so patients may get different advice from different people. In some cases community care teams did not know when someone was being released into their care.
- Under-funding can cause problems if there are not enough community care programmes or sheltered accommodation, and staff are over-stretched. This will impact on the patient's recovery, and may even make them worse.
- One study in London (Leff, 1994) concluded that the balance between hospital and community services was inappropriate. There weren't enough hospital beds for those that needed them and not enough community residential places for patients when they had been released from hospital.
- Where you live also has an impact on the quality of the care in the community. Kuno et al. (2005) carried out a study in America and found that white affluent areas had a higher quality of care than low-income African American areas.
- Lora et al. (2001) found that the intensity of schizophrenic symptoms and the burden on the family determined which service patients used. Those who had relatively mild psychiatric symptoms but were a moderate burden on the family tended to use community services. Those who had severe positive symptoms, with the family suffering distressing burdens, used both hospital and community services, whilst those who had severe negative symptoms and were a moderate burden on the family tended to use the hospitals more than community services.

Other options

Another social therapy is family therapy. This assumes that psychological problems come from family interactions, and therefore the whole family needs to be involved in the treatment, not just the patient. The therapist looks at both what the family members say and how they communicate with each other, with the aim of improving how they relate to each other so they are more able to deal with their problems.

Examiner's tip

If you are asked to evaluate a therapy, you do not need to give any description about what the therapy involves. No marks will be available for description, and you will be wasting time.

◆ Rational Emotive Therapy (Cognitive Approach)

The Cognitive Approach assumes that mental disorders are caused by an early experience causing a dysfunctional belief (faulty schema). An event in adulthood may then activate this dysfunctional belief, or faulty schema, which leads us to process information according to that schema, and ignore information that does not fit the schema. This biased processing then leads to the symptoms of the mental disorder. Rational Emotive Therapy (RET) aims to changes these patterns of irrational thinking and replace them with more rational thinking patterns. For more details on how this is achieved, see page 116.

Other options

The alternative cognitive therapy that you can study is Cognitive Behaviour Therapy. Details on this can be found in books such as Davision and Neale, *Abnormal Psychology*, other general psychology textbooks and on the Internet.

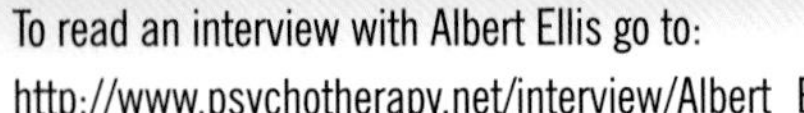

Taking it further

To read an interview with Albert Ellis go to: http://www.psychotherapy.net/interview/Albert_Ellis

◆ Evaluation

Strengths

- Several studies have shown the effectiveness of RET. Engels (1993) found that it was more effective for anxiety disorders than systematic desensitisation, or a combination of RET and another therapy.
- Silverman et al. (1992) reviewed 89 studies and found that in 49 of them RET was the most effective treatment, whilst in the other 40 it was just as effective as other treatments.
- One study looked at how effective RET was compared with drug therapy for depression and found that RET was significantly more effective than drugs in the treatment of depression (David et al., 2008).
- Emmelkamp (1991) found that RET was as successful as *in vitro* therapy for obsessive compulsives, and that both were equally effective six months later.
- It has also been found to reduce depression and anxiety in patients awaiting an operation, both before and after the operation (Osinowo, 2003).
- Most of these studies have been done on adults, but it has also been found to be effective for children. Gonzalez et al. (2004) found that it was effective in dealing with disruptive behaviour in children and adolescents – though it was more effective for children than adolescents – and the longer the therapy continued, the greater the improvements.
- One reason it may be effective for younger patients is that it does not have a moral judgement. The therapist questions whether a bad act makes the person a bad person, with the rational answers being that no, it doesn't.

Weaknesses

- One problem with the assumption that faulty processing causes mental disorders is that the person is not usually seen until they have a mental disorder, so it is impossible to study their thinking processes before the disorder.
- One problem with most of the studies that look at the effectiveness of RET is that they only look at the short-term effects, and not the long term to see if it is still effective.
- In a 15-month follow-up study, Sandahl (1998) found that patients who had had psychodynamic therapy were more likely to still be abstaining from alcohol compared with those who had had cognitive therapy.
- What seems an irrational belief to the therapist may be a rational belief to the patient. For example, the therapist may think it is irrational to think you can hear voices from the dead; however, in some cultures the belief that the dead can talk to you is perfectly rational.
- A psychoanalyst would argue that RET does not work, as the therapist is just changing the belief systems of the patient. What is really needed is to look at the unconscious causes of those belief systems.

◆ Dream analysis (Psychodynamic Approach)

The Psychodynamic Approach sees mental disorders as coming from the unconscious mind, usually due to repressed thoughts or emotions from childhood. In order to treat the mental disorder the analyst must therefore access the patient's unconscious mind. One way of doing this is through dream analysis. When we sleep our ego's defences are more relaxed, so material that usually stays in our unconscious enters our conscious in the form of a dream.

However, because the material is still threatening to our peace of mind it cannot be allowed into our conscious in its actual form. The material is disguised, and symbols in dreams represent the real content of the dream. The content of the dream that we remember is called the **manifest content**, whilst what the dream actually means is called the **latent content**.

◀ Dreams allow us to access our unconscious thoughts and desires.

It is the analyst's job to uncover the true meaning of a patient's dream. This can take some time, as the analyst needs a number of recorded dreams rather than just one. One way to analyse the dream is via free association, where the patient talks about the thoughts and emotions that the dream created, rather than the content of the dream. For more on free association, see page 117.

Examiner's tip

If asked about treatment of a mental disorder, be sure to link to a disorder and, for example, not to just describe what dream analysis is.

◆ Evaluation

Strengths

- Heaton et al. (1998) found that clients who had therapists interpreting their dreams felt they got more insight and depth from the interpretation than when they had to interpret their own dreams. They also found that 88% of clients preferred the therapist to interpret their dreams, so dream analysis does seem to offer clients help.
- Kolchakian and Hill (2002) found that females in heterosexual relationships gained more insight into their relationships through dream interpretation, and so improved their own well-being and their relationship, when compared with females who didn't have dream interpretation. However, dream interpretation did not have any effect on improving the quality of relationships for men.

Weaknesses

- Dream analysis is subjective, with the interpretation of the dream dependent on the analyst. Different analysts may have different interpretations of the same dream.
- The client may not tell the analyst the whole dream – they may have forgotten bits of it, and these could be the important bits, or they might edit the dream for the analyst. The interpretation may therefore not reflect what was actually in the unconscious.
- The Eysenck (1952) review looked at early studies on psychoanalysis, which includes dream analysis, and found that psychodynamic therapy was no more effective than having no therapy or treatment at all. However, there have been criticisms of this review, and Bergin and Garfield (1978) found that the rate of improvement for those receiving no treatment was 30–43 % and those receiving psychoanalysis was 83% when they reanalysed the data.
- Espostio et al. (1999) analysed the dream content of people suffering combat-related post-traumatic stress disorder (PTSD) using 18 Vietnam veterans. They found that about half the participants' dreams included features from combat, and that 79% of the participants had distorted elements of combat in their dreams. This disputes the theory that we symbolise material that would distress us in our dreams.

Other options

The alternative psychodynamic therapy is free association. This is described on page 117. Remember, you need to be able to describe and evaluate all the therapies you study.

Studies in detail

What you need to know

- Describe and evaluate Rosenhan (1973) 'On being sane in insane places'.
- Describe and evaluate two other studies. One study must focus on schizophrenia and the other on another disorder.

Examiner's tip

The studies can be of your own choice, as the ones named in the specification are only examples, but the studies must focus on specific disorders.

How staff responded to patients' requests

Response	% making contact with the patient	
	Psychiatrists	Nurses
Moves on with head averted	71	88
Makes eye contact	23	10
Pauses and chats	2	2
Stops and talks	4	0.5

Taking it further

For a recent replication of Rosenhan's study by Lauren Slater, read her book *Opening Skinner's Box: Great Psychological Experiments of the Twentieth Century.*

On being sane in insane places (Rosenhan, 1973)

◆ Aim

To see if the sane could be distinguished from the insane using the DSM classififcation system and, if they can be differentiated, how sanity can be identified.

◆ Procedure

Rosenhan sent eight pseudo-patients to 12 different hospitals. The group consisted of three women and five men. All gave false names, and those in the medical profession gave a false occupation. Each pseudo-patient said that they could hear an unfamiliar voice of the same sex saying 'empty', 'hollow' and 'thud'. Apart from these details, all the information the pseudo-patients gave was true, including details about their relationships, childhood and education.

As soon as they were admitted to a psychiatric ward, the pseudo-patients stopped any abnormal symptoms, though some did later admit to acting in a nervous manner at the start of the study, partly because they thought they would be exposed as frauds. They took part in ward activities, spoke to staff and fellow patients as they would normally and responded to instructions from staff. Some wrote down their observations about the ward, the patients and the staff. If asked how they felt, they said they felt fine and no longer had any symptoms. In some hospitals the pseudo-patients approached members of staff with a request such as 'Pardon me, could you tell me when I am likely to be discharged?'

◆ Results

All the pseudo-patients were admitted, and none was detected as being sane. All but one of them had a diagnosis of schizophrenia in remission. They stayed in hospital for between seven and 52 days, with the average being 19 days. In three hospitals, 35 out of 118 patients were suspicious about the insanity of the pseudo-patients.

◆ Conclusion

Rosenhan concluded that staff in psychiatric hospitals were unable to distinguish those who were sane from those who were insane, and that DSM was therefore not a valid measurement of mental illness at that time.

◆ Evaluation

Strengths

- The study was carried out in actual psychiatric hospitals, using real staff who were unaware of the study, so it has ecological validity.

- As a range of hospitals was used from around the country, including old and new and using different methods of funding, the results could be generalised to other psychiatric hospitals at the time.
- The number of days the pseudo-patients stayed in hospital is an objective measurement, and the fact that the pseudo-patients could see what life was like from a patient's perspective adds validity.

Weaknesses

- Whilst the pseudo-patients' observations would try to be objective, some subjectivity and the emotions of the pseudo-patients could have influenced these observations.
- There are ethical problems, as the hospital staff were deceived about the patients' symptoms. Nor did they know they were in a study so were unable to give consent. However, Rosenhan did not name any staff or hospitals so there was no risk of identification.
- Another problem is that all doctors, either of physical or mental illness, tend to play safe and go for the most serious or common diagnosis before ruling it out, rather than immediately trying to see if the patient is faking it. Psychiatrists have to be especially careful, as if they release someone with a mental disorder there can be serious consequences (for them or for others).
- The pseudo-patients insisted on being admitted to the hospital, which is an important symptom in itself, so the voices were not the only symptom they presented. Nor was their behaviour totally normal once they were admitted, as they didn't say that they were in fact normal and insist on being released (which is what most normal people would do).
- Psychiatrists point out that DSM has been revised since Rosenhan's study, and such results are less likely. Another study now is therefore unlikely to replicate the results.
- Spitzer argues that the diagnosis of schizophrenia in remission was in fact due to how the pseudo-patients behaved and not to the fact that the psychiatrists couldn't tell they were normal, as it is a very rare diagnosis for real patients. Therefore, he argues, the psychiatrists recognised there was something different about the pseudo-patients.

Examiner's tip

When asked to *describe* a study, read the question carefully. If the question asks for a specific part of the study, such as the procedure, make sure your answer focuses on that. If you include everything you know about the study, some of it will be irrelevant.

Gender differences in the course of schizophrenia (Goldstein, 1988)

◆ Aims

To see if there is any significant difference in the age of onset of schizophrenia between the two sexes, and to see if women have a less severe course of the disorder than men.

◆ Procedure

The sample consisted of 199 women and men. In the 1970s all had been diagnosed with schizophrenia on admittance and on discharge from psychiatric hospital, where they had stayed for less than six months. They were all expected to live with a family member, either parents or spouse, and all were aged between 18 and 45 years. None of them had any organic brain disorder such as epilepsy, and none had any drug problem, including alcohol abuse.

They were re-diagnosed 10 years later using the revised version of DSM. Of the original 199 patients, 169 were re-diagnosed with schizophrenia using the revised version, 30 were deemed not to be schizophrenic according to the revised version of DSM (i.e. they had been misdiagnosed). Of the 169 who were re-diagnosed, 52 were first-time admissions and 38 had had only one previous hospitalisation in the 1970s. The remainder were the patients studied by Goldstein.

Outcome	Mean
Number of re-hospitalisations	
0-5 years	
Men	1.4
Women	0.59
0-10 years	
Men	2.24
Women	1.12
Length of hospital stay (days)	
0-5 years	
Men	267.41
Women	129.97
0-10 years	
Men	417.83
Women	206.81

How well the patients could function in everyday life was measured by looking at marital status, occupational status, peer relationships, isolation and interests. The course and severity of the illness was measured by looking at the number of times the patients had been in hospital, and how long the hospital stays had been over a 10-year period.

Results

As can be seen in the table of results on the left, the researchers found that schizophrenic women had a significantly lower number of re-hospitalisations, and that they had shorter stays in hospital over the 10-year period. The difference in gender was even stronger when looking at a five-year period, possibly because the severity of schizophrenia does not worsen after five years. Differences in premorbid functioning, such as isolation, peer relationships and interests, affected re-hospitalisations. Social functioning, such as marital and occupational status, affected the length of stays.

Conclusion

Gender differences in the course of schizophrenia are present in the early stages of the disorder, with poorer **premorbid functioning** in men being responsible for a poorer outcome.

Evaluation

Strengths

- Whilst this was a longitudinal study, it did not suffer from the problem of participants dropping out, as data on their functioning was collected at the start of the study, and data about their hospitalisation was obtained from the New York State Department of Mental Health.
- The men and women were well matched in terms of marital status, age, education, religion and socio-economic status.
- Two experts who did not know the aim of the study tested the reliability of the re-diagnosis; there was an inter-rater reliability rate of 80%, showing that there was good reliability.
- The sample size was 169, as they added people who had previously had one hospital stay before the start of the study to increase the sample so that it was more generalisable to all schizophrenics.
- Other studies support the findings of this study. Gittelman-Klein and Klein (1969) found that men do tend to have poorer premorbid histories than women, and Huber et al. (1980) found that those with a poorer premorbid history had a poorer outcome when it came to schizophrenia. Angermeyer et al. (1987) carried out a larger replication of this study and found the same results. This increases the reliability of Goldstein's study.
- The data is objective and unbiased in terms of the number of hospital stays and length of the stays, as it came from an outside agency that accurately recorded these details.

Weaknesses

- Whilst the men and women were matched for employment status, the type of employment varied. The women mostly had clerical or sales jobs or were housewives, whilst the men had more blue collar jobs. There were also more unemployed men than women.
- There are problems with generalising the results, as all the participants returned to their families after hospitalisation. The same results may not be true for schizophrenics who do not return to their families. However, all these patients were in the early stages of schizophrenia at the start of the study, and it has been found that most early-stage schizophrenics do rely on family help after hospitalisation, so this may in fact be representative.

AS check

To remind yourself of the strengths and weaknesses of longitudinal studies, look at AS pages 78–79.

Examiner's tip

Remember that you can evaluate a study by evaluating the method used to carry it out, as long as you refer to the actual study.

- Another problem with the sample is that the age limit was 45 years. Nine per cent of schizophrenic women have their first schizophrenic episode after 45 and have more paranoia, whilst very few men do, so this may have biased the sample in favour of finding the gender differences. However, in the current version of DSM, people must be under 45 to be diagnosed with schizophrenia, so those over 45 would be diagnosed with a different disorder.
- If you argue that DSM is not a valid measurement of mental illness, this brings into question the validity of the diagnosis of schizophrenia.

Other options

You do not have to study Goldstein's study. You can choose one of your own, as long as it relates to schizophrenia. One such study is Sexual Dimorphism, Brain Morphology and Schizophrenia by Lewine et al. (1990). The abstract of this study can be found at: http://www.ncbi.nlm.nih.gov/pubmed/2374880

Taking it further

To enhance your understanding of any study you could order a copy of it (or ask your teacher to order a copy) from the British Library. Read the whole article then highlight what you think are the key points in each section. Use your highlighting to write up the study in your own words. To order a copy you will need to know the name of the article and the journal, which volume and number it is and the page numbers. These should be found in the reference section of books using that study, or with the abstract on the Internet.

Increased prevalence of bulimia nervosa among Asian schoolgirls (Mumford and Whitehouse, 1988)

◆ Aim

Based on the fact that very few cases of anorexia or bulimia were reported in non-whites, the aim was to see if eating disorders do actually occur fewer times in British Asian schoolgirls than in their white counterparts.

◆ Procedure

The researchers studied girls aged 14 to 16 from four different schools in Bradford. The total sample size was 559 – 204 Asians and 355 whites. The girls were given an eating attitudes test and a body shape questionnaire. In both the test and the questionnaire, the more abnormal the girls' attitudes were to eating or body shape. Those who scored over 20 on the eating attitudes test, or over 140 on the body attitude questionnaire, then went to an interview, where details of their eating history were collected and they were examined to see if they had an eating disorder. Altogether, 22 Asian girls and 32 white girls were interviewed. An eating disorder was only diagnosed after a discussion between the researchers.

◆ Results

They found a significant difference in the scores from the eating attitudes test, with the Asian girls having a mean of 10.6 and the white girls having a mean of 7.7. However, there was no significant difference in the scores from the body shape questionnaires, with the Asian girls having a mean of 73.3 and the white girls a mean of 70.3. Of those who went for the interview, seven Asian girls and two white girls were diagnosed with bulimia, a significant difference. Anorexia was diagnosed in one Asian girl and no white girls. The mean scores are summarised in the following table.

Ethnic origin	Mean score from eating attitudes test	Mean score from body shape questionnaire
Asian	10.6	73.3
White	7.7	70.3

◆ Conclusion

They concluded that bulimia nervosa was more prevalent amongst Asian schoolgirls than white schoolgirls, which is not what they expected to find. They also found that Asian schoolgirls were more concerned about their weight and the amount of food they ate than their white counterparts.

◆ Evaluation

Strengths

- The sample was large – 559 completed the original questionnaires and 54 went for the interview, so the results can be generalised to other schoolgirls.
- The reliability of the diagnosis of an eating disorder was high, as the researchers came to a joint decision and so had to agree, rather than coming to individual decisions.

Weaknesses

- A very limited age range was studied and it is not possible to say whether the same results would be found if older women were studied, or indeed younger girls.
- The original questionnaires were administered in the girls' classroom by their teachers, which may have affected the results. Perhaps because eating disorders are perceived as more of a white issue, the white girls may have been more careful about how they answered, especially if they did have some issues with food.
- There was no independent verification of the diagnosis from someone not involved in the study, and there may have been an experimenter effect, as both knew what the study was about. This would be reduced by the fact that they thought there would be fewer instances of eating disorders in Asian girls.
- They used the DSMIII-R version to diagnose, which may not be a reliable measure of eating disorders. Nicholls et al. (2000) found that DSM was not a reliable measure of eating disorders in children (see page 106).

Summaries of other options

You may choose your own studies rather than those described in detail here, but one of them must be a study on schizophrenia.

◆ Sexual dimorphism in brain morphology and schizophrenia (Levine et al., 1990)

Aim: To see if understanding **sexual dimorphism** in the brains of male and female schizophrenics could help understand the different types of schizophrenia.

Procedure: The researchers compared schizophrenic and non-schizophrenic patients and a control group with no psychiatric illness. Each participant had a physical examination, an EEG, ECG, and a medical records check. Most were given a semi-structured interview to check their psychiatric history and any current problems. The doses of chlorpromazine in the schizophrenics was checked to ensure there was no significant difference in the dosage used by males and females. An MRI was used to take images of the brain, focusing on the corpus callosum. A questionnaire determined left and right-handedness.

AS check

To recap on MRI scans, see AS page 102.

Results: Nine men and no women had an MRI scan that showed a clear abnormality. Being left- or right-handed had no effect. There was no significant difference in the corpus callosum area of the brain between male and female schizophrenics, though schizophrenics did have a smaller area than non-schizophrenics.

Conclusion: There are brain differences between schizophrenics and non-schizophrenics, and some difference in brain function between male and female schizophrenics.

◆ Social support, self-esteem and depression (Brown et al., 1986)

Aim: To see if the level of self-esteem and the amount of social support available to a person can predict the risk of depression for up to a year after a stressful event.

Procedure: The participants were working-class women with at least one child at home. The first interview asked questions about self-esteem, their personal ties with their partner, friends and relatives, and any psychiatric illness in the previous 12 months. A year later, a second interview looked at any stressful events that had occurred over the year, the amount of social support they had during any stressful event and any psychiatric illness that had occurred.

Results: Of the four women who had depression during the follow-up year, 91% had had a severe life event in the preceding six months. Of these women, 33% had low self-esteem. Women who were married and had had a severe event had received a reduced risk of depression if their partners gave them support after the event, especially emotional support.

Conclusion: An increased risk of depression is associated with low self-esteem and a lack of support, especially at the time of crisis.

◆ Observational conditioning of fear-relevant versus fear-irrelevant stimuli in rhesus monkeys (Cook and Mineka, 1989)

Aim: To see if rhesus monkeys can learn fear through observing it in other rhesus monkeys.

Procedure: Rhesus monkeys were shown a large brown rubber toy snake, two smaller toy snakes, and three pairs of silk flowers or wooden blocks of different sizes, shapes and colours. They saw videos of other monkeys reacting fearfully to the snakes and non-fearfully to the wooden blocks, or reacting fearfully to the flowers and non-fearfully to the wooden blocks. Fear was measured by the monkeys' willingness to reach over the objects to get a food reward.

Results: Before seeing the video, equal numbers of monkeys were afraid of the flowers and the snakes. After seeing the video, more than 60% of the monkeys developed a fear of snakes, whilst the number of monkeys afraid of flowers remained constant.

Conclusion: Rhesus monkeys can learn fear through observing other monkeys when the stimuli is fear-relevant.

Evidence in practice

What you need to know

- Describe one key issue in clinical psychology using the topics you have studied.
- Prepare a leaflet using secondary data for a particular audience about the key issue. Include a commentary on the leaflet explaining why decisions were made, who the audience was and what outcomes were intended.

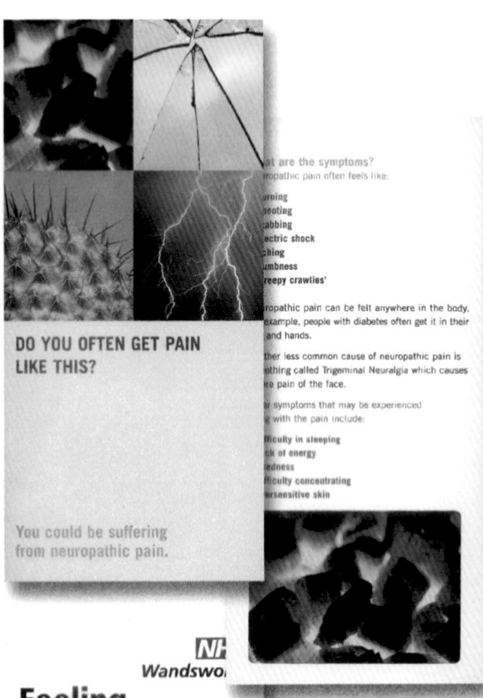

Feeling unwell?
Treat yourself right

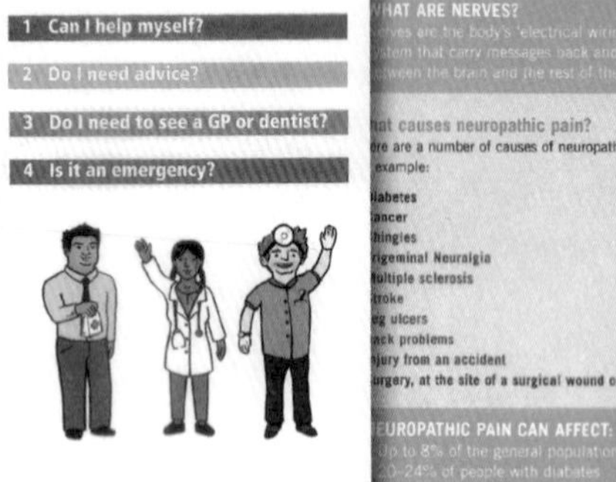

▲ Leaflets like this are commonly found in mental health advice centres and GPs' surgeries.

Key issue: Understanding schizophrenia

Schizophrenia is defined as a psychotic disorder which involves loss of contact with reality and typically involves hallucinations and/or delusions.

Somewhere between 0.2% to 2% of the population will develop schizophrenia. Some recover fully, but many suffer recurring episodes for the duration of their lifetime.

Males are most likely to develop the disorder between the ages of 16 to 25, then diagnosis trails off sharply. Women are most likely to develop schizophrenia in their 20s, but it trails off more gradually, so from 35 onwards, onset is higher in women than men.

The DSM IV distinguishes between positive symptoms (behaviours which are additional to normal behaviours, such as hearing voices) and negative symptoms (behaviours which appear to be absent from normal behaviours, such as loss of drive).

◆ Preparing a leaflet

Imagine you work for a local health authority and specialise in mental health. Your job is to raise awareness amongst the public about schizophrenia, in particular by creating a leaflet to put out in the community.

You can get ideas about what the leaflet should look like from ones in your local GP's surgery or library, etc. Alternatively, a websearch will provide lots of examples like the one above.

The front of the leaflet should engage your target audience and provide a brief outline of its purpose. Remember your target audience here are those who may think they have signs of schizophrenia (or know someone who has) and those who have already been diagnosed with the disorder. In this way you are helping current and potential sufferers and their families, friends and colleagues.

Inside the leaflet you should have the key facts of the disorder summarised, with its features and symptoms. So, for schizophrenia, useful headings might be:

- What is schizophrenia?
- What are the symptoms of schizophrenia?
- What causes schizophrenia?

When talking about the symptoms, you could include some helpful advice for people who live, work or are at school with someone who has schizophrenia – how they can best help them, for example.

In the last section you could draw a simple diagram highlighting physiological, psychological and social explanations.

This could be followed up with a section on treatments. Useful sections might include:

- What different treatments are available?
- What are the most effective and appropriate treatments?

Here you could list the different types of therapy and a brief outline of the procedures involved. In this section you are giving your audience a chance to look at the strengths and weaknesses of the different therapies.

The final pages of your leaflet should deal with advice on what to do next. This could include useful links to podcasts, websites, etc.

◆ Commentary on your leaflet

Get your leaflet evaluated by others (peers, parents, etc.). How effective and appropriate was it? Did it suit your target audience?

◆ Over to you

Use a different mental disorder you have studied and design a leaflet based on the principles described here. You could work in a group and design leaflets for different disorders such as depression, phobias and obsessive compulsive disorder.

Key issue: Supporting someone with a mental disorder in the home

Families and parents in particular may indirectly contribute to the onset of an eating disorder. For example, mothers who complain about their own weight or appearance or who criticise the looks of other people set a poor example of a healthy body image to their children, especially young girls.

When a member of the family develops an eating disorder, it can have an enormous impact on the whole household. Emotions that family members may experience when an eating disorder is present include overprotection, guilt and anger.

◆ Family therapy

Because of the frequently close relationship between eating disorders and family life, therapy sessions often involve the whole family. During family therapy sessions, a therapist will, for example, show the family members specifically how to deal with the disruptions caused by the eating disorder and teach them more about the disorder so that they can understand it better.

Dysfunction among the family is a key component addressed at family therapy. Forming solutions and determining roles in the home may help to relieve this dysfunction and ease the stress brought into the home through the eating disorder.

◆ What to look for

The main signs to look out for include:

- skipping meals and avoiding social activities which involve eating
- obsessive perfectionism about all things, especially food
- wanting to cook for others and encouraging them to eat more
- worrying that others are watching them when they eat
- reducing the range of foods eaten
- calorie counting.

◆ Ways of supporting the family member

1 Be aware of the eating disordered person's condition and progress, but respect their privacy.

2 Don't be 'helpful' by pointing out which foods are healthy and which aren't – and never try to force someone to eat. Recovery is a long and slow process, and if you try to cram meal after meal down a person's throat, you will only make them feel even more guilty and upset, which can lead to purging (getting rid of food from the body, usually by inducing vomiting). Mealtimes should be as comfortable and friendly as possible.

3 Talk about other things – it will probably come as a welcome relief for someone who spends an inordinate amount of time obsessing on these things already. Suggest new activities, such as art classes, volunteering, music or yoga. It is important to replace the unhealthy, disordered eating behaviours with healthy interests. Young people struggling with eating disorders often have a small number of activities based on dieting, weight regulation and exercise. It is difficult to break away from these patterns.

4 Research the disorder, as it shows the person that you're genuinely interested and helps you understand their struggles.

5 Eat together and treat the person as an active participant in their recovery. Meals and snack times are often the most difficult parts of the day. Eating itself may cause anxiety and often requires support and supervision. If someone they trust eats with them, the experience of eating is more comfortable.

6 Be a good role model by cooking and shopping together. Check out new foods and set a goal to try one new food each week. People with disordered eating often have a small list of 'safe foods' that they can tolerate eating. Usually, these foods are low in calories, carbohydrates and fat. During recovery, it is important to increase food choices. A nutritionist is very helpful with setting these goals.

WHY CAN'T THEY JUST DO AS THEY'RE TOLD?

All children misbehave at times. Impulsive behaviour, inattention and fidgeting are all perfectly natural in young children and you will often be reassured that they'll "grow out of it".

But what if they don't? What if you still dread picking them up from school every day – partly because you're worried that their teacher will want a word with you AGAIN and partly because you just don't know how you'll cope with them when you get home?

Well firstly, you should not blame yourself. There can be many reasons for a child's extreme behaviour but "bad parenting" is not usually one of them.

And secondly, it may be useful to get some help. Behaviour problems in children can have a number of causes which your doctor will be able to discuss with you in more detail. One such cause could be a medical condition known as ADHD (Attention Deficit Hyperactivity Disorder). This is a relatively common condition which affects about 1 in 20 children and, once diagnosed, there are a number of treatments available.

If you are in any way concerned about your child's behaviour it is always worth speaking to your doctor about it. They will be able to give you a realistic idea of what is considered normal behaviour for that age group, put you in touch with local parenting groups and also refer you to a specialist if they suspect that your child has ADHD or any other type of behavioural disorder.

◆ Preparing a leaflet to help explain the key issue

Your audience here is primarily families and friends of the sufferer and your aim is to help by suggesting practical everyday solutions and activities in and around the home. You could design a leaflet which incorporates all the above, giving a step-by-step guide of what to do with the sufferer. You may wish to have some facts about eating disorders at the start of the leaflet and some possible causes.

You could even make up a case study of someone with an eating disorder, giving quotes about how the support from families has helped them recover. For example:

> ***'My family did lots of research for themselves and me which was vitally important in the next stage of recovery. We now use an approach called solution-focused therapy, which concentrates on all the positive points of the recovery route.'***

You might decide to make separate sections especially for parents and siblings, offering separate advice, for example:

Parents
- Your child is caught between wanting independence and needing to be cared for. You will need to communicate to them that they can have both.
- Try not to let the needs of the child with the eating disorder overshadow the needs of siblings.
- Seek support for yourself whenever you feel overwhelmed.

Siblings
- Try to remember that your brother/sister has not stopped caring about you.
- Accept that you may have strong conflicting feelings towards your brother/sister.
- Try not to stop shared activities with them.

Summary of one other key issue

◆ The way that mental illness is portrayed in the media

According to international research, mental illness tends to be portrayed negatively in both news and entertainment media. The presentation of negative images of mental illness in hospital dramas like *ER* and *Casualty* results in the development of more negative beliefs about mental illness, which in turn may lead to stigma and discrimination. Major films such as *American Psycho*, *The Bone Collector*, *Seven* and *Natural Born Killers* all reinforce negative stereotypes about 'crazy' people.

◆ Preparing a leaflet

Your audience here is the general public and the aim is to raise awareness of real mental illness and dispel the myths that come from the media.

Your leaflet could include examples of characters from films and TV who are mentally ill and portrayed negatively. You might then wish to give psychological explanations of where their particular disorder comes from. So, for example, Hannibal Lector in *Silence of the Lambs* may have a biological imbalance in the brain causing increased levels of dopamine to explain his behaviour. Try and do the same for other characters but using different physiological, psychological and social explanations for their disorders.

▲ Hannibal Lecter was portrayed as a 'psycho' in the *Silence of the Lambs* movies.

You could be quite creative and hard-hitting by including items such as:
- Should we watch martial arts movies so we can learn how Asians behave?
- Should we watch gangster movies so we can learn how Italians behave?
- Why, then, should we watch 'psycho' movies to learn how people labelled mentally ill behave?

You may also want to give some advice to the media in the leaflet about how they should portray mental illness. Ironically, in a great majority of the films mentioned here, the psycho is actually the psychiatrist. Maybe this needs to change?

You might also offer comparison with the more accurate accounts of mental illness given in films such as *A Beautiful Mind* and *One Flew Over The Cuckoo's Nest*.

Summary

Clinical psychology focuses on mental illness and aims to explain what causes mental disorders as well as offer possible ways of treating the disorder. The explanation and treatment vary according to the approaches.

Look back at the list of key terms for clinical pyschology on page 97 and check you can use them all effectively.

◆ Methodology

- Tell the difference between primary data and secondary data, and evaluate them.
- Talk about reliability and validity and relate them specifically to clinical psychology. It may be issues to do with classification or with specific studies.
- Describe and evaluate the research methods of twin studies and animal experiments in the context of schizophrenia.

◆ Content

- Describe and evaluate the use of both the statistical definition of abnormality and the social norm definition.
- Comment on issues that arise from the use of the DSM, including issues of validity, reliability and cultural issues.
- Know what the symptoms of schizophrenia and anorexia are, and two possible explanations. For schizophrenia that is the biological explanation, looking at the effect of genes and neurotransmitters, and the cognitive explanation, i.e. the faulty thinking patterns and how they affect the positive and negative symptoms. For anorexia that is the learning explanation, how anorexia is caused by environmental factors using conditioning theories, and the biological explanation, which looks at the role of the hypothalamus and genes using twin studies.
- For both disorders, describe and evaluate two treatments or therapies. For schizophrenia you looked at the effect of drugs on reducing the symptoms and how Cognitive Behavioural Therapy can change how schizophrenics think by challenging their assumption. For anorexia you looked at RET as a treatment and free association, how confronting your unconscious can help.
- Describe and evaluate one treatment from each of the five approaches. These included:
  - care in the community from the Social Approach
  - RET from the Cognitive Approach
  - dream analysis from the Psychodynamic Approach
  - ECT from the Biological Approach
  - systematic desensitisation from the Learning Approach.

◆ Studies

- Describe and evaluate, in depth, Rosenhan's study which looked at the validity of DSM, and two other studies that focused on a specific mental disorder. The two covered in this book are:
  - Goldstein (1988) Gender differences in the course of schizophrenia
  - Mumford and Whitehouse (1988) Increased prevalence of bulimia nervosa among Asian schoolgirls.

◆ Evidence in practice

- Describe one key issue in clinical psychology using areas covered in this application. Suitable examples include understanding a mental disorder and the way mental illness is portrayed in the media.
- Design a leaflet using secondary data about the key issue.

Examzone

*1. Describe the procedure of Rosenhan's (1973) study. (5 marks)

*2. Sarah has been referred to you, a cognitive therapist, for treatment. She is nervous about what the treatment entails, and asks you to explain it to her.
Explain to Sarah what is involved in a cognitive therapy that you have studied. (4 marks)

*3. Evaluate **one** cause of schizophrenia. (6 marks)

4. (a) Outline the symptoms of one disorder you have studied in clinical psychology other than schizophrenia. (4 marks)
(b) Describe one explanation for the disorder you outlined in (a). (5 marks)
(c) Evaluate the explanation you gave in (b). (5 marks)

5. Describe and evaluate one treatment/therapy from the Learning Approach. (12 marks)

6. Issues and debates

This chapter is the final part of the course and draws together much of what you have covered so far. It is a synoptic section, which means you are expected to draw on more than one area of the course. There are six parts to the chapter.

Contributions of psychology to society

You are asked to describe and evaluate two contributions to society from each of the five AS approaches, plus one contribution each from the three A2 applications you have covered.

Humans, animals and ethics

You need to be able to describe five ethical guidelines for using human participants and five for using animals. Then you need to be able to evaluate ethical issues in psychology (humans and animals), as well as two studies in terms of their ethics.

Research methods

Seven research methods are specified and you have to be able both to describe and evaluate each of the research methods as well as to describe and evaluate one study from each. You have to be able to make suggestions to improve studies and to plan a study of you own.

Key issues

In the course you prepared eight key issues – one each for the five AS approaches and one each for the three A2 applications. You need to review these eight and be ready to describe and explain them using appropriate concepts and ideas.

Issues and debates

There are four parts to this section.

- **Culture:** Ethnocentrism and possible bias in cross-cultural research is considered. The psychology you have studied has been largely British or from the USA, and it is important to take a more global view.
- **Psychology as a science:** This includes considering whether psychology should be called a science and how far each of the five AS approaches can be called scientific.
- **Psychology and social control:** This is about social control and considering ethical and practical considerations with regard to using psychological knowledge as a form of social control. Issues to look at include the use of drug therapy, token economy programmes, classical conditioning and the influence of the therapist or psychologist in treatment(s).
- **Nature-nurture:** The fourth debate is nature-nurture and the question of how far someone's characteristic or behaviour is due to their nature (biology) or their nurture (environment and upbringing). You need to consider how far the five AS approaches relate to either or both, and also what evidence about the debate is covered in the applications you have studied, including clinical psychology.

▲ Social control can be in the form of therapy or using medication – psychology can inform such practice and there are ethical and practical issues to consider.

Applying psychology for yourself

This final section asks you to be ready to apply your knowledge and understanding of psychology to new situations – to be ready to 'talk psychology' with the examiners.

Contributions to society: Social and Cognitive Approaches

What you need to know

- Two contributions to society for each of the Social and Cognitive Approaches.
- Strengths and weaknesses of each contribution.

Examiner's tip

You can choose any two contributions for each approach. The ones here are chosen to fit in with what you have covered. However, there are many others.

AS check

You have already defined the Social Approach, so use that material here, as well as other relevant material from the approach.

▲ A sports team will form an in-group and will be prejudiced against any other team. To reduce prejudice between them two teams could combine against a third team.

Taking it further

Find out other ways of reducing prejudice that have been suggested by psychological studies, for example having high-status role models from an 'out-group', or equal status groups.

Reducing prejudice – the Social Approach

Reducing prejudice is about interactions between people, including group behaviour, so it is the Social Approach which offers suggestions about it.

Social identity theory

Tajfel's (e.g. 1979) social identity theory suggests that prejudice is formed because people identify with members of their in-group and, to raise their self-esteem, denigrate members of the out-group. You would see the group that you belong to as useful, good, relevant or successful, for example. You would be prejudiced against the out-group, and believe the opposite because that would boost your in-group. This explanation of prejudice would suggest that in-groups and out-groups need to merge in order to reduce prejudice.

Social conflict theory

Sherif's (e.g. 1954) social conflict theory goes further and says that not only are two groups likely to be prejudiced against one another but that prejudice also arises because groups are in conflict over resources. In order to reduce prejudice the two groups need to work together to solve a common problem – called a superordinate goal.

Evaluating the contribution

Strengths

- Sherif (e.g. 1954) found that two groups where he had instilled prejudice worked together to solve common problems and then claimed more friends in the opposing group than they had before – evidence that working towards superordinate goals reduces prejudice.
- Studies have used either laboratory (e.g. Tajfel) or field (e.g. Sherif) experiments where there are clear controls and measurable independent and dependent variables, so reliable cause and effect conclusions can be drawn.
- Both these theories suggest that it is the formation of groups that leads to prejudice and the removal of group delineation that reduces it, so they support one another.

Weaknesses

- It is not easy to remove in-group/out-group behaviour as it is a feature of society that people have different affiliations. Even if some groups merge, they are likely then to be hostile to another group.
- It is likely that many different circumstances have to come together to reduce prejudice, as well as merging groups and having common goals. For example, it depends on the status of the groups, and on cultural norms that lead to stereotyping.

Understanding obedience – the Social Approach

Milgram (1973/74) explained obedience using the agency theory, where he suggested that people act as agents in society to authority figures, obeying orders from people in power rather than acting autonomously. Hofling et al. (1966) found that nurses obeyed someone they thought was a doctor even when what they were told to do went against their training. They obeyed an authority figure. Understanding such issues about obedience, and that the situation (such as being in the role of a nurse) can affect whether people obey, helps to understand brutal acts such as have happened recently to prisoners of war.

Evaluating the contribution

Strengths

- Many studies have shown evidence of blind obedience to an authority figure, such as Milgram's and Hofling et al.'s studies, as well as studies in other cultures. Participants were obedient even when it went against their own moral code.
- Studies have used laboratory (e.g. Milgram) or field (e.g. Haney et al.) experiments where there are clear controls and measurable variables, so reliable cause and effect conclusions tend to be assumed.

Weaknesses

- Obedience is a complex issue. Factors such as the setting, the presence of the authority figure, what task the 'obedient' person has to carry out are all important. It is hard to measure 'obedience' in one way, so hard to research it validly.
- Although obedience has been found in studies such as Milgram's, there is often a lot of disobedience as well (35% in Milgram's main study, though only one of Hofling et al.'s nurses). Thus reasons for not obeying must also be studied.

The cognitive interview – the Cognitive Approach

Elizabeth Loftus and others have found that eyewitness testimony can be unreliable, for example because leading questions can affect someone's account of a situation. A witness's memory can be altered by how they are questioned, by the time that has lapsed since the incident, and by their own schemas (ways of looking at the world). The cognitive interview has been developed from research by Geiselman (and others) into problems with memory. For example, a **cognitive interview** can start from any one of a sequence of events so that the witness can tell the story in their own way. It can also take place at the scene so that cues present at encoding are also present at retrieval. This links to cue-dependent forgetting.

Evaluating the contribution

Strengths

- Studies such as Loftus and Palmer (1974), which showed how just the change of a verb could affect a witness's judgement of speed (see page 20), showed that more than 'just' questioning was needed to get accurate eyewitness testimony. Therefore, a technique that took into account the power of words was needed – the cognitive interview was developed from well-evidenced theory.
- Evidence that led to the cognitive interview came from well-controlled laboratory experiments, which were replicated and found to be reliable, such as in Loftus's many studies.

Examiner's tip

Note how the strengths for both contributions here are the same – one is citing the evidence and the other is showing how experiments can give cause and effect reliable conclusions. Giving evidence is a useful way of indicating a strength, and giving a strength of any methodology can be useful.

Taking it further

Use your learning of a therapy from the Social Approach, which you covered within Clinical psychology, to explain that as a contribution of the Social Approach.

Taking it further

Look up Haney et al., often known as Zimbardo's study.

Taking it further

Find out more about a cognitive interview. Look up the work of Geiselman, and search for CIT, which is the cognitive interview technique.

AS check

Use what you learned about cue-dependent forgetting as well as other theories of memory (e.g. Bartlett's).

Examiner's tip

A key issue for the Cognitive Approach is the question of the reliability of eyewitness testimony (AS page 58). Use the information there to discuss a contribution of the Cognitive Approach.

Weaknesses

- Milne (1997) found that the cognitive interview did not seem to lead to the recall of more material than other techniques did.
- Memon et al. (1997) found no greater effect when asking the witness to recall from different places in the sequence of events than asking for recall more than once from the start. Perhaps asking the witness to start in different places does not have much effect.
- The enhanced version of the cognitive interview (Fisher and Geiselman, 1992) includes many different features. It is hard to test it to see which features are effective.

▲ CBT can help change negative thoughts, such as a phobia of shopping or crowds, in order to change maladaptive behaviour.

Cognitive behavioural therapy – the Cognitive Approach

Cognitive behavioural therapy (CBT) is used for depression and other mental health problems (see page 112). Many counsellors now use CBT, which has been found to be successful at least in the short term, with clients finding relief from symptoms quite quickly. CBT focuses on how thoughts lead to feelings that in turn lead to behaviour, which has consequences. Learned experiences can trigger **negative automatic thoughts**, giving patterns of thoughts and responses that can be **maladaptive** for an individual.

◆ Evaluating the contribution

Strengths

- The therapist works with the client to help them learn new strategies to cope with negative automatic thoughts. The client does homework focused on their thinking and behaviour, so learning tools that can help them in the future. They are in charge of the therapy – which means it is likely to last quite a long time even without the therapist's support.
- It has been said that CBT is a scientific approach because it draws on **empirical** evidence. From that evidence the client draws their own conclusions about their thoughts and feelings. There is objectivity in that the therapist explores the client's meanings and does not impose their own frames of reference.

Weaknesses

- A client has to be able to consider their thoughts, carry out homework and remember their early experience. They have to be cognitively able to do these things, so the therapy may not work for everyone.
- If the client believes the therapist is responsible for the outcome, CBT might not work. A study in Switzerland (Delsignore et al., 2008) looked at 49 people suffering from social anxiety disorder. At a three-month follow-up, clients who felt they were responsible for their progress were more likely to feel the continued benefits of CBT than those who thought the therapist was responsible. Long-term outcomes of CBT seem to depend on the expectations of the client as to how far they are responsible for their own improvements.

Taking it further 

The government has funded CBT strongly in 2008 because it appears to be successful, delivered in a short time, and fairly cheaply (needing just one therapist and no other equipment or medication). The government funding is part of their aim of Improving Access to Psychological Therapies (IAPT). Find out more about CBT and IAPT.

Examiner's tip 

You covered a therapy from the Cognitive Approach when studying clinical psychology. You can use that therapy as a contribution to society from the Cognitive Approach.

Examzone

1 Outline two contributions to society from the Social Approach. (6 marks)
2 With reference to one contribution to society from the Social Approach and one from the Cognitive Approach, evaluate those contributions. (6 marks)
3 Using one contribution to society from the Social Approach and one from the Cognitive Approach, in each case explain why they are said to be from that approach. (6 marks)

Contributions to society: Psychodynamic, Biological and Learning Approaches

What you need to know

- Two contributions to society for each of these approaches.
- The strengths and weaknesses of each contribution.

Success of psychoanalysis – the Psychodynamic Approach

The psychodynamic approach is about **psychoanalysis** and Freud's ideas about the power of the **unconscious** and the need to make unconscious thoughts conscious. It is a therapy to help those who are mentally ill, so helps society to maintain mental health.

Evaluating the contribution

Strengths

- Psychoanalysis is still used over 100 years later, and the theory continues to be built on, by the **object relations school**, for example. The idea has led to other practical applications and theories.
- Unlike other therapies, such as drug treatments or some counselling, psychoanalysis involves very in-depth probing of an individual's whole life and background, which can have value when trying to help them to live more successfully from their own viewpoint.

Weaknesses

- Psychoanalysis involves intensive visits for a long time so is time-consuming and expensive. CBT, for example, is more accessible, often free and can be limited to under ten weeks.
- It is hard to measure the concepts involved, such as the unconscious and dream symbols, so the therapy does not rest on scientific foundations. This makes it hard to test and show to be effective.

Understanding gender – the Psychodynamic Approach

The Psychodynamic Approach explains that boys learn their gender behaviour from identifying with their father in the **phallic stage** through the **Oedipus complex**. Girls, in a similar (but different) way, identify with their mothers and copy their behaviour. It helps society to understand gender differences in behaviour such as why a woman may choose as a partner a man like her father.

Evaluating the contribution

Strengths

- The Little Hans study has been used as evidence for the Oedipus complex and the need a small boy has to identify with his father.
- There is evidence (e.g. Connor and Brown, 2007) that girls have later relationships with (or marry) males like their father and boys have later relationships with (or marry) females like their mother. This is evidence for the Oedipus complex and the idea of identification.

Examiner's tip

You can choose any two contributions for each approach. The ones here are chosen to fit in with what you have covered but there are many others.

AS check

Use material that you studied as part of your work on the Psychodynamic Approach.

Taking it further

Find out more about psychoanalysis by searching for the views of those who have undergone such therapy.

Examiner's tip

You covered a therapy within the Psychodynamic Approach when studying clinical psychology and you can use that therapy as a contribution of the approach to society.

AS check

As well as gender behavior, you probably also studied how the Psychodynamic Approach can help explain issues such as homosexuality. You can use that learning here to explain the contribution.

Weaknesses

- It is hard to test ideas such as the Oedipus complex as the ideas are not measurable in a scientific way.
- The therapy is long, expensive and a huge commitment – in some cases someone has to attend every day for psychoanalysis – so it is not a therapy that society can easily fund and recommend.

> **AS check**
>
> You may have studied Raine et al. (1997) within the Biological Approach. This study used PET scanning (see AS page 102).

PET scanning evidence – the Biological Approach

The Biological Approach has contributed **PET scanning** evidence to society. PET scanning involves generating computerised pictures of the brain by using a radio-active tracer to highlight areas of activity. This helps society to contain mental health problems by better understanding them. Health problems are expensive and do not help productivity, as well as causing individual stress.

> **Examiner's tip**
>
> 
>
> If you studied health psychology, you may choose to consider the contribution of understanding drug addiction.

Evaluating the contribution

Strengths

- PET scanning is objective in that another person can check the printouts from the scans to make sure there is no subjectivity.
- A PET scan is repeatable so can be tested for reliability. This makes it a scientific method with scientific standing.

Weaknesses

- PET scans only show certain areas of the brain to be active but cannot pinpoint precise areas of this very complex organ.
- It is hard to say whether brain changes cause a certain behaviour or whether that behaviour causes changes in the brain. Raine et al.'s (1977) study is evidence of this difficulty.

> **Examiner's tip**
>
> 
>
> One way of evaluating a method is to contrast it with a different method. If the other method proves more useful, that indicates a weakness of the method being evaluated (and vice versa). MRI scanning would serve that purpose here.

Understanding gender – the Biological Approach

The Biological Approach explains gender through hormones and genes. Males are **XY** and are more governed by **androgens** and females are **XX**, governed by **oestrogens**. The Biological Approach points out that some people are XXY, or wrongly sex assigned at birth. This allows society to help such people, if that is appropriate, to maintain good mental health.

Evaluating the contribution

Strengths

- The findings about gender are measurable and testable, so results of studies have objectivity – the results do not need interpretation.
- Those with sex differences with regard to genes and/or hormones, such as **Turner's syndrome**, have consistently similar observable differences, suggesting that the explanation is **reliable**.

Weaknesses

- There are other explanations for gender development, such as from the Learning and Psychodynamic Approaches, that show a role for **nurture** and the environment. The Biological Approach does not take nurture into account to the same extent.
- Some studies are done with animals, such as injecting testosterone into female mice to see the effect, and findings from animals may not be validly **generalised** to say they are true of humans.

Systematic desensitisation – the Learning Approach

Systematic desensitisation (SD) is a treatment used for phobias (see page 119). It works by linking relaxation instead of fear to something that causes a phobia.

Someone is taught to relax deeply and then to maintain that relaxation state whilst gradually being introduced to the phobic situation. The treatment follows classical conditioning principles. Therapies are useful to society to help avoid health problems, which can be expensive in terms of work lost and individual dissatisfaction and stress.

AS check

Use your understanding of the principles of classical conditioning when explaining SD as a contribution to society.

◆ Evaluating the contribution

Strengths

- SD is a therapy that gives the client some control over what they agree to and it is a gradual therapy. This means that it is ethical in the sense of having informed consent and allowing the right to withdraw.
- SD can be self-administered and does not need a therapist, which means it is free and can be undertaken in someone's own time and at their own pace.

Weaknesses

- SD is not suitable for clients who are unable to relax well or to imagine scenarios where their phobia might occur. It is limited to people with insight and some control over their thoughts and emotions.
- It is better for specific phobias rather than for free-floating anxiety or social phobia. This is because a specific issue needs to be broken down into a hierarchy which is not as easy with general phobias.
- SD may not be as effective for phobias that might have a survival element, such as fear of closed spaces and dangerous animals. It is more effective for learned phobias, as classical conditioning would predict.

Token economy – the Learning Approach

The token economy programme (TEP) is used in schools, prisons and other institutions to control behaviour and to achieve required behaviour. The required behaviour is rewarded by some sort of token that can later be exchanged for time watching TV, sweets, or any other reward. Gradually, required behaviour can be shaped in this way. The programme follows operant conditioning principles. It is useful in helping control behaviour so that society's members comply with norms and rules and the majority can feel safe and comfortable.

AS check

Use your understanding of the principles of operant conditioning when explaining TEP as a contribution to society.

◆ Evaluating the contribution

Strengths

- The TEP can be run by people who are not therapists, although they must be trained. The training can be done in-house and is not very expensive. This is more cost-effective and less time-consuming than using trained therapists.
- Behaviour of people who find it hard to be involved in therapies that require analysis and concentration can be shaped using token economy programmes, so it is useful for those with less insight than other therapies need.

Weaknesses

- It can be hard to transfer the learning from the institution to the 'outside' world as the environment is different.
- Ethically, there is an issue about the power of the people running the programme as they can both reward and punish. Such a power must be carefully controlled and supervised to protect the individuals concerned.

Examzone

1 Outline two contributions to society from the Biological Approach. (6 marks)

2 Explain how the Psychodynamic Approach has helped society in its functioning. (3 marks)

***3** With reference to one contribution to society from the Learning Approach and one from the Biological Approach, evaluate those contributions. (6 marks)

Contributions to society: applications of psychology

What you need to know

- One contribution to society for each of two applications from criminological, child, health and sport psychology (criminological and child psychology are covered here).
- One contribution to society from clinical psychology.
- Evaluation of each of the three contributions.

Examiner's tip

You can choose any contribution for each application you studied, and you can choose any contribution from clinical psychology. The contributions chosen here are key issues from two of the applications. You are likely to have studied them in a lot of detail so use that detail when learning about contributions to society.

AS check

In many cases you may already have studied the following contributions as key issues, so use your past learning.

Taking it further

Investigate the case of the Railway Rapist, in particular to see how offender profiling was used. Find other examples as well.

▲ David Canter is probably the best-known person in offender profiling in the UK.

Offender profiling – criminological psychology

Offender profiling is a relatively recent development in criminological psychology and is carried out when there is a crime that is repeated so that a pattern can be identified to help to catch the criminal. David Canter is a well-known name in the development of offender profiling, and the case known as the Railway Rapist case is a famous example of the usefulness of offender profiling. Society benefits from catching criminals of course, so offender profiling is an important contribution.

Evaluating the contribution

Strengths

- Offender profiling is done in cases where the police need as many clues and hints as possible to follow up. The cases involved are usually ones where there is an urgency to stop another similar incident. Offender profiling can help to reduce the field of suspects, saving police time.
- Offender profiling takes all aspects of the case into account, from the crime scene to possible psychological aspects of the criminal. This makes it a holistic way of looking at a crime and details are less likely to be missed than if each aspect were looked at one at a time.

Weaknesses

- It is hard to show that offender profiling is effective as it is just one element in the search for the criminal and the profiler cannot come up with the name of the criminal. This also makes it hard to show its usefulness to society, which has made it suspect by some as a method.
- Approaches to offender profiling differ (e.g in the UK and in the US with the FBI). This means it can be idiosyncratic, which is not scientific and so might not be seen as useful.

Understanding daycare – child psychology

Daycare has been researched a great deal by psychologists, not least because parents want to know what is good or bad for their child, as does government. If daycare is bad for a child, and a child has problems in later life as a result, then society would have to deal with possible anti-social consequences. If daycare is good for a child and it allows both mother and father to work, for example, then society would benefit. Studies show positive and negative effects, and in general the conclusion seems to be that the right quality of daycare in the right amounts can be beneficial but that poor quality and too much daycare (particularly perhaps when very young) can have negative effects.

Evaluating the contribution

Strengths

- There is evidence that daycare is beneficial, including from Swedish studies and studies such as the EPPE study in the UK. And although some researchers, such as Jan Belsky, have said that there can be problems with daycare, they tend to find that not all daycare is bad.
- Studies tend to include data from a range of methods, such as questionnaires, observations and interviews, so there is an attempt to cover the many different variables that affect the situation and to find valid information.

Weaknesses

- There are many variables in a daycare setting – the staff, the child's background, gender, temperament, family, previous experiences and interactions, and the actual physical setting itself. It is very hard to carry out a study taking all these variables into account.
- Daycare has been researched in the UK and the US and in other countries, with different findings. Studies in Sweden are more likely to show that daycare is beneficial than studies in other countries, so there might be something about society in Sweden that helps daycare to be successful.
- If studies gather in-depth information to make the findings valid and about real life they are likely to be hard to replicate because of lack of controls so findings tend to either lack validity or reliability (as well as generalisability).

Examiner's tip

Only use this contribution if you studied child psychology. You will have looked at two studies about day care, use them when explaining this contribution. (The same applies for the other applications.)

Taking it further

Look at the work of Andersson in Sweden, who found that, in general, day care is good for a child.

Understanding schizophrenia – clinical psychology

If a mental health disorder can be treated, this helps the individual, the family and society as a whole. When behaviour mirrors the norms and rules of a society, the members of society are generally happy. There is also a cost element in that mental health disorders are often expensive to treat and deal with. Schizophrenia can be at least partially controlled by anti-schizophrenic drugs, and the dopamine hypothesis seems to explain at least some forms of schizophrenia.

Examiner's tip

If you studied health or sport psychology, prepare your two key issues from those applications.

Evaluating the contribution

Strengths

- In about a third of cases drug treatment controls schizophrenia as long as the medication is taken. People are then able to function in society rather than in an institution, which has benefits for them and for society.
- Other treatments such as care in the community, which gives support to someone with schizophrenia (page 120), have also been developed from psychological explanations, such as labelling and the need for social support. Taken with drug treatment, care in the community, with its strong focus on the individual, is likely to be socially responsible from an ethical point of view.

Weaknesses

- Medication does not work in all cases, though if it has a calming effect perhaps that qualifies as 'help'. The problem is that many people say that being 'drugged' is not a successful treatment because the person is no longer 'themselves'. Perhaps society benefits rather than the individual and their family.
- There are different forms of schizophrenia such as catatonia, reactive and paranoid schizophrenia. These might have different causes, which makes explaining the illness difficult.

Examzone

1. What does it mean to ask about a contribution to society? (3 marks)
2. Evaluate two contributions to society that have come from applications of psychology. (6 marks)

Ethical issues in the treatment of participants

What you need to know

- Five ethical guidelines relating to human participants and five relating to the use of animals.
- Evaluation of ethical issues.

AS check

The Social Approach included five BPS guidelines for humans (AS page 10) and there was evaluation of ethical issues when looking at Milgram's study (AS page 15). The Learning Approach included discussion of studies and assessing the ethical guidelines for human participants (AS page 130). The Biological Approach discussed evaluation of the study of animals, including ethical issues (AS page 103). Another guideline that you will have covered is confidentiality (AS page 74), so you could use that too.

▲ Consent is not needed to observe people in a public place.

Examiner's tip

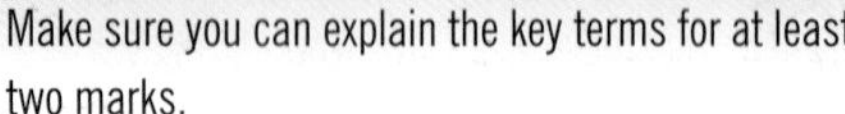

Make sure you can explain the key terms for at least two marks.

Five ethical guidelines when using humans

1. Informed consent

Getting informed consent is important, though it is not needed for observations in a public place. Consent must be informed, though the participants may not always be fully informed if that will jeopardise the study. In that case, they must be fully informed at a debrief. For example, in Godden and Baddeley's (1975) study, the divers needed fairly fully informed consent because they had to know what to do, but the main point about the environment for learning and recall was not explained, to avoid affecting the findings.

2. Deceit

Deceit should be avoided as far as possible, but is sometimes necessary for the success of the study. Again, this should be put right in a debrief. Hofling et al.'s (1966) nurses study deceived the participants when a 'doctor' gave fictitious orders. However, the point was to see if nurses would obey so they could not be told that the orders were not real.

3. Right to withdraw

Participants must have the right to withdraw at any time. They must also have the right to withdraw their data after the study is finished. Milgram's (1963) study included verbal prods to make the participants carry on, so the right to withdraw was compromised (although they could still refuse to continue).

4. Debrief

To make sure the participant leaves the study in the same emotional state as they arrive, they must be **debriefed** and everything revealed to them. Milgram's (1963) study included a thorough debrief.

5. Competence

A researcher must be **competent** to carry out the study and must check with colleagues if there is doubt – or not carry it out. Hofling et al. (1966) showed their competence, for example, in the setting up of observers to make sure the nurses were safe and debriefed.

Five ethical principles when using animals

1. Cost-benefit consideration

Cost-benefit analysis involves considering the costs of the study, including the cost to animals compared with potential benefits from the findings.

It is also important to take account of how sound the findings are. If the costs outweigh the benefits, the research can go ahead.

2. Suitably qualified researchers

Research must be carried out by researchers who are **suitably qualified** and competent – and they must make sure that everyone they supervise on the study has the appropriate skills. In the UK, the researcher must have a personal licence, be part of a licensed project and the study must be done in the place specified on the licence.

3. Using non-animal procedures if possible
The research can only be done using animals if alternatives using non-animal procedures have been considered.

4. Keeping discomfort to a minimum
Where a protected animal has been used in a study and has suffered pain and distress they must not be used again. Pain must be minimised.

5. Using suitably equipped premises
Premises must be suitable and licensed. Caging must be suitable for the species, for example, and there should be provision for anaesthetic procedures.

Evaluating ethical issues with human participants

Advantages of ethical guidelines

Psychological research must be ethically carried out, for three main reasons:

- Participants must feel safe.
- Society's moral standards must be maintained.
- Vulnerable participants need protection.

Problems with ethical guidelines

Ethical guidelines can restrict studies. Three restrictions are:

- Not being able to do a covert observation of private behaviour. A covert observation can be difficult to set up because it is hard to get informed consent from participants and observations are only exempt from informed consent if they concern public behaviour.
- Not being able to study violent or aggressive behaviour experimentally. It is not possible to set up real violence in an experimental situation.
- Not being able to report on all aspects of a case study. Important information from a case study may not be reported because of confidentiality.

Evaluating ethical issues with animal participants

Advantages

Clearly ethical guidelines for animals are there to protect the animals. The key advantage is in adhering to society's moral standards so that people are comfortable with the research that is being carried out. Having ethical guidelines for using animals means that research can be carried out that will benefit humans without feeling that the cost of such findings is too high. (There are still those who feel, however, that the cost is too high and that no animals should be used in research.)

Disadvantages

Guidelines can hinder research because of restrictions. For example:

- Endangered species cannot be used, so some research is not possible.
- The smallest possible number of animals must be used, which can mean findings are less reliable as too few animals were used.
- Replication can also be prevented by ethical principles, as the same study cannot be carried out repeatedly.
- Getting the right licences from the Home Office and finding suitably qualified researchers can take time and be expensive, which limits the research.

Examzone

1 Outline two ethical guidelines that need to be paid attention to when using human participants and for each give an example. (6 marks)
2 Outline two ethical issues that are important when using animals in psychological research. (6 marks)
3 Evaluate with regard to ethical issues using animals in research in psychology. (6 marks)

Taking it further

Bateson developed the idea of cost-benefit analysis, so is a name to start with when researching this area.

Examiner's tip

To remember the five principles, use the following: cost-benefit, qualified, non-animal, discomfort and equipped.

Examiner's tip

Don't use ethical guidelines for humans when answering a question on non-human animals. For example, don't say animal studies are wrong because they cannot be given the right to withdraw, as having the right to withdraw is not an ethical principle when using animals.

Taking it further

Using the BPS website, read the *Code of Ethics and Conduct* (2006) and *Guidelines for Psychologists Working with Animals* (2007) to find out more. Look up the Animals (scientific procedures) Act as well.

Examiner's tip

Prepare enough so that you can write about ethics with either humans or animals for a whole essay (prepare for more than 12 marks). You can use the examples of studies from the following pages or from any other part of your course. You would need to be able to describe and evaluate.

Two studies in terms of ethical considerations

What you need to know

With regard to two studies you need to know:

- The aim(s), procedure(s), results and conclusions of each.
- The strengths and weaknesses of each in terms of ethical considerations.

Examiner's tip

Make sure in the exam that you only evaluate in terms of ethics if that is what the question demands – avoid other evaluation points even if you know them.

Milgram's (1963) study of obedience

Milgram's (1963) study of obedience in the USA is probably very familiar to you by now and is not described in detail here. He set up an experiment where participants thought they were giving another participant an electric shock and he wanted to see what level of 'shock' they would go up to. All the participants went to 300 volts, a very high level indeed and 65% went up to 450 volts. Milgram concluded that people obey authority figures even when they very strongly do not want to.

Evaluation of ethics

Strengths

- Milgram carried out a full **debrief** that included a questionnaire to make sure the participants were all happy to have taken part; most said they were.
- He checked with colleagues to make sure the study was ethical and they agreed it was, so he showed **competence**.

Weaknesses

- The participants were very much affected by the study, including one having a seizure and others getting very distressed.
- They were not given the **right to withdraw** properly. When they wanted to stop the experimenter gave verbal prods (four times) to push them to continue.

Meeus and Raaijmakers (1986) study of obedience

Meeus and Raaijmakers (1986) studied obedience to replicate Milgram's (1963) study, though they made some important changes. Instead of the participants having to give shocks (as the participants really believed they were doing), this study used psychological violence, where the participants had to make stress remarks whilst a 'participant' (who was a confederate) completed a job application. The study found higher obedience than Milgram did – 91.7% carried on with all 15 stress remarks as opposed to 65% giving the highest shock level.

Evaluation of ethics

Strengths

- Meeus and Raaijmakers (1986) toned down the punishment as making stress remarks may have been less stressful than giving electric shocks; to that extent the pressure was less and the study was more ethical.
- The researchers obtained consent that was more informed than in Milgram's study because they told the participants they would be making stress remarks. They did not have to lie about the reality of the 'shocks' as Milgram did – so the consent was more informed.

Weaknesses

- The researchers knew that Milgram's participants had suffered a great deal of distress so replicating the study, even slightly differently, meant an almost deliberate lack of ethical considerations.
- The participants were **deceived** because they thought that the job applicant was applying for a real job that was important to them, whereas in reality the applicant was a confederate.

Skinner's (1948) study of superstition in pigeons

Skinner (1948) carried out a study of eight pigeons. Each was put separately into a cage, with food being swung in and out for them at intervals governed by the researcher. Two observers watched the behaviour of the pigeon to see what they did whilst waiting for the food. With six of the pigeons, they found that, whatever the pigeon was doing when the food was swung in, they continued to do until the food arrived again. It was concluded that the pigeons had somehow connected their activity to the arrival of the food and so had made an association between the two.

▲ The pigeons in Skinner's study were to an extent well looked after, though they were still caged, starved to 75% of their body weight and tested.

Evaluation of ethics

Strengths

- The experiment used only eight pigeons whereas more would have been possible. To some extent that therefore adheres to the requirement of using as few animals as possible – though the study was in 1948 and the Animals (Scientific Procedures) Act not until 1986.
- Pigeons are not an endangered species, so are a suitable species to use according to the guidelines.

Weaknesses

- Such a study could possibly be carried out using humans to see if superstitious behaviour was found when humans were operantly conditioned to behave in some way for a reward. Guidelines for the use of animals say that alternatives should always be sought.
- Each pigeon was starved to 75% of their body weight. This could be said to cause undue distress since, as long as the bird wanted food, the study could have been carried out at their normal feeding time.

Examiner's tip

You can use any studies that you know, as long as you have sufficient detail and can evaluate them thoroughly in terms of ethics.

Examzone

1 Describe one psychological study in psychology that you can evaluate in terms of ethics. (5 marks)
2 Evaluate one psychological study in terms of ethics. (6 marks)
3 Explain the ethical weaknesses of two psychological studies. (6 marks)

Research methods

What you need to know

- With regard to research methods, you need to be able to describe and evaluate:
- Laboratory, field and naturalistic experiments
- Observations and questionnaires
- Interviews and content analysis
- You also need to be able to describe and evaluate an example of each method as used in a study.

Laboratory, field and naturalistic experiments as research methods

Describing the experiments

Laboratory experiments: involve a study in an artificial environment using careful controls.
Field experiments: involve using careful controls in a natural environment or setting.
Naturalistic experiments: involve a study with an independent and a dependent variable where the independent variable is naturally occurring.

Evaluation of the experiments

Laboratory experiments: These can be shown to be reliable because they are replicable – controls and variables are carefully noted and the study can be repeated. There is objectivity because of operationalisation of variables. However, they tend to lack validity because tasks are usually unnatural and they often also lack ecological validity because the setting is unnatural.
Field experiments: These can be shown to be reliable if controls are sufficient and clearly documented. They are also more ecologically valid than laboratory experiments as the setting is natural.
Naturalistic experiments: As the independent variable is naturally occurring, such experiments are valid with regard to what is being measured. They are hard to replicate as they tend to be one-off situations, so it is hard to say the findings are reliable. Being about one-off situations, it is often also hard to generalise the findings from them.

Examiner's tip

Don't use bullet points in an exam answer. You have to communicate clearly and effectively, which bullet points rarely do.

Examiner's tip

Methodological terms are deliberately included here to remind you what they all mean. You have come across most of them before – many times. Make sure that you are completely sure about their meaning.

Examples of the experiments

Study	Example of methodology	Application/ Approach	Page
Pickel (1998)	Laboratory experiment	Criminological	14
Yarmey (2004)	Field experiment	Criminological	16
Loftus and Palmer (1974)	Laboratory experiment	Criminological	20
Charlton et al. (2000)	Naturalistic experiment	Criminological	22
Cottrell (1968)	Laboratory experiment	Sport	89
Milgram (1963)	Laboratory experiment	Social	12 (AS)
Skinner (1948)	Laboratory experiment	Learning	136 (AS)

The observational research method was covered in more detail in child psychology (see page 28).

The observation as a research method

Describing the method

There are structured observations and naturalistic observations. Structured observations involve careful controls and a set-up situation that can be repeated. There is often more than one observer and observations tend to be carried out through a one-way mirror to avoid affecting the situation. Naturalistic observations take place in a natural setting. They can be overt or covert. They can also be either participant or non-participant.

Evaluating the method

- **Structured observations** can be repeated and tested for reliability. They are carefully controlled so that findings can be analysed and compared. Tallying, for example, is often used, or more than one observer is used so that their findings can be correlated. However, they take place in a controlled setting and, therefore, can be said to lack validity.
- **Naturalistic observations** tend to have validity as they take place in a natural setting. However, if they are non-participant observations, the observer may somehow alter the behaviour of those being observed, which would mean a lack of validity. There are many variables that can affect behaviour in a natural setting so a naturalistic observation can be hard to replicate, which also affects validity.

Examples of observations

You need to be able to describe and evaluate one example of an observation and it is likely that you have not covered one during your studies. Mary Ainsworth used structured observations so if you looked at child psychology you will be familiar with her work (see page 34). During your course you might not, however, have looked at a naturalistic observation, so an example follows.

An observational study – Melhuish et al. (1990)

Melhuish et al. (1990) looked at four types of daycare to see how children's development was affected. The four types were: relatives, child minders, a nursery or remaining at home. The data was gathered using observations of the children individually, in the home or setting. The study involved 255 families in London, who also completed a questionnaire giving information about themselves. The observation reported here was carried out at age 18 months but the children were also visited at 36 months, five years and 11, so this is an example of a longitudinal study. There were two separate one-hour observations of the children in their daycare setting. For the children not at home during the day, observations were also carried out in their homes. The observer watched during free play sessions and recorded the child's activity every 10 seconds. Some behaviours were one-off and were recorded once, others were recorded by including their start and end time. More than one observer was used and, if the observers did not agree 70% or more of the time, that observation was discarded.

Example of a laboratory experiment

Loftus and Palmer (1974) is chosen as the study here because if you have studied the criminological application, you will have covered it already. If you chose a different application you could revise a different laboratory experiment here.

Loftus and Palmer (1974) carried out a laboratory experiment to look at the effect of leading questions (or changing the wording of a question) on memory (or judgement) of an event. After watching film of a car accident, participants were asked how far the cars were going when the car 'hit' or 'smashed' (and there were other verbs). The results were that 'hit' led to estimate of a lower speed than 'smashed', and the conclusion was that just one word – the verb in this case – led to a different estimate of speed.

Some of the results were that:

- The home and relatives groups showed more responsiveness than the nursery group.
- The home group was also more responsive than the childminder group.
- The nursery group showed fewer affection responses than the other groups.
- Aggression was generally low but there was more aggression in the nursery group.
- The nursery group also produced the fewest language utterances.

It was concluded that the four types of daycare gave different outcomes with regard to specific behaviours, such as responsiveness, affection, aggression and language.

Evaluation of Meluish et al. (1990)

Strengths

- There is inter-observer reliability and where this does not occur the data was not included in the results.
- The children were observed during free play when they could choose their own activities, which should have led to fair comparisons between the four groups. If the observations were of structured sessions this might have affected the child's behaviour.

Weaknesses

- The nurseries were privately owned and not well-resourced. Other better-equipped and resourced nurseries may not give the same findings.
- The researchers point out that the observations all watched 18-month-old children, so findings might only generalise to that age group.

The questionnaire as a research method

Describing the method

Questionnaires usually involve gathering both qualitative and quantitative data. Closed questions gather quantitative data and open questions gather qualitative data. Open questions allow a respondent to give some opinions and closed questions offer only a forced choice of answer.

Personal data such as age, gender, work situation and other required information are also asked.

Evaluating the method

Questionnaires can be sent out by post to large numbers of people. This might seem to be an advantage, but the response rate does tend to be low. In general, however, they can gather a lot of data by reaching a large number of people. Also, the inclusion of instructions and information on the questionnaire means they can be ethical – for example, the respondent knows what they are being asked to do and can be given the right to withdraw. However, respondents can lie because they want to look good, which is a type of social desirability. There can be a lack of validity because of this.

Examples of questionnaires

During your course you have probably looked at a study where a questionnaire was used as a research method. Some examples from within this book are listed opposite.

Examiner's tip

Notice that you can evaluate a study by looking at generalisability, reliability, subjectivity or validity but that there are also evaluation points which are specific to the study, such as the type of nursery in this study. Make sure that the point relates to the study rather than being a general point about the research method.

Final numbers in the observation:
44 – home group
19 – relative group
59 – childminder group
34 – nursery group

Examiner's tip

You need to know enough about a study in this section to be able to describe different aspects of it, such as the procedure or the results separately. Make sure you know enough.

AS check

Questionnaires are explained in detail in the Social Approach (and in sport psychology if you chose that area in the second year).

Boyd and Munroe (2003) used two questionnaires in their study to look at how climbers and athletes use imagery. This is the compulsory study for sport psychology so if you chose that application you will already be familiar with it (see page 88).

Study	Example of methodology	Application/ Approach	Page
Boyd and Munroe (2003)	Questionnaire	Sport	88
Mumford and Whitehouse (1988)	Questionnaire	Clinical	127
Koivula (1995)	Questionnaire	Sport	90

The interview as a research method

Describing the method

There are three types of interview that you have looked at:

- A structured interview uses a set of questions that are fixed for each respondent.
- An unstructured interview has a schedule of questions but the interviewer can divert from them to investigate areas that arise or that the respondent chooses to address.
- A semi structured interview is a combination of a set list of questions and some room for exploring areas.

Evaluating the method

Interviews are one-to-one, so any questions can be explained or areas of interest explored. Theoretically, therefore, data should be more valid. However, respondents can still not tell the truth for some reason, which would put the validity in question. Structured interviews are more replicable than unstructured ones and responses from structured interviews are more comparable.

Examples of studies using the interview method

A list of such studies from this book is shown below.

Study	Example of methodology	Application/ Approach	Page
Levine et al. (1990)	Interview	Clinical	128
Brown et al. (1986)	Interview	Clinical	129

Content analysis as a research method

Content analysis as a research method has not been covered within this book. This section is therefore covered in more detail than for other research methods.

- When analysing the content of a media story or topic, references to that topic or to some aspect of it are counted – this is content analysis.
- Often, categories relating to the topic are set up and agreed beforehand so that it is known what is to be counted.
- A researcher goes through the material – a newspaper, a series of programmes or children's books, etc. – and counts the number of times each category is mentioned. This is tallying.
- When writing up the analysis it is very important that the categories are clear, so that what is covered in each case is overt and wrong conclusions are not drawn. For example, if going through children's books looking for references to jobs and gender, the categories are probably clear, but if looking for acts of aggression, a clear definition of 'act of aggression' will be needed.

AS check

Interviews were covered in detail in the Social Approach (see AS page 9).

Examiner's tip

There are three types of interview, each with strengths and weaknesses, so if you are asked to evaluate interviews in general you can choose one type to give a strength or a weakness and work through them in turn.

One area which is often studied using interviews is depression.

Examiner's tip

Make sure in an exam answer that you make your point very clearly. For example, if you say an observation can be overt make it clear that you know what it means. You need to show knowledge but also that you have knowledge with understanding.

Examiner's tip

It is worth considering strengths and weaknesses of covert, overt, participant and non-participant observations separately so that you can be clear about the different types of observation and how useful they are.

Taking it further

If you studied depression as part of clinical psychology you will have looked at a relevant study in detail. If this was Brown et al., (1986) you have already covered an interview and can use that here. If it was another study using an interview, that would be useful too. If you have not studied depression, you might like to explore this area looking at some of these other studies.

Examiner's tip

You will have carried out a content analysis as part of a practical for one of the applications of psychology that you have studied. Use your learning there when describing and perhaps evaluating this research method.

Examiner's tip

If you give as two strengths the ideas that content analyses are ethical and uncover novel data, you might not gain marks. Remember to expand on your points so that you show clearly what you mean and why this is a strength, as is done here.

Examiner's tip

If you have studied health psychology you can link this study to your coverage of the misuse of drugs.

- Alcohol scenes: 12 per hour
- Smoking-related scenes: 3.4 per hour
- Drug-related scenes: 1.7 per hour
- 4% of scenes featured none of the above.
- Of the main characters, drinkers made up 37% and smokers 4%. These percentages were not found in the other characters.
- 84% of the messages about alcohol were neutral rather than positive or negative.

Evaluation

Strengths

- Content analyses involve collection of data from sources that already exist, so few ethical issues are involved. There might be some issues of confidentiality but there should be no deceit and informed consent should not be necessary.
- Even though a content analysis is likely to study data that already exists, it does so in a novel way and is likely to highlight a fresh interpretation of such data, which is unlikely to be found another way.

Weaknesses

- Content analyses require interpretation of data quite often because sometimes a detail might be hard to 'fit' into a category. To be scientific content analyses (as other research methods) need to avoid **subjectivity**.
- If categories are set up that do not represent what is being studied – if categories do not cover what is commonly thought of as aggression, for example – then the data will not be valid.

Example of content analysis

Cumberbatch and Gauntlett (2005) carried out research for Ofcom, the regulator of the UK communications industry. 'A Broadcasting Code requires under 18s to be protected from unsuitable broadcasting. The aim was to look at programmes targeted at or watched by 10 to 15-year olds to see how drugs, smoking, solvent abuse or alcohol were treated. The top 10 programmes watched by the age group were chosen. Over a three-month period in 2004, 256 programmes were watched, 70% of which were soaps and were broadcast before the 9pm watershed. The analysis noted all scenes where alcohol, smoking or drugs were mentioned, whether legal or illegal use. Altogether, 2099 scenes were noted. See left for results.

Evaluation

Strengths

- If Ofcom wishes to know the frequency of certain types of behaviour on TV, or references to it, content analysis – which involves counting the number of such incidences – is the obvious way of collecting the data.
- There is nothing unethical about analysis of programmes that have been broadcast. The programmes were not even 'real' so there was no need for any ethical considerations, though the researchers would need to make sure they were competent to carry out the study.

Weaknesses

- The categories would need to be set to make sure a 'scene' was clear. It sounds straightforward, but it might be hard in practice to decide where one 'scene' started and another ended. For example, how should they count a long scene in a pub? This would need to be clarified so that data is reliable.
- Although the top 10 programmes were chosen, there are many other programmes shown in three months that 10 to 15 year-olds would watch. The study took a 'snapshot' of what was being shown. This could mean that the findings cannot be generalised to a different period or a different year. Having said that, the programme sample was large and three months is quite a long time for a study.

The correlation as a research method

Describing what is meant by a correlation

Correlations are really a form of analysis because they involve two scores generated by one person and then compared. If enough people are asked, their scores on one variable (such as reaction time) can be correlated with their scores on another variable (such as their age) and a test can be done to see if age and reaction time show a relationship. A positive correlation would be a score from the test of towards +1 and a negative correlation would be a score of towards –1. The closer to 1, the greater the relationship is.

Evaluating correlational analysis

A correlation is the only way of showing a relationship between two variables and a test is a good way of showing how great a relationship there is. This is advantageous, as finding a relationship is often the first step in linking one variable with another to see the effect. For example, smoking seemed to correlate with heart disease and studies have since suggested that there is a causal link. One problem, however, is that correlations do not in themselves show that cause and effect link.

Examples of correlational analyses

You will have looked at correlations during your course. There is also one that you can revise or learn on page91 in sport psychology (Craft et al., 2003).

▲ There are fears about 10 to 15 year-olds watching TV scenes about smoking, alcohol or other substance misuse, and content analyses have shown that alcohol features significantly in such scenes.

Taking it further

Look back through your study of applications and find a correlational analysis. Review your own correlation as well, that you carried out when studying the Psychodynamic Approach, but make sure you know a published study.

You are likely to have come across more than one study that uses correlational analysis. If you studied sport psychology, you might have looked at Craft et al. (2003) who carried out a meta-analysis looking at the relationship between different types of anxiety and self-confidence. It is summarised very briefly here.

The case study as a research method

Describing the method

Case studies are in-depth studies of one person (or perhaps a small group of people in a unique situation) and many different research methods under the case study umbrella can be used. For example, there are case studies of brain-damaged people done to see what different parts of the brain do. There are case studies to uncover unconscious wishes and desires and to try to help someone with a neurosis. Others include studies of feral children who have been privated and not socialised, carried out to see the effect on their development.

Evaluating the method

Case studies gather in-depth detailed information, often from a variety of sources, so the data is likely to be valid and real-life. Much of the data will be qualitative. Case studies are, however, not often replicable and the unique individual or situation means that generalising is not possible either.

Examples of case studies

Study	Example of methodology	Application/ Approach	Page
Freud (1909) (Little Hans)	Case study	Psychodynamic	86 (AS)
Axline (1964)	Case study	Psychodynamic	88 (AS)
Money (1975)	Case study	Biological	110 (AS)
Curtiss (1977)	Case study	Child	46

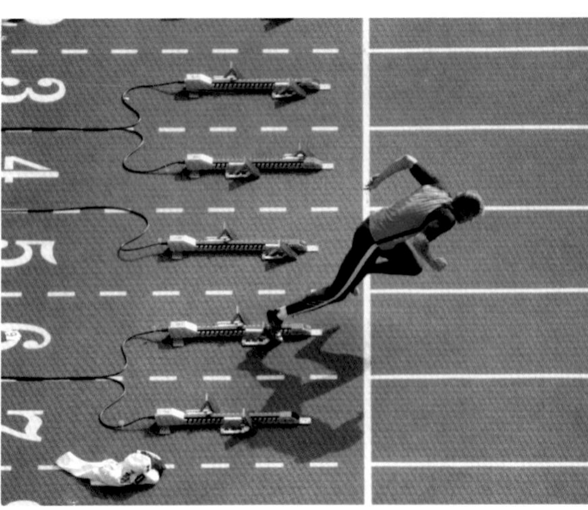

▲ It has been found that self-confidence links strongly with sporting success. Self-confidence might link with motivation to train, too.

Examzone

1 Explain one main difference between a laboratory experiment and a field experiment and one main difference between a laboratory experiment and a naturalistic experiment. In your answer, use an example of each research method when explaining each difference. (6 marks)

2 Compare observations and questionnaires in terms of validity. (4 marks)

***3** What is meant by content analysis as a research method? (2 marks)

4 Outline the procedure of one study that used correlational analysis. (3 marks)

Key issues: Social and Cognitive Approaches

What you need to know

- One key issue from the Social Approach and one from the Cognitive Approach.
- For each key issue, the concepts, theories and research to explain them as relevant (including ethical and methodological issues).

Social Approach: The massacre at My Lai, Vietnam

Up to 500 women, children and old men were killed on 16 March 1968 by US soldiers following orders. The soldiers went through the village killing everyone they saw, and without provocation. It was later found that three villages suffered a similar fate but My Lai was the one focused on when everything first came to light. The orders were to search and destroy – but they referred to Vietcong soldiers who were thought to be hiding in the village. The US soldiers spread out and it is thought that once shots were heard the killing spree started, though it seems that no shots were fired at the US soldiers. It was not 'just' killing – there were many acts of brutality that shocked the world. The leader of the group, Lieutenant Calley, was sentenced to life imprisonment but only served four and a half years because the appeal board thought that he genuinely had felt he was obeying orders.

Explaining the issue using social psychology

- Milgram found blind obedience to an authority figure when his participants continued to give what they thought were strong electric shocks to a person they thought was another participant. The soldiers in My Lai, acting (as they thought) under orders, would have been in a similar situation perhaps.
- Milgram developed the idea of agency, suggesting that people in a society act as agents for authority figures and to do this they give up their **autonomy**. This is **agency theory**. The soldiers in My Lai may have been acting as agents rather than under their own moral code.
- Philip Zimbardo spoke in defence of US soldiers, this time concerning brutal acts in Iraq, in the Abu Ghraib prison. He suggested that the situation, not their 'evil' personalities, led to their behaviour. The same could be said of the soldiers in the My Lai situation. This is a practical application of psychological research.
- Milgram and Zimbardo drew their conclusions from laboratory studies and simulations rather than from real-life situations like My Lai or Abu Ghraib. It could be said that their findings lack validity because of the unnatural nature of the studies they carried out.
- Claiming that soldiers like Calley and those involved in Abu Ghraib are 'only' acting under orders, and that anyone else in the same situation would do the same, raises ethical issues. The question is whether they are responsible for their actions or not. In practice, courts have not yet fully accepted the claim by psychologists that there is no personal responsibility in such situations.

AS check

You may have used the My Lai massacre, or the Abu Ghraib brutality, as the key issue in your study of social psychology.

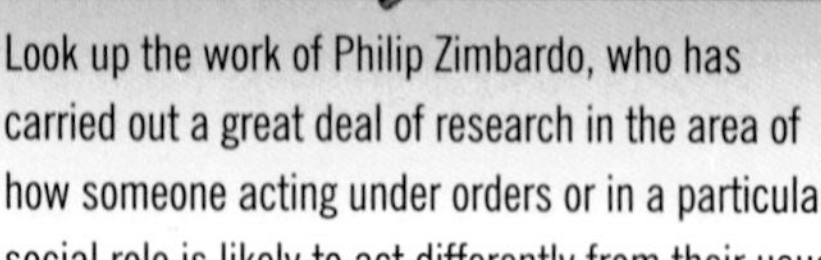

Taking it further

Look up the work of Philip Zimbardo, who has carried out a great deal of research in the area of how someone acting under orders or in a particular social role is likely to act differently from their usual moral code.

Cognitive Approach: The unreliability of eyewitness testimony

On the face of it, if someone has seen something, they will know exactly what happened so others take notice of what they say. However, there is doubt as to whether memory is so reliable. It appears to be far from precise and detailed. There have been a series of convictions that have been overturned because they relied solely on the testimony of eyewitnesses and that testimony was found to be unsafe (often through DNA testing). In 1982, Julius Earl Ruffin was convicted of rape and sentenced to life in prison, his conviction resting on the identification by his victim. It was 21 years later that DNA evidence finally showed that he was innocent and he was set free. He has written a book, *Why Me? When It Could Have Been You?'*. It is not suggested that the eyewitnesses in such cases are lying or in any way perverting the course of justice – just that such testimony can be unreliable.

Explaining the issue using cognitive psychology

- Reconstructive memory theory suggests that a memory, far from being an exact replica of an event, is reconstructed from bits of memories that are interpreted using existing schemas and experiences to form a coherent story.
- Cue-dependent forgetting theory suggests that, unless there are the right cues for recall, forgetting is likely because memories rely on reconstructing the cognitive environment when the memory was laid down.
- There are state-dependent cues, which are about the emotional or physical state of someone, and there are context-dependent cues, which are about the situation at the time.
- Another issue with memory is that the way in which a memory is elicited can affect it. Elizabeth Loftus carried out many studies from the 1970s onwards looking at leading questions, for example, and the effect of cues in a question. She found that key words can affect testimony, such as whether a verb is strong (e.g. smashed) or weak (e.g. hit), which can affect how fast a 'witness' judges a car as going.
- Loftus, and others, at first used mainly laboratory experiments because of the good controls so that clear cause and effect conclusions could be reached, leading to scientific understanding. This was desirable because the issue of the unreliability of eyewitness testimony is so important in many convictions and there are practical applications of the material.
- Later studies have used field experiments, however, trying to maintain the reliability of the experiment whilst testing the validity of the claims.

Examzone

1 Describe one key issue you have studied that can be explained using concepts and theories from the Social Approach. (4 marks)

2 Using concepts and theories from the Cognitive Approach, explain one issue that is of interest to society. (6 marks)

Taking it further

Find other cases where a conviction resting on eyewitness testimony has been found to be unsafe and has been overturned.

AS check

You may have used eyewitness testimony as the key issue in your study of the Cognitive Approach.

Examiner's tip

The effectiveness of the cognitive interview technoque and the effectiveness of CBT are other key issues you could consider.

Examiner's tip

When preparing material about a key issue remember to consider ethical and methodological issues concerning the evidence you are using.

Key issues: Psychodynamic and Biological Approaches

What you need to know

- One key issue from the Psychodynamic and one from the Biological Approach.
- For each key issue, the concepts, theories and research to explain them as relevant (including ethical and methodological issues).

Psychodynamic Approach: false memories and psychoanalysis

False memories can apparently arise during therapy, as will be discussed here. However, false memories can also come from other sources, such as hearing a conversation about an event in one's childhood, which can then give us the 'memory' of that event being true. Memory is not infallible.

False memories that come from memories recovered during therapy may involve 'remembering' abuse in childhood that did not happen. Clearly, families are severely affected by such recovered memories, and this is the issue discussed here. The British Psychological Society looked at the issue of memories recovered during therapy and suggested that 'recovering' childhood memories of abuse could be self-fulfilling and that 'recovered memory' work was unscientific. It was found that it could take four months or more for recovered memories to occur during analysis.

If these memories are about abuse in childhood, they are about very traumatic experiences. However, other studies have shown that those who are abused remember the experience only too well. The issue is whether false recovered memories are a feature of analysis. Is the analysand–analyst relationship biased in power such that the analysand is open to the suggestions of the analyst?

Explaining the issue using the Psychodynamic Approach

- During psychoanalysis the client (the analysand) talks and the analyst listens, using research methods such as dream analysis, case history and free association. The analyst needs a great deal of information in order to begin any analysis, so a relationship is built up between the analyst and the analysand.
- There can be transference, where the analysand transfers feelings of love or hate onto the analyst, for example, and there can be counter transference, where the analyst transfers feelings back. These are features of the therapy.
- Both the above points suggest a strong power relationship between the client and the analyst, with the analyst being in the position of power.
- From an ethical point of view, the therapist must not abuse their power, and there are issues about confidentiality.
- The analysand will be spending a lot of time with the analyst. They will explore the analysand's life in great detail and suggestions will be made during analysis. These elements – time spent and power of the relationship – illustrate how a suggestion from the analyst could be strong enough to eventually become a memory for the client.

Examiner's tip

Be ready to give points from the approach to explain your key issue and include some methodology points and ethical points where relevant. A useful way to prepare for the exam is to use the essay title 'Describe one key issue from the XX approach and explain the issue using concepts and theories from the approach'. Assume 12 marks are available, with additional marks available for the balance of the essay and how far you use terms appropriately.

- Loftus showed that overhearing a story about childhood can lead to someone accepting the event featured in the story as being real. False memories have been shown to be planted using experimental methods. There is therefore evidence to support this theory.
- Ethically, false memories are potentially very damaging to the client and others involved.

Biological Approach: Is autism an extreme male brain condition?

Autism is a condition that affects boys more than girls. It is a developmental disorder that affects a child's ability to relate to other people and their ability to build any relationships, including with their parents. It is often diagnosed at the age of about two but parents tend to report having noticed differences and difficulties before that, so it is generally accepted to come from birth not from environmental factors.

In 2005, it was suggested that features of autism – problems with understanding emotions, preference for order and stability, difficulties with language – are features of a male brain and Baron-Cohen suggested that perhaps autism is an extreme form of the male brain. It is worth noting that females can have a 'male brain'; what is referred to here is the standard finding of what a male brain tends to be like compared with a female brain. (See also Chapter 2.)

▲ Simon Baron-Cohen has been researching autism for a great many years and has developed understanding of biological aspects of the condition, including fairly recently suggesting that autism is an extreme male brain condition.

Explaining the issue using biological psychology

- Male brains are heavier than female brains and those with autism have an even heavier brain than a normal male brain. Male brains also grow more quickly, as does the brain of someone with autism. These pieces of evidence support the idea of a link between autism and an extreme male brain.
- Males are said to be better at spatial tasks such as map reading than females, so are better at systems – which is what autistic people focus on. Females are better at language tasks, which those with autism have difficulty with. Here again are two pieces of evidence that autism might be an extreme male brain condition.
- There is evidence against the theory as well, however, as male brains are said to show more lateralisation than female brains – females tend to use both hemispheres more. It might be thought, therefore, that those with autism would be extremely lateralised with regard to brain functioning, but this is not the case.
- There might be a link with testosterone (which females also produce though to a lesser extent, explaining why there are females with autism) and that might relate to difficulties in interpreting the emotions of others. Females are found to be better at interpreting emotions in studies showing facial expressions. Those with autism find interpreting the emotions of others difficult, if not impossible.
- There might be a genetic element to autism or an environmental cause and other theories have been put forward to explain it.
- Explanations of characteristics and conditions such as autism must be backed by evidence and carefully put forward as there are ethical issues involved. The idea of autism being an extreme male brain condition does not blame parents, so can be put forward as an idea whilst evidence is gathered. Some years ago, when it was suggested that schizophrenia came from patterns of family communication, there was strain put on families who believed that if a child developed schizophrenia it was their fault. This shows the importance of using psychology to explain real-life conditions.

Examzone

Describe one key issue from the Psychodynamic Approach and explain it using concepts and theories from the approach. (12 marks)

Key issues: Learning Approach and criminological psychology

What you need to know

- One key issue from the Learning Approach and one from criminological psychology.
- For each key issue, the concepts, theories and research to explain them as relevant (including ethical and methodological issues).

Examiner's tip

You have already covered contributions from the approaches and applications that you have studied in psychology. Questions such as whether those contributions are useful or how they work are key issues in society.

Examiner's tip

Remember that the Learning Approach offers three main theories about how people learn: classical and operant conditioning and Social Learning Theory.

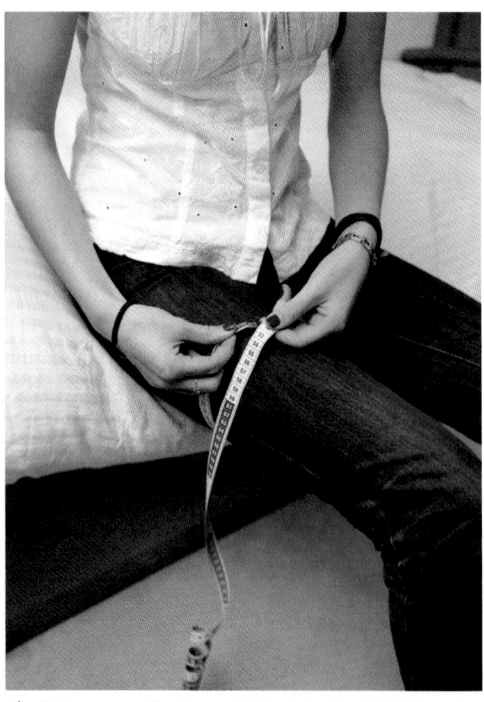

▲ It is generally thought that in the UK there is an obsession over weight, which could lead to anorexia if it is caused by imitating 'size zero' role models.

Learning Approach: Is anorexia caused by role models?

The trend for 'size zero' role models has been commented on frequently in the news. On the one hand there are continued reports about the UK having a nutrition problem because of obesity; on the other there are reports of 'stick thin' models and celebrities. It seems that on both sides there are criticisms. Children and young people look up to their role models and copy them, as can be seen in young boys imitating their favourite footballer or young girls dressing like their pop idol. Anorexia is an illness where someone is well under their desirable weight and does not realise it – in fact, they think they are fat. Anorexia has been growing over the same time that models in the media have been shrinking, and it is suggested that one cause of anorexia is that young children – perhaps girls in particular – are copying their role models.

◆ Explaining the issue using the Learning Approach

- Bandura showed that children exposed to aggressive role models were more likely to copy that aggression than if they were exposed to passive role models. This suggests that children imitate behaviour they see in adults.
- Bandura also showed that, if a role model is seen to be rewarded for a behaviour, it is more likely the behaviour will be imitated. So, if models in the media seem to be praised for being thin/slim, which in general they are, then that behaviour is more likely to be imitated. This underlines the practical implications of psychological research.
- Female role models in the media are more likely to have their appearance commented on – such as being criticised if they have not lost weight after having had a baby – and girls are more likely to imitate female role models. This could link to the fact that there are more girls diagnosed with anorexia than boys.
- However, male models and role models also have their looks (including their weight) commented on, and anorexia amongst boys is growing.
- Bandura's work has included laboratory experiments, which are useful because they are replicable and the controls can help to show a cause and effect link between observing behaviour and imitating it.
- However, laboratory experiments can lack validity so it is possible that what is replicated in an artificial setting does not happen in real life.
- The media recognise the responsibility they have to their viewers/readers, however, and the government, too, has taken steps against inappropriate role models being put forward for children (via the 9 o'clock watershed, for example). There are ethical issues here.

Criminological psychology: How successful is offender profiling?

Offender profiling was used many years ago when people looked at patterns in crimes committed by mass murderers like Jack the Ripper (1888). For example, the murderer was assumed to have some medical or physiological knowledge because of what he did to the bodies, and he was assumed to be local because of his knowledge of the area (Whitechapel in London). The idea behind offender profiling is still the same – to draw conclusions from the crimes and the crime scenes about what sort of person was committing the crimes. A famous case is that of the Railway Rapist. In the 1980s, a series of rapes on young women at railway stations took place and eventually one of the young women was murdered so the Railway Rapist became the Railway Killer. The police gathered what information they could but they called in a psychologist working in the field of geography at the time, David Canter. He used geographical clues such as suggesting that the perpetrator (in fact, there were two – two friends) lived near the railway and also suggested other features of the killer. This was the start of offender profiling as a formal method used to help police. Jack the Ripper was never caught but the Railway Killers were both caught in the end.

Explaining the issue using criminological psychology

- Offender profiling works on a practical basis. For example, if victims are all attacked at night it is assumed the attacker must either be working at night so their absence isn't noticed, or that he or she lives alone.
- Issues such as strength and skills are also considered. For example, if a heavy body is moved, the attacker is likely to be male.
- Geography seems to be important as the person concerned is going to choose places with which they are familiar. It can therefore be assumed that they live in the area or somewhere very similar. In one case the person clearly understood all about a block of flats – but did not live in that block, just in one identical.
- It can be seen that habits are predictable to an extent and that learning is important. These ideas come from an understanding of behaviour and underline the practical applications of psychology.
- The profiler can make other estimates about the individual from the type of crime, such as whether they live alone, are male or female, how old they are or whether they work. However, these are only guesses. A profile does not find the criminal; rather, it helps inform the direction of police investigations.
- Ethically, profiles must be as accurate as possible and everyone involved has to be protected, including victims and possible criminals.
- Offender profiling draws on evidence from the crime scene, so empirical evidence is used.
- In some cases, offender profiling uses evidence from known criminals and patterns of crime to draw likely conclusions.

Key issues: Child and health psychology 

What you need to know

- One key issue from child psychology and one from health psychology.
- For each key issue, use the concepts, theories and research to explain them as relevant (including ethical and methodological issues).

Child psychology: Does daycare help a child's development?

Some studies show that daycare is good for a child's cognitive and social development as well as their personal development, and some studies suggest that being at home is better. Measures of development have included language development and interpersonal relationships. Daycare refers to when a child is taken care of by someone other than a relative during the day. It includes day nurseries, child minding and playgroups. In the UK over the last 10 years, the government has funded daycare, presumably because they thought either that daycare is better than parenting for some children's development, or that mothers are needed in the workplace. Parents would like to be reassured that daycare is good for their child. The issue is whether that is the case.

Examiner's tip

The issue of daycare was suggested as a contribution from child psychology and a study looking into daycare was also outlined as the example of an observation in this chapter (see page 149).

Explaining the issue using child psychology

- Melhuish et al. (1990) suggested that daycare is not beneficial for the child and that the children looked after at home in their study were more responsive. They found that day nurseries had children who showed the least number of affectionate responses.
- Belsky has studied daycare in more than one study and in general has suggested that good quality daycare for some children is better than staying at home, as social and cognitive development is enhanced. By 'good quality' is meant a high ratio of staff to children and good stimulation of the children. The children who benefit are those who receive less stimulation at home.
- Belsky suggests, however, that too long spent in daycare each week has a negative effect for those under the age of one.
- Studies in Sweden, such as those by Andersson, tend to find that daycare is beneficial for a child's development, possibly because of the nature of Swedish society. In another culture it might be less successful because of different social factors.
- Ethically, it is very important to research into daycare to find out about its effectiveness. Children's development up to the age of five is rapid and includes developing personal, social and cognitive skills they need for school and beyond. This development affects their life chances.
- Research tends to use observation and survey, both of which have weaknesses as research methods. A key problem lies in separating out factors for study, as a child's development is complex and includes so many different variables that it is hard to take them all into account. Age, gender, social background, temperament, position in the family, religion of the family and ethnicity can all affect a child's development.

Health psychology: using drug treatment to treat drug abuse

Methadone is used as a replacement drug for heroin to reduce or stop the withdrawal symptoms. It has to be prescribed by a doctor, and the individual usually attends a clinic once a day to get their treatment. Without the strong withdrawal symptoms, and because the effects of methadone last longer than heroin, the drug helps someone to stop taking heroin altogether. Some addicts stay on methadone long term, which is called maintenance, but the use of methadone can help them to avoid the 'drug scene' and this is another useful part of the treatment.

In general, the treatment is found to be successful, although by no means all heroin users on methadone treatment successfully come off all drugs. This is usually thought to be because of the level of commitment needed from the individual and because of the need to avoid the 'drug scene' to avoid being drawn back into heroin use. Neither is easy. Work has been carried out to find a similar replacement drug for other recreational drugs, such as cocaine. Disulfiram has been used to help treat alcoholism and has been found to be effective for cocaine. Anti-depressants and a drug called selegeline have also been trialled for use with cocaine.

It is sometimes difficult to assess how effective a particular substitute drug is, because of polydrug use, which means an addict uses more than one drug.

Explaining the issue using health psychology

- Blättler et al. (2002) carried out a study looking at those who used both heroin and cocaine and then had methadone treatment. They found that, after 18 months of treatment, cocaine use had decreased from 84% to 48%. From 16% not using cocaine at the start of the methadone treatment, 52% did not use cocaine at the end.
- It was found that the drug treatment for heroin helped those who also abused cocaine – unless prostitution, illegal income and contact with the drug scene were also factors, in which case the treatment was much less likely to have been successful. Economic factors also affect the success of the treatment. This is why often counselling is offered as well as drug therapy. Psychological findings have important practical applications.
- Those on maintenance, who have to keep taking the methadone, may not feel they have successfully stopped being a heroin addict, and there are also ethical issues involved in making sure that the individual knows the whole situation and what is likely to happen.
- Without help to establish different living conditions and different support groups it seems unlikely that drug treatment alone will prove to be successful, especially as it is hard for someone on a maintenance programme to earn money.
- Learning theory can be used to explain why the drug scene needs to be avoided, as associations with the paraphernalia of drug taking can trigger renewal of the addiction.

Key issues: Sport and clinical psychology

What you need to know

- One key issue from sport psychology and one from clinical psychology.
- For each of key issue, the use concepts, theories and research to explain them as relevant (including ethical and methodological issues).

▲ Netball is seen as a female sport, with basketball as the masculine equivalent. In society sport is gendered, which is part of social norms.

Sport psychology: how gender influences sporting choice

Sport psychology raises many issues for society because it focuses on key features of social interactions such as the motivation to act, anxiety about interacting with others and the arousal required for a good sporting performance. And sport itself is a socialising influence.

If someone in the UK is asked to 'gender' a sport they usually can – for example, that netball is for girls and football for boys. Some sports are less 'gendered', such as tennis. The point is that sport is not 'gender-free'. Not only is it thought that sport can be suitable for a specific gender but it is possible that learning about gender comes through sport. Often this is through school but also through out of school activities. Little girls tend to be pointed towards dancing and gymnastics and little boys are more likely to take up a form of martial art training or football. Although the child may asked to do a specific activity, it is more likely perhaps that parents choose the activity for their child, at least when they are very young.

Explaining the issue using sport psychology

- Koivula (1995) looked at the gender appropriateness of participating in sport and used a survey to ask participants to 'gender' sports. The results were fairly consistent, showing that sports are seen in 'gender' terms.
- Koivula (1995) also found that, although the majority of sports were rated neutral with regard to gender, after that there were many more 'masculine' sports than 'feminine' ones. This reflects the general trend in the media, with male sport being shown a lot more often than female sport. There is a stronger link between sport and masculinity, perhaps, than between sport and femininity.
- It is possible that male traits in society that are encouraged, such as power, confidence, strength, stamina and energy, are those more often seen in sport, and so sport is seen as more masculine. This could be through Learning Theory and operant conditioning, where positive reinforcement is given to children who display what is seen as appropriate behaviour. Boys might be more highly praised for sporting behaviour than girls. There can be useful practical applications of such understanding.

- Ethically there is criticism from feminists that stereotyping of women leads to less participation by females in certain sports. Women sportspeople are also in general less well known than male ones because of lack of media coverage – again reflecting socialisation norms.
- Studies that look at sport and gender tend to use self-report data via questionnaires. Such data can lack reliability, which could be a problem with the studies.

Clinical psychology: how mental illness is portrayed in the media

Clinical psychology focuses on mental health and mental illness, both of which have great relevance to society. Media coverage of news items is often sensationalised to entice the reader into the story and coverage of mental health issues is no different. When Frank Bruno was admitted into a psychiatric hospital, *The Sun* started their headline 'Bonkers Bruno...' but misread their readership and soon changed it to 'Sad Bruno...'. The media portrayal of a murder committed by someone with mental health problems also leads the public to associate the two, even though this is true of only 5% of murders.

Mind (1996) carried out a survey looking at how people think the media portrays mental illness and found that 60% of those asked who had a mental illness felt that mental illness was portrayed unfairly. Many said it had affected them directly, and how others treated them. Someone with paranoid schizophrenia may go 'mad' with an 'axe', which is indeed frightening, but the media can counter the story a little by explaining about paranoid schizophrenia. In 1997, the Health Education Authority found that more than half the references to mental health in the media were linked with violence and criminality. A survey also found that 40% of the British public linked mental health to violence.

Explaining the issue using clinical psychology

- There are different types of schizophrenia and not everyone with schizophrenia has the paranoid form. The word 'schizophrenia' therefore covers a great many different symptoms and situations, and should be portrayed as such.
- For many, schizophrenia is controlled by medication most of the time. There may be times when the individual needs more help and support, but someone with schizophrenia is far from unable to function all the time. Practical applications of psychological research have importance for individuals.
- Depression is a mental health disorder that in the UK at least is common rather than rare, and mental health disorders are likely to affect many members of society at some time or another during their lives. It is thought that around one in four people will have some form of mental health problem at some point. Such evidence itself goes against the idea that mental illness is always linked with violence.
- Bandura has shown that people imitate and learn from media images, so if mental illness is shown as being associated with violence and crime, then those with mental health problems are likely to be treated as violent and criminal. This is discrimination and comes from stereotyping and prejudice.
- Ethically, society has a duty not to label one sector of society in such a way that they are likely to be mistreated or misjudged.

Taking it further

Look up the work of Mind and investigate how they view the role of the media in portraying mental health issues.

Debates in psychology: ethnocentrism

What you need to know

- Describe and evaluate ethnocentrism in psychological research, including the potential effects of cultural bias and in the interpretation and application of cross-cultural studies.

Introduction to the debates

For this part of your course you have to look at four debates including ethnocentrism, psychology and science, issues around social control and nature-nurture. These debates are not separate ones – for example, one reason why ethnocentrism is called a bias is that it is not scientific, and cross-cultural studies are used very often in evidence for or against a nature-nurture argument. The four debates are largely presented separately here but the idea of ethnocentrism is used both when looking at different cultures in research and also when considering psychology and science.

Ethnocentrism

When someone is said to be ethnocentric they are said to be focusing on their own culture and seeing their own cultural ways as the right ways. It therefore tends to be a criticism, just as saying someone is prejudiced or biased. Certainly it is a type of bias, because if research is interpreted from the view of one culture it might not be appropriate for a different culture.

Cultural relativity

You will have come across the idea of cultural relativity when studying clinical psychology because in the field of mental health it is often said that mental illness must be relative to the culture being discussed. Hear voices in the UK or the USA and, like Rosenhan's pseudo-patients, you are likely to end up at least temporarily in a mental institution. Hear voices in a different culture and you may be hailed as having spiritual powers. **Cultural relativism** means being sure that findings from research are understood in the culture from which they came, including those norms and beliefs.

The idea of ethnocentrism and the idea of cultural relativism both rest on the claims of those such as Kant, who showed that there cannot be knowledge separate from the cultural beliefs and norms of the researcher. For example, language was studied, and it was found that if a culture had no word for a particular colour – such as green – they did not see 'green'.

Cross-cultural studies

Cross-cultural studies were covered in child psychology. However, if you did not study that area of psychology it is important to know something about how cross-cultural studies must be carefully interpreted because of our tendency to be ethnocentric and the need to acknowledge cultural relativity.

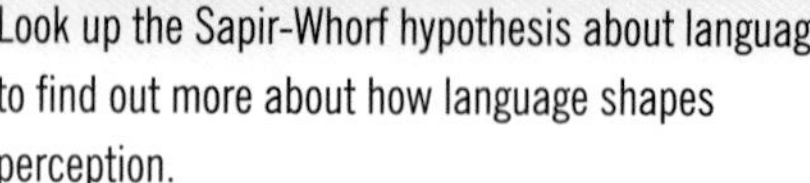

Look up the Sapir-Whorf hypothesis about language to find out more about how language shapes perception.

AS check

When you studied Milgram in the Social Approach, you will have looked at one study of obedience that was done in a country other than the USA. When you compared Milgram's findings with the findings of the other study, you were making cross cultural comparisons.

Example of a cross-cultural study: True et al. in Mali, West Africa

True et al. (2001) studied attachment interactions between mothers and infants in the Dogon people of Mali in West Africa. They used the **strange situation test**, which involves the mother and infant interacting and then various stages of leaving the child with a stranger. The main focus is the subsequent reunion of the mother and child. The child's behaviour is observed and categorised into one of three or four types of attachment bond. These include securely attached, anxious avoidant, anxious resistant and disorganised (this last one being added later). The strange situation was developed in the USA by Mary Ainsworth and has been used across different cultures to compare attachment types (see page 36).

True et al. wanted to look at how infant attachment security is linked to the quality of mother–child communication and also whether mothers of secure infants respond more sensitively than mothers of insecure infants. In addition, they looked to see if the disorganised attachment type is linked with frightening or frightened behaviours. They studied 27 mothers and infants and found that 67% of the pairs showed a secure attachment, none were avoidant, 8% were resistant and 25% disorganised. Ainsworth, who developed the strange situation technique, also found over 60% secure attachments (see page 34) so, to an extent, True et al.'s cross-cultural study confirms that the strange situation test is appropriate across different cultures.

The security of the attachment in the Dogon people was related to the quality of the mother-infant communication and there was also some correlation between security of attachments and maternal sensitivity. Disorganised infants did have mothers who were either frightened or in some way frightening. There are many similarities here with findings in the US, although also some differences, which may be because of Dogon child-rearing practices. This study suggests that the tools for studying attachment types can work across the different cultures but that cultural norms and beliefs are important when interpreting the findings. Cultural relativity is an issue here. Without taking into account the Drogon's own cultural practices, there could be bias in interpretation of the results.

▲ Psychological studies are carried out in particular cultural settings and findings must be interpreted with those special settings in mind. This is to avoid ethnocentric bias.

Evaluation

True and her colleagues tried to make the strange situation test culturally appropriate. For example, they used a Dogon woman as the stranger and asked for help from a Malian researcher to interpret the reunion behaviours. However, the researchers say that they would try harder to incorporate the cultures beliefs into the categories if they did the study again. For example, many babies die before the age of five years old. If a mother had recently had a baby die, that may account for different type of mothering and a disorganised attachment type. These issues are important and must be noted to avoid ethnocentric bias in assuming that Dogon mothers are in some way more frightened or frightening that mothers in the 'West' – which is why such conclusions are not drawn from the findings and it is emphasised that findings must be interpreted in the light of cultural relativism.

Examzone

1. Outline what is meant by cultural bias. (2 marks)
2. Describe two examples of the application of cross-cultural studies in psychology. (8 marks)
3. Explain the potential effect of cultural bias in interpretation of cross-cultural studies. (6 marks)

Debates in psychology: science

What you need to know

- Describe the debate over what science is, including how far psychology fits the definition.
- Evaluate whether psychology should be called a science, including where ethnocentrism and cultural relativity fit.

Prejudice	Operant conditioning
Obedience	Social Learning Theory
Memory	Eyewitness testimony
Forgetting	Attachments
Oedipus complex	Drug misuse
Gender	Motivation
Genes	Anxiety
Hormones	Schizophrenia
Neurons	Depression
Classical conditioning	

Psychology and scientific subject matter

There are two ways of asking whether psychology is a science – by considering either the subject matter or the processes involved, and how scientific either is.

The subject matter of science is something people would say they know about. Look at the list on the left, for example. If someone were asked to select the terms they think relate to science, they would probably tick 'genes', 'hormones' and 'neurons', and possibly 'drug misuse', 'schizophrenia', 'depression' and 'anxiety'. These are all terms from psychology, so as far as subject matter is concerned, at least some of psychology is science – the Biological Approach, healthy psychology and clinical psychology being the most scientific areas.

Psychology and 'doing science'

Is psychology done in a scientific way? Is this important? Which parts of psychology are more 'scientifically' done than others? Is there value in non-scientific research? These are the questions considered in this section.

There are official terms involved when discussing 'doing science'. You will have come across at least some of these, so here is a summary:

Term	Explanation	Example
Hypothesis writing	Drawing an idea from something and making a statement (hypothesis) about what is then expected from it.	Noticing lots of white swans. Hypothesis = All swans are white.
Empirical testing	Testing the idea against reality and showing it to others.	Setting out to look at lots of swans and check if they are white.
Falsification	Trying to prove a hypothesis is false.	No matter how many swans you see, you can't prove they are all white, only that they aren't – if you see a black one.
Reductionism	To make something measurable against reality (to do empirical testing), complex issues may have to be reduced to very small parts.	The actions of a drug are tested on a focused area of the brain only.
Controlling to avoid bias	To make sure that only what is being measured can cause what is being looked at, there must be no bias in either setting up the study or interpreting the results.	Biases include experimenter effects, situational and participant variables and wider issues such as ethnocentrism.

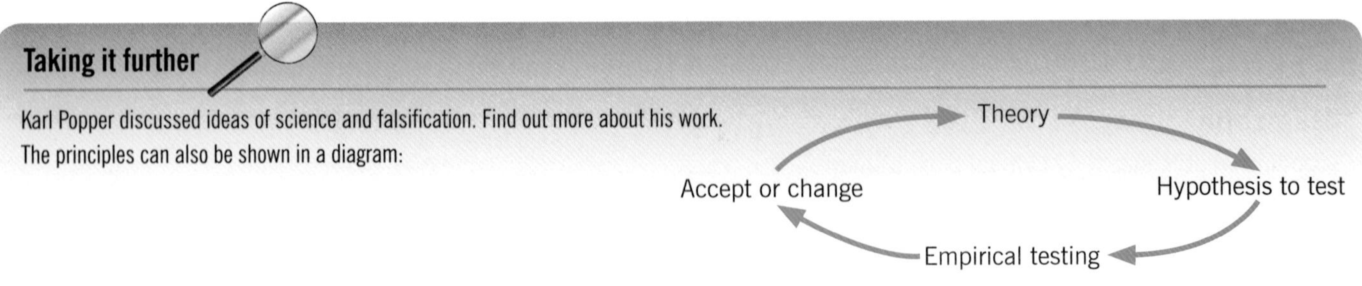

Reasons for not 'doing science'

There are arguments against 'doing science' when undertaking research:

- Holism means that the person or complex event is studied as a whole, the idea being that the whole is more than the sum of the parts. For example, our brains may not just be the sum total of different neurotransmitter functioning and different brain organisation because the relationship between all the parts is likely to affect our behaviour as well.
- Humanistic psychologists such as Maslow and Rogers turned to a new approach they called 'humanism' because they did not want to have to rely on theory and testing. They just wanted to consider individuals with their individual needs, such as the need to self-actualise.
- Scientific controls and careful measuring of data tend to give replicability and, therefore, reliable data. However, you can do a study many times and get the same results without them having any validity. For example, a questionnaire can find over and over again that as self-confidence rises anxiety falls (e.g. Craft et al., 2003) but that does not mean we know any more about what self-confidence is or whether it has any link with anxiety.
- Qualitative data cannot easily be gathered scientifically because it involves stories, attitudes and opinions – all of which are about people who are changeable, unsure and can be swayed by others.

Social constructionism

The idea of social constructionism is that so much of what is studied in social science is a construct. Think of a construct as being the opposite from a universal. If something is generally accepted as true, such as that water boils at 100°C, it is true everywhere. However, according to social constructionism, very little of what is known is a universal. Most of what we study are constructs. Gender, for example, can be seen as a construct because gender behaviour is different between cultures. Obedience has been found in different cultures to different degrees (according to Milgram and other studies) so is perhaps a universal, as Milgram suggested in his Agency Theory. Social constructionism is anti-science and suggests we should not look for universals because they only tell us very basic facts about people and interactions. Instead we should study constructs, which will identify bias such as ethnocentrism, and will tell us more about 'real life' (valid) behaviour within a specific social and cultural setting.

Taking it further

Investigate the work of the Murphys, anthropologists who studied the Mundurucu tribe, who have different parenting and family structures from the West. Consider why a scientific study of them would not have worked while an anthropological one did.

Examzone

1 Describe what is meant by scientific method. (4 marks)
2 Give one example each for when psychology uses a scientific approach and when it does not. (4 marks)
3 How can ethnocentric bias be useful in finding data? (3 marks)

Debates in psychology: science and the approaches

What you need to know

- For the five AS approaches, consider how scientific they are.
- Use this evidence to decide whether psychology is a science or not.
- Continue to evaluate whether psychology should be called a science.

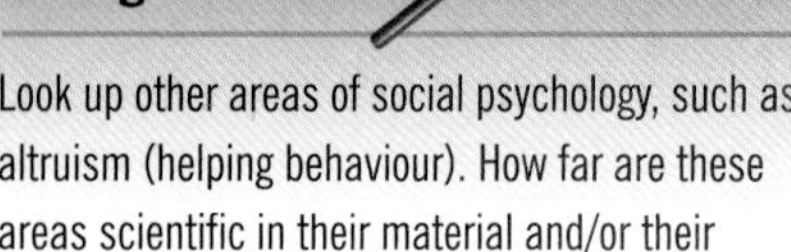

Taking it further

Look up other areas of social psychology, such as altruism (helping behaviour). How far are these areas scientific in their material and/or their methodology?

The Social Approach and science

With regard to the subject matter, social psychology tends to be seen as non-scientific. However, there are elements of science, such as in suggesting that societies evolved to have agents and followers (Agency Theory). Evolution theory is part of science.

With regard to methodology, however, there is a lot about social psychology that is scientific. Milgram used experimental methods as did Hofling et al. (1966). Tajfel et al. used laboratory experiments, and Sherif used field experiments. In other areas of social psychology as well, such as when looking at helping behaviour, field experiments are a popular research method (e.g. Piliavin). Even when surveys are carried out (e.g. Adorno), questions are piloted and care is taken to avoid ambiguity and to gather at least some quantitative data. There are hypotheses and there is empirical testing.

The Cognitive Approach and science

With regard to the subject matter, cognitive psychology does contain biological principles. Memory and forgetting, for example, are about information processing and, when considered in more depth, can involve scanning the brain and considering neuroscience.

With regard to methodology too, cognitive psychology follows scientific research methods, including laboratory experiments, scanning and brain imaging. Craik and Tulving carried out a laboratory experiment with careful controls and Godden and Baddeley carried out a well-controlled field experiment. There are hypotheses, there is empirical testing, and statistical testing with regard to results.

The Psychodynamic Approach and science

With regard to subject matter, the Psychodynamic Approach studies the unconscious and its power over conscious thoughts. As the unconscious is not empirically measurable, the subject matter of the Psychodynamic Approach is not scientific – though Freud does talk about energy and instincts, which are biological aspects of the person.

With regard to methodology, the Psychodynamic Approach is the least scientific because it focuses on case studies and unique research methods such as dream analysis and free association. Qualitative data is gathered, not quantitative data, and far from having controls over their behaviour, participants are required to generate data freely and without control. There are no hypotheses to test using empirical data, more that data drive the analysis.

Freud hoped to build a scientific theory so he made sure he could give examples and evidence for all his claims. For example, in the Little Hans study he only took notice of what Hans's father said that came directly from Hans, and he checked back with Hans where possible to see if his analysis was appropriate. However, the Oedipus complex, unconscious, ego and id are not measurable or testable, so the Psychodynamic Approach is seen as non-scientific. This does not in itself make its conclusions wrong, however.

The Biological Approach and science

The subject matter in the Biological Approach is clearly scientific, as it includes things like genes, hormones, brain lateralisation and synaptic functioning. Methodology is also scientific, including laboratory experiments, PET scans, MRI scanning and using EEG measurements. Hypotheses are rigorously set up, with clearly operationalised variables, and empirical testing takes place to confirm or amend them.

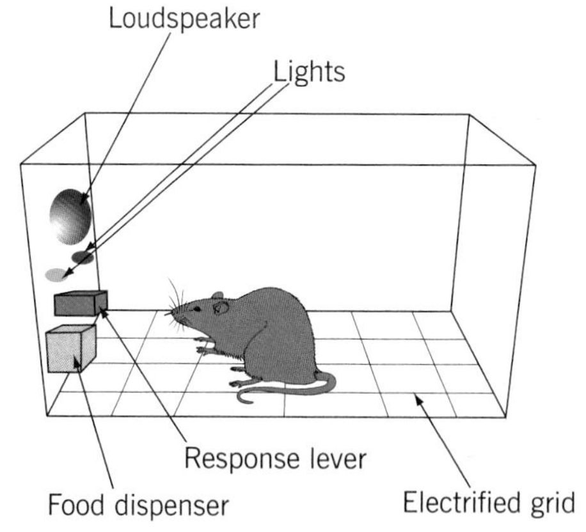

▲ The Learning Approach involves the scientific study of behaviour, at first often involving using rats in laboratory experiments.

The Learning Approach and science

The subject matter of the Learning Approach is behaviour, and only measurable and observable behaviour is considered in a bid to make the approach scientific. Particularly at first, the approach focused on stimulus and response – both of which could be observed and tested. By reducing behaviour to separate parts for study – such as a rat pressing a lever to get a reward of food – the subject matter was claimed to be scientific.

With regard to methodology, scientific research methods such as laboratory experiments and using animals were adopted from the start, with the aim of making the study of behaviour scientific. It was social learning theory that started to move away from such a strong scientific background, although Bandura began with carefully planned experiments. He later considered motivation and memory, which are aspects of thinking. When he moved to look at issues such as self-efficacy, which involves considering how far our feelings about being able to succeed affect our performance, the research methods and subject matter began to be less scientific.

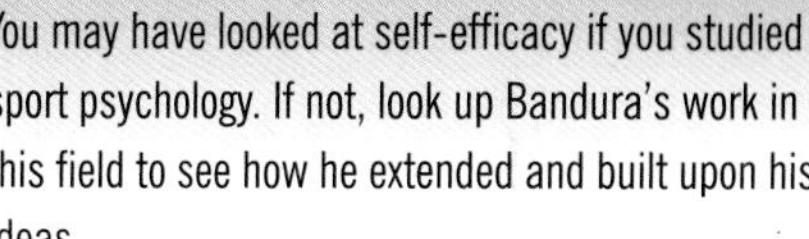

Taking it further

You may have looked at self-efficacy if you studied sport psychology. If not, look up Bandura's work in this field to see how he extended and built upon his ideas.

Is psychology a science?

With regard to subject matter in general, social and psychodynamic psychology are thought to be the least scientific but the Cognitive, Biological and Learning Approaches are thought to be scientific – at least to some extent – in that they look at brain and behaviour.

With regard to research methods, except for psychodynamic psychology, scientific methods are used as far as possible. Hypotheses are generated, empirical testing takes place and statistical testing is used to see how far any findings might be due to chance.

The five approaches are also compared in terms of how scientific their content and methods in the context of how much emphasis they place on nature and nurture (see pages 174-175).

Examzone

1 With reference to one approach in psychology, describe two ways in which it is scientific. (4 marks)

2 Explain why you think psychology is not scientific. (6 marks)

Debates in psychology: psychology and science; drug therapy as social control

What you need to know

- Compare how scientific the five AS approaches are.
- Continue to evaluate whether psychology should be called a science.
- Examples of using psychological knowledge as a means of social control, including the use of drug therapy.
- Assess ethical and practical implications of such control.

Psychology and science
Reductionism
Experiments
Biology and brain
Hypothesis testing against reality
Measurable data
Falsification and statistical testing
Experiments using animals
Paradigm
Observable facts
Psychology and non-science
Holism
Case studies
Humanism and self-actualisation
Focusing on individuals
Unconscious/personality
Human stories and detail
Ethology to study animals naturally
Pre-paradigm
Socially constructed discourses

Paradigms are ways of understanding the world and representing large theoretical frameworks within which we try to find out more. For example, we currently believe that the earth has a series of plates that move (plate tectonics), but it took some time after the idea was put forward before it was accepted. Plate tectonics had to replace a different paradigm.

Psychology and science

A summary table can help to show the scientific nature of psychology (see left).

Falsifiability

This is the idea of testing data using inferential statistics to see how far results can be said to be due to chance and yet still be accepted. The point is to set up the idea, called the null hypothesis, that there is no difference as predicted by the original hypothesis and then see if there is enough of a difference to say that the null hypothesis is not true. This is attempting to deal with the idea of falsifiability. In psychology, it is rare that people always conform to a hypothesis. Inferential testing can help to show how far any results might be due to chance.

Paradigms

It has been argued that psychology is pre-science because there is no single paradigm in which psychologists are working. Behaviourism can be called a paradigm, as can the Psychodynamic Approach and the Biological Approach. Or it could be claimed that psychology works within a science paradigm accepting, for example, Darwin's ideas about evolution, and the general idea of scientific methodology being the way to discover truths about the world. The question itself being considered here – whether psychology is a science – strongly suggests that psychology's paradigm is 'science'.

Discourses

A different way of looking at people and their behaviour is considering discourses. Discourses are socially constructed views of the world. As long as you are having a discussion with someone sharing the same discourse, you will probably have good understanding. If, however, you are not sharing views of the world or meanings of terms and words, there is likely to be poor understanding. For example, I might say that I talk too much, and you could reasonably conclude that I am self-aware and would like to talk less. However, I might mean that I tell people *too much about myself*. To understand people it is necessary to understand their meanings, and this is often not what is done in a laboratory situation.

Drug therapy as social control

All societies have rules, norms and customs, which people learn through socialisation. In general, people are expected to conform to such rules without any 'social control' (they have internal social control) but there are occasions when social control – a more formal way of making someone adhere to society's rules – is thought to be needed. Psychology has been used to inform methods of social control.

Drugs can help to control behaviour and are used by those that are 'normal' to make those more 'abnormal' be more like them. Rosenhan's study about being sane in insane places (see page 124) showed how his pseudo-patients were prescribed drugs to control their 'schizophrenia' (not that they took the drugs and in fact the pseudo-patients reported that other patients appeared not to be taking the medication either). Usually, those with schizophrenia are prescribed and presumably take such drugs – an example of psychological knowledge being used as social control.

Drug therapy is also used as social control when prescribed for heroin addiction. Methadone is a substitute for heroin and does not give the strong withdrawal symptoms so is more likely to be taken by an addict.

Taking it further

Judith Butler discusses the importance of discourse – a term that came from Foucault. Research further in this area.

Ethical issues and the influence of the practitioner

The main ethical issue is about who has the power to make a decision to control someone else's behaviour. The individual might be thought of as not able to make decisions for themselves. Their family might feel they can make the decisions – but should they? Do they have knowledge to make such decisions? Are their motives unselfish enough?

It is often thought that professionals are in a better position to make such decisions. Often there is multi-agency working, which means a group of professionals – GP, social worker, health visitor, perhaps someone from a voluntary agency, carers and others – have case conferences to make decisions. Such conferences can help to ensure ethical practice, however the question of power over an individual still remains.

There are special guidelines for dealing ethically with the mentally ill, not only when researching but also in mental institutions. Issues tend to focus on confidentiality and consent.

Examiner's tip

Note that the influence of the practitioner is one of the implications of social control that you need to know about, as well as assessing ethical and practical implications of such control.

Taking it further

Look up ethical rules for dealing with mentally-ill patients, both as participants in research and as patients needing treatment.

Practical issues

One problem with drug therapy is checking whether a person is taking the drugs that are prescribed. Schizophrenia, for example, can often be controlled using drug therapy but, once controlled, there is a tendency for the patient not to continue with the drug therapy so there is often a relapse. This relapse often means re-hospitalisation and is distressing for the patient. Newer anti-schizophrenic drugs have been developed that have fewer side effects and also are more likely to avoid the psychotic episodes that tend to lead to a relapse.

Drug therapy for drug addiction is widely thought to be effective but only in conjunction with other forms of treatment. No single treatment seems to be appropriate for everyone. Any treatment has to focus on the individual's lifestyle and problems not 'just' on their drug addiction. As the individual's needs change, their treatment plan needs to be reviewed too. Drug therapy is more effective alongside counselling, other behavioural therapies and care in the community.

▲ From an ethical and practical viewpoint it is likely to be better if a group of professionals is involved in a case conference about the drug therapy and care of an individual.

Examzone

1 Discuss the idea that psychology should be called a science. (12 marks)
2 Describe the use of drug therapy as a means of social control. (4 marks)
3 Assess both ethical and practical considerations of using drug therapy as a treatment. (8 marks)

Debates in psychology: token economy and classical conditioning as social control

What you need to know

- Examples of using psychological knowledge as a means of social control, including token economy and classical conditioning.
- Assess the ethical and practical implications of such controls.

Examiner's tip

In your course, token economy has been mentioned as part of criminological (page 18), health psychology (page 54) and clinical psychology (page 118), which is an indication of the range of its usefulness.

AS check

Token economy was also one of the suggested treatments or therapies when looking at Social Learning Theory (AS page 139).

Examiner's tip

Note that for this section you have to know about drug therapy, token economy, classical conditioning and the influence of the practitioner but that you can also use other examples of social control that you know about. For example, in clinical psychology you had to know at least one treatment or therapy from each of the five AS approaches – and all such treatments or therapies are means of social control.

Examiner's tip

Use the terms from operant conditioning to explain the token economy idea – including positive reinforcement and shaping.

An example of systematic desensitisation

Muscle control (UCS)	→	Relaxation (UCR)
Flying (NS/CS) + Muscle control (UCS)	→	Relaxation (UCR)
Flying (CS)	→	Relaxation (CR)

Token economy as social control

Token economy is used in schools, prisons and other institutions to help control behaviour. Required behaviour is identified and is then broken down into steps that are achievable and observable. When the required behaviour is observed, it is rewarded using a system of tokens, which can, at an agreed time, be exchanged for something the individual desires. The principles are: rewarding required behaviour; ignoring undesired behaviour; offering positive reinforcement; using shaping.

Ethical issues and the influence of the practitioner

As with drug therapies, one problem is the question of who has the power to control someone else's behaviour. To help mitigate this, individual staff should not stand out as having power in the programme – the system of rewards must be very clear, predictable and reliable for the programme to work. It must also be very clear what the required behaviour is, why it is desired, and by whom.

Practical issues

- Token economy can be difficult to use outside the institution where it is set up. The person's behaviour might slip back into what is undesired once outside the institution.
- A very careful system has to be set up, where required behaviour is always reinforced, at least at first. This is labour-intensive as members of staff have to be very much involved in the programme. As shifts change, for example, behaviour can be missed.
- It is sometimes difficult to sort out what the tokens should 'buy' for the individual. The rewards must be real for that individual and tailored to their needs or the programme will not work.

Classical conditioning as social control

Systematic desensitisation and aversion therapy are both treatments or therapies that use classical conditioning principles.

Systematic desensitisation (SD)

SD works for anxieties such as specific phobias where there is a particular stimulus that gives problems. The response of fear can be replaced with a response of relaxation, and this is the aim of the treatment. For example a fear of spiders can be replaced with a relaxation response on seeing a spider.

Ethical issues and the influence of the practitioner

SD is ethically sound because the client is in charge of the process, lists the hierarchy, gets themselves into relaxation mode, and can say if their anxiety gets too much to manage. Although to an extent the therapist still has the power to make suggestions and push the client into going further up the hierarchy, this power is not as strong as in other treatments and therapies, such as when a psychiatrist prescribes drugs to someone statemented as mentally ill.

Practical issues

- SD is good for certain anxious situations such as where there is a clear stimulus causing the anxiety so that it can be worked on.
- The treatment works best with a client who can learn to relax sufficiently and can maintain relaxation when required to.
- The client needs to be able to transfer their learning when in a different situation.

Aversion therapy as social control

Aversion therapy is used in cases such as alcoholism. A person who drinks alcohol and wants to stop takes a drug that will make them feel sick (an emetic). If that drug is paired with alcohol, then alcohol will make them feel sick and that should be enough to stop them drinking (at least for a while).

An example of aversion therapy

Emetic drug (UCS)	→	Feeling of sickness (UCR)
Alcohol (NS/CS) + Emetic drug (UCS)	→	Feeling of sickness (UCR)
Alcohol (CS)	→	Feeling of sickness (CR)

Ethical issues and the influence of the practitioner

This can be quite a strong form of social control, as someone can be made to undergo it. For example, some time ago homosexuals were made to undergo various forms of 'treatment' for what was then seen as a disorder. Treatments based on classical conditioning principles would today only be considered appropriate if the individual is the one asking for the treatment and is in control of it.

Practical issues

In practice, it is not easy to carry out a treatment using classical conditioning principles as the association has to be made very clear. For example, in the treatment for alcoholism it would be important for the person to drink water and soft drinks without the drug, or they may become conditioned not to drink at all. One method now used is to incorporate cognitive principles, so the client would be given a drug they *think* will make them feel sick if they drink alcohol and will only discover that it does not have that effect if they try alcohol with it. They are unlikely to do that, so the treatment can be just as effective – at least until they do try a drink and discover no harmful effects and then the association, which was a mental one, would not work any more.

Ethical issues in therapy and treatment involve:
- Setting boundaries
- Documentation and forms
- Fees and gifts
- Communication
- The client/practitioner relationships

Examzone

1 What are two practical problems with a token economy programme? (4 marks)
2 Explain how a token economy programme could be said to be a form of social control. (4 marks)
3 Outline two ways that classical conditioning principles have been used as treatments or therapies. (6 marks)
4 Explain one ethical and one practical problem with regard to using classical conditioning principles as therapy. (4 marks)

Debates in psychology: nature, nurture and explaining human behaviour

What you need to know

- The roles of nature and nurture in explaining human behaviour, drawing on material studied in psychology.
- Evaluation points about whether nature or nurture helps to explain human behavior.

AS check

You will already have looked at the role of nature in explaining human behaviour, starting when you looked at the Biological Approach.

AS check

The Psychodynamic Approach looks at nature when claiming that we all have a large unconscious which holds wishes and desires of which we are unaware but which guide our behaviour. So it is not just the Biological Approach which suggests that nature underpins human behaviour and development.

▲ Studies suggest that arousal up to a certain level means better sporting performance but that too much arousal and anxiety leads to a worse performance, so there is an optimal level of arousal. Arousal is about someone's biology – their nature.

The role of nature

'Nature' refers to what we are born with, including any processes that develop as we mature, and any effects on ourselves as an organism before birth. It is about our biology. As human beings we are genetically programmed to look in certain ways, to behave in certain ways, some say to die in certain ways. Our genes dictate release of hormones, for example, and hormones dictate our gender. Alongside that, neurotransmitter functioning sends messages around the brain and between neurons. All this is to do with our nature. Our brains function in certain ways, such as the hippocampus laying down new memories and the amygdala focusing on aggression.

Summary of the influence of nature

This table summarises the points covered throughout the course.

Approach/application	Nature aspect of the material
Biological Approach	Genes Hormones Brain lateralisation Brain functioning
Psychodynamic Approach	The unconscious which guides us The id, ego and superego Psychosexual stages of development
Criminological psychology	Personality and criminal behaviour
Child psychology	Evolutionary aspects of attachment
Health psychology	Processes involved in drug addiction
Sport psychology	Arousal, anxiety and the inverted U
Clinical psychology	Biological explanations of mental health issues Biological treatments for mental health issues (e.g. drug therapy)

The role of nurture

'Nurture' refers to the effect of environment on us as we develop and grow. The biological environment that affects us before birth and after conception is still part of nature, but all other environmental influences are nurture. There will be nurture influences before birth if we take into account what we hear from outside the womb, for example. In practice, separating nature from nurture is probably neither possible nor useful, as will be discussed later.

Social psychology focuses on nurture, for example when we are influenced by members of groups to which we belong so that we become prejudiced towards others. Cognitive psychology focuses on nurture when considering the importance of cues in the environment for retrieving memories or when showing how the wording of a question can affect what we think we remember about an event. The Psychodynamic Approach considers nurture in focusing on how desires for the mother and guilt towards the father can affect how a son behaves towards his parents at the time of the Oedipus complex and how this leads to male behaviour for the boy. The Biological Approach focuses mainly on nature, but it is the Learning Approach that focuses completely on nurture.

The Learning Approach holds that some learning takes place through classical conditioning, where a stimulus is associated with a response and causes that response to happen. The stimulus is in the environment and linked to the environment, though the response is involuntary and biological.

Operant conditioning is another way in which the Learning Approach explains learning. This time both the response and the stimulus are in the environment. Operant conditioning suggests that any behaviour that is rewarded will be repeated to get the reward.

The final learning theory is Social Learning Theory – which suggests that learning comes from modelling and imitation. Behaviour that someone sees (in the environment) is copied, particularly if it was rewarded. This is to do with nurture and learning – and socialisation into social norms and customs.

AS check

Think of blinking the eye to a puff of air. If the puff of air is associated with a certain noise, soon the noise will cause the eye blink. The eye blink is natural and the noise (and puff of air) is in the environment (so nurture).

Summary of the influence of nurture
This table summarises the points covered throughout the course.

Approach/application	Nurture aspect of the material
Social Approach	Learning social norms and rules through socialisation. Developing hostility through group membership.
Cognitive Approach	Using aspects of the environment as cues for recall. Allowing aspects of a situation such as words used when being questioned to affect recall.
Psychodynamic Approach	Focusing on interactions between mother, father and child in the phallic stage to learn about gender behaviour.
Learning Approach	Classical and operant conditioning focus on learning through environmental influences. Social Learning Theory involves observing and copying role models – who act in the environment.
Criminological psychology	Social learning theory and/or self-fulfilling prophecy can explain anti social behaviour.
Child psychology	Privation and deprivation can affect a child's development and later adult functioning. Daycare can affect a child's progress.
Health psychology	Learning theories can help to explain and treat substance misuse.
Sport psychology	Socialisation can affect both choice of sport and sporting performance.
Clinical psychology	Mental disorders can both be explained and treated using learning theory principles, which suggests a strong role for the environment.

The AS approaches and nature-nurture

Some approaches involve both nature and nurture in their explanations:

- The Social Approach looks at interactions between people and individuals and so is likely to focus more on nurture and the effects of the environment. It does, however, consider some in-built tendencies such as the tendency to form into groups and the tendency to act as an agent for a society.

Examiner's tip

When making a point about some feature being nature, nurture or both, end your point by linking to the debate to make your point really clear.

- The Cognitive Approach looks at information processing and how the brain takes in information, processes it and produces an output. The processing is likely to be a feature of our nature and what is processed is likely to come from our environment, so is from nurture. The Cognitive Approach, therefore, also takes both nature and nurture into account.
- The Psychodynamic Approach looks at the role of the unconscious and the importance of the first five years in a child's development. These two features are seen as being innate and coming from a human's nature. However, the experiences that lead to fixation, for example, or to what is stored in the unconscious, are from nurture. This approach also takes both nature and nurture into account when explaining human behaviour.
- The Biological Approach is the one most focused on nature to explain human behaviour. Genes, hormones, brain lateralisation, neuronal functioning, brain structure and other features of being human all help to explain human behaviour. However, the environment is often needed to trigger certain behaviours within the organism and there is an element of interaction between the two that is important for good understanding. The Biological Approach asks you to look at twin studies as well as scanning, so involves methodology that can uncover nature or nurture as guiding human behaviour.
- The Learning Approach is the one deliberately focused on nurture because of the desire to experiment using observable features of human behaviour. It does acknowledge biology, such as that we have involuntary behaviours such as fear, but it focuses much on learning and nurture.

The A2 applications and nature-nurture

- Criminological psychology is interested in nature in so far as there are biological explanations for anti-social behaviour and crime. It is also interested in examining what background or environment is more likely to lead to anti-social behaviour or crime. There are elements of both nature and nurture in the explanations of criminological psychology.
- Child psychology is interested more in what happens to a child after birth, focusing on their attachment experiences and the type of mothering they experience. The focus is firmly on the nurture of the child. However, there is also interest in a child's innate temperament and on any possible developmental disorders that will affect them, such as ADHD or autism.
- Health psychology in this course focuses on substance misuse – though there are many other areas that health psychology involves. Substance misuse has a strong biological element as it involves how drugs work and features of addiction. However, there are nurture elements to becoming a drug addict, including the role of modelling drug taking and the influence of friends and other socialising influences.
- Sport psychology also involves both nature and nurture. Sport involves biological aspects – not only physical ones but mental ones as well, such as motivation and anxiety. However, there is also a nurture influence, with certain sports being thought of as 'male', for example, and others as 'female'. There is also the discussion about whether someone is socialised into sport or whether sport socialises children. Probably there is an element of both.
- Clinical psychology focuses on mental health issues. These are shown to have biological explanations such as the dopamine hypothesis for schizophrenia. They are also shown to have biological treatments, such as drug therapy or electroconvulsive therapy (ECT). However, there are nurture explanations for mental health issues too, for example stress in the environment and lack of social support. These can worsen mental health problems. Clinical psychology, as with all the other applications, has elements of both nature and nurture in its explanations for human behaviour.

Evaluation of the role of nature or nurture when explaining human behaviour

- The main evaluation point would be that most explanations involve an element of both nature and nurture when explaining any aspect of human behaviour as has been suggested.
- If behaviour is reduced to parts (reductionism) and not looked at as a whole (holism) then it is likely that either nature or nurture could be pinpointed as a cause separately, such as when looking at the role of genes.
- However, this would have taken away the aspect of looking at human behaviour as a whole, which would be a criticism of focusing on either nature or nurture and not both.
- A nomothetic view of learning is to look for general laws about behaviour and it is hard to do that without reducing behaviour to some particular part to draw a universal law from. So when taking a scientific view – and searching for general laws of behaviour – it is possible that either nature or nurture would be the focus. A nomothetic focus tends to mean drawing on quantitative data.
- However, an idiographic view of learning is to focus on individual behaviour that is whole and real for a person, which is likely to mean taking both someone's nature and their nurture experiences into account together. An idiographic focus tends to mean drawing on qualitative data.
- This does not even mean looking at both, but it means that the two cannot be separated from human behaviour enough to be studied separately at all.
- One evaluation point is that the debate about nature-nurture is in a way not a debate at all, as the two simply cannot be separated for study whilst still studying meaningful human behaviour.
- Research methods can help to uncover influences from nature and nurture. One such method is to look at twin studies to see if identical twins who share their nature are more similar than non-identical twins who do not. However, identical twins are also more likely to share their nurture, as they look exactly alike and non-identical twins do not. And no characteristic is 100% the same in identical twins so nature does not seem to have any example of being the sole influence on human behaviour.
- Another research method that can help to uncover nature and nurture influences is cross-cultural research. If differences are found between cultures, such behaviour is likely to be down to nurture because in general it is thought that humans are similar in their nature. If similarities are found between cultures then these are likely to be due to nature, as in general humans are thought to be similar across cultures. The problem is that there are nature differences between people of the same culture just as there are nurture similarities between people of a different culture (such as that gender is often seen as important, and that children are usually brought up in some form of family).

Examzone

1 Drawing on material from your course, explain how both nature and nurture are usually involved in aspects of human behaviour. (6 marks)

*2 With regard to the AS approaches for your course, explain how one approach focuses mainly on nurture and one approach focuses mainly on nature. (6 marks)

3 Evaluate the role of nature and nurture in explaining human behaviour. (6 marks)

Reductionism is when something is reduced to a small part in order to study it, as opposed to **holism**, which is the idea that something is more than the sum of its parts – it includes the relationship between the parts.

Examiner's tip

If you use reductionism as a criticism of experiments, you need to explain why it is a criticism.

Taking it further

Look up the terms holism, nomothetic and idiographic and make sure you can define them. Find out more about the four approaches.

▲ A child inherits genes from their parents and grandparents, and they learn from their parents and grandparents too. Their biological make up and their environmental experiences are inextricably linked – both nature and nurture contribute to behaviour.

Research methods: planning and evaluating studies

What you need to know

- How to plan a study, including the aim, hypothesis, design, procedure, ethics, analysis of results and evaluation.
- Evaluation studies with reference to research methods, including making suggestions for improvements such as controls, changing the methodology, and/or improving the reliability or validity.

Planning a study

You need to be able to plan a study when asked to. For example, you could be given a context/idea and asked to plan a study using a particular research method, such as a survey. Here is an example of a planned study to research whether males or females are better at recognising facial expressions.

Aim: To look at gender differences in interpretation of facial expressions.

Hypothesis: Females are better than males at allocating emotions from a list to a set of eight photographs of faces showing these emotions.

Design: Independent groups, as gender is the independent variable.

Procedure: An opportunity sample of 20 male and 20 female participants were tested separately. They were given a list of eight emotions – happy, sad, tired, worried, questioning, laughing, calm, angry. Each emotion had a letter allocated to it. The participants were then shown eight photographs, numbered, all of females, with eight different facial expressions. They were asked to allocate the eight emotions to the eight faces. The number of correctly-allocated emotions was noted for each participant, with their gender.

Ethics: The participants were given the right to withdraw, told that the study was about judging faces and informed that the findings would be confidential.

Analysis of results: The number of correctly-allocated emotions for each participant was put into two lists based on gender. A Mann Whitney U test was carried out because this is an experiment, the data ordinal (number of correct emotions out of 8) and the design independent groups. A mean average of the two lists was also worked out and the two means compared.

Strengths of the study:

- There were strict controls because the participants all saw the same list of emotions and the same photographs, so the study was replicable and can be tested for reliability.
- Ethics were attended to by giving the right to withdraw, confidentiality and seeking informed consent.

Weaknesses of the study:

- Looking at photographs and allocating an emotion from a list is not perhaps representative of decoding facial expressions in a live situation, so validity can be questioned.
- Some ethical issues and detail were missed, such as who was photographed, which is an ethical consideration, and how the photographs matched the emotions, which is important with regard to validity too.

Evaluating a study

You might be asked to evaluate a study that is given to you and you might also be asked to suggest improvements. An example follows.

Oswald and Rablen (2007) looked at whether social status could affect someone's lifespan. Nobel Prize winners in physics and chemistry between 1901 and 1950 were compared with a control group of scientists who were nominated for the same years but did not win. There were 524 male scientists, of whom 135 won a Nobel Prize. Winners of the Nobel Prize were found to live an average of 77.2 years and the nominated group lived on average 75.8 years – a difference of 1.4 years.

Suggestions for improvements:

- Information could be included about the family status of the participants, because it is possible that those with social support lived longer. It is possible the Nobel Prize winners had more social support.
- It could be that social status improves lifespan for scientists only, because in science social status has more importance than in other research or work areas. Other prize winners should therefore also be considered.
- Another analysis could be carried out using a less wide gap of years so that fewer other changes would be found, such as two World Wars and many other social changes.

Changing choice of method: A laboratory experiment could be carried out to see if participants who had been told they had been very successful on a test, did better on a subsequent test, compared with participants who were told they had not been successful. This would check whether status had improved performance.

Improving validity: Comparing real Nobel Prize winners with others who had actually been nominated meant that there was high validity in the sense that it was real social status that was compared. However, those nominated would have quite high social status as well. Perhaps comparing with another lower social status group would be a more valid measure.

Improving reliability: It would be hard to replicate this study using a completely different group without waiting a number of years and then there would be many other factors that might affect lifespan – differences in norms and cultural attitudes, as well in medical care and health habits. However, a different group of people of higher and lower status over the same years could be used to compare the findings with this study, for example directors of companies compared with middle managers.

Examzone

The General Social Survey carried out in 2004 by the National Opinion Research Centre in Chicago has found that people who score highly on altrustic love are more likely to rate their marriage as very happy. An example of 'altruistic love' is agreeing with the statement, 'I would rather suffer myself than let the one I love suffer'. About 50% of those who did not agree said their marriage was very happy, compared with 67% of those who did agree. The researchers concluded that there is a link between altruistic behaviour and romantic love.

1 Outline two improvements you would suggest with regard to this above study. (6 marks)
2 Explain how you could find out whether the results of the study are reliable. (3 marks)
3 Explain one way in which the study has validity and one way in which validity could be improved. (4 marks)

Evaluating a new issue

What you need to know

- Evaluate previously unseen material concerning an issue.
- Use psychological concepts, theories and/or research from different applications and approaches as appropriate to evaluate previously unseen material.

AS check

See pages 18-19 for Social Identity Theory and pages 24-25 for realistic conflict theory.

Unseen material: Example 1

An internet headline in January 2009 explained that violence had erupted at the Australian Open, with rival fans launching chairs and missiles at one another. It was said that dozens of Serbian and Bosnian fans fought after the match between Novak Djokovic and Amer Delic. The fighting began in a garden outside the main centre court arena.

Explaining the issue

This example links clearly to the social identity theory, which explains that in-group members become hostile to out-group members. This is because members of a group categorise themselves as part of the group and their self-concept is enhanced by group membership. To enhance their self-concept more, they will denigrate the out-group – which brings prejudice. Use what you know about social identity theory (Tajfel) as well as realistic conflict theory (Sherif) if you have covered that. You could also draw on what you know about ethnocentrism (page 164) to show how people centre on their own culture and this gives bias in their views and opinions.

Unseen material: Example 2

In the *London Lite*, 13 January 2009, it was reported that a man accused of robbing a driving instructor was set free by the judge because the female driving instructor was such a good, clear, convincing witness. She identified the man and was certain about her identification. The problem that the judge saw, however, was that because she was such a convincing witness, the man might be found guilty as a result of her credibility rather than based on the evidence.

Explaining the issue

Cognitive psychology explains that memory is not like a tape recorder. According to reconstructive memory theory, people use schemas based on their own experiences and do not remember in exact detail. Just because someone is a very credible witness, due to their certainty about their evidence, does not mean that their memory is exact and precise. This does not, of course, suggest that the driving instructor was wrong, just that the conviction needed to be because of evidence not witness credibility. According to the cue-dependent theory of forgetting, cues are needed at recall to reinstate the cognitive environment the person was in when encoding the memory. The witness may have used cues to identify the robber but they may not have been accurate ones. It was not reported that there was a reconstruction, for example. Time had passed between the original incident and identification and the court case, so original memories could have been lost as their trace decayed. Identification in court is then likely to rely not on the incident itself but on subsequent information.

Note that if you have studied criminological psychology you will be able to add more detail here.

Exam advice

For AS you have learned about injunctions (the wording of the questions such as 'describe', 'evaluate'), assessment objectives (whether you are being asked to show knowledge or ability to comment, for example), and revision techniques. You have learned the types of question asked and probably how they are marked (some point by point and others using levels or banding, which look at quality as well as content). These same issues apply at A2. This section focuses on the structure of the units. It is followed by the answers to some of the questions within the book, with commentary.

Assessment objectives

The A2 question papers test three assessment objectives (AOs).

- AO1 is about showing knowledge and understanding of psychology. You will be asked to outline, describe, name or identify some material such as a theory, study or psychological term. You must express yourself clearly.
- AO2 is about evaluating psychology including giving strengths or weaknesses, comparison points (similarities or differences) and other comments such as giving evidence to back up a theory.
- AO3 is about methodology and doing psychology, including consideration of ethical issues.

Exam overview

Exam paper	Availability	Time	Marks	% of the exam
Unit 3	January and June	90 mins	60	40% of A2
Unit 4	June	120 mins	90	60% of A2

Unit 3 paper structure

- Covers four applications of psychology, of which you will have studied two. The paper is presented application-by-application – criminological, child, health and sport.
- You have to answer the whole question for each of your two applications.
- Each application question involves AO1, AO2 and AO3.
- For each question there will be short-answer questions (e.g. to describe a study) for four or five marks and a piece of extended writing (e.g. to describe and evaluate a theory) for 12 marks.

Unit 4 paper structure

- Covers two sections, clinical psychology and issues and debates.
- The clinical psychology question has both short-answer questions and a piece of extended writing, and involves AO1, AO2 and AO3.
- The issues and debates question also includes both short-answer and extended writing questions, with extended writing questions at the end.
- However, the piece of extended writing is longer than for the applications and there is also likely to be a choice of question for it.
- The issues and debates piece of extended writing is likely to involve 12 marks as with other essays but with another 6 marks available for the structure of the essay, the coverage and the terms used.

Marks and grades

- In all A level papers an E grade starts after getting 40% of the marks for the paper and an A grade starts after 80%.
- Psychology A level, therefore, has 400 UMS marks available because there are 4 units.
- UMS marks are not the same as raw marks. For example, for Units 1 and 3, 60 raw marks are converted into 80 UMS marks in each case, Unit 2 has 80 raw marks converted into 120 UMS marks and Unit 4 has 90 marks converted into 120 UMS marks.
- The final AS level grade involves adding the UMS marks for Unit 1 and Unit 2 together so getting a total out of 200 UMS marks.
- The final A level grade involves adding the UMS marks for all four units to get a total out of 400 UMS marks.
- For the overall A level, an E grade is awarded for 160 or more UMS marks and an A grade for 320 UMS or more marks. The other grades are given by mathematical calculation between the E and A grades.

A*

An A* is awarded for the overall A level if:

- You have 80% or more of the 400 total UMS marks.
- And you have 90% or more of the 200 A2 UMS marks.

Examzone answers

Criminological psychology (page 26)

1. *Define the following terms:*
   i Recidivism
   ii Anti-social behaviour
   iii Crime *(3 marks)*

i Recidivism is when someone commits a crime again.
ii Anti-social behaviour is a criminal offence. It is when someone upsets another person or causes harm.
iii Crime is a legal term used to describe a behaviour that leads to imprisonment.

Commentary
The definition of recidivism is technically correct and should get 1 mark. It could have also referred to a criminal who has been convicted of a crime, released and then is re-convicted of a crime.

Anti-social behaviour is only a criminal offence if it breaks a law or causes distress to members of the public. An example, such as excessive noise or littering, would have added detail to the definition.

The definition of crime is not accurate. It may lead to imprisonment, but not necessarily. It could just lead to a financial penalty, for example. The student should have described crime as a violation of a legal boundary or maybe even discussed the relative nature of crime across time and cultures.

Examiner's tip
These are AO1 marks as they ask for knowledge of the terms.

2. *Outline how a field experiment is used as a research method to investigate witness effectiveness.* *(3 marks)*

A field experiment is a study that is done in a natural setting to look at normal behaviour. It is set up by a researcher to study a variable.

Commentary
This is an accurate, although limited, description, but the question specifically asks the student to describe the field experiment as a research method to investigate witness effectiveness. The answer could have been simply rephrased as: 'A field experiment is a research method that is done in a natural setting to look at the recall of witnesses after experiencing an incident in a realistic environment. It is set up by a researcher to study a factor, such as weapon focus, that might affect witness effectiveness.'

The first answer is likely to get no marks but one mark might be given for a general point about field experiments. It is best to focus much more on the question.

Examiner's tip
This is a question focusing on AO3 because it is about methodology.

3. *During your course you will have studied one study into eyewitness testimony. Identify this study and describe its findings.* *(2 marks)*

Loftus and Palmer found that leading questions had an effect on witness recall. Participants recalled faster speeds when asked a question containing the word 'smashed'.

Commentary
This answer is fine in terms of its content. Note that the student has outlined the conclusion as a finding – which is perfectly acceptable. The results described are a little limited, and could have been made clearer by stating that the speed was of a car before a collision, and that other key verbs were used. A more detailed answer may have even stated the average speed of the car (smashed 40.8mph), or that the difference between smashed and contact was an average of 9mph. This would have been a better answer, worth both marks.

Examiner's tip
This is a question focusing on AO1 because it is about understanding of a study.

Child psychology (page 50)

1. *Define the following terms:*
   i Attachment
   ii Deprivation
   iii Privation *3 marks)*

i Attachment is a close emotional bond between an infant and caregiver.
ii Deprivation is the loss of a formed attachment with a caregiver.
iii Privation is when an attachment between child and caregiver is never formed.

Commentary
All these answers are fine as simple definitions worth one mark each.

Examiner's tips
This question has one mark for each term but revise enough so that you can define terms for two marks and perhaps even three marks, in which case an example would be useful. These are AO1 marks as they ask for knowledge of the terms.

2. *Ainsworth classified different attachment types using the strange situation. Describe the behaviour of the children she observed in each attachment type, making it clear which type you are referring to.* *(6 marks)*

Type A/Anxious-avoidant attachment type: the child is upset a lot.
Type B/Secure attachment type: the child cries when the mother leaves the room, is not consoled by the stranger and enjoys being reunited with the mother.
Type C/Anxious-resistant: The child does not know whether it likes its mother or not.

Commentary
This answer clearly states the three attachment types found by Ainsworth, but needs an accurate description. The first description of the child's behaviour is very limited and not specific to type A as type B children cry when they are left and type C when they are reunited. The description of type B is much better, and clearly explains the behaviour of the child in relation to the episode of the procedure, so two marks are likely to be given here. The description of type C is almost there. The answer indicates knowledge of resistant behaviour but should really relate this behaviour to the mother-child reunion. This is likely to get one mark.

Examiner's tip

In general, a mark is given for a point that is clearly made and answers the question. If you are not sure that you have made your point clearly enough, an example can help demonstrate your understanding.

Health psychology (page 74)

1. *Describe the mode of action at the synapses of one drug other than heroin.* *(4 marks)*

Nicotine is a powerfully addictive drug affecting the central nervous system and the peripheral nervous system. It works at nicotinic receptors. Nicotine inhibits the function of specific acetylcholine receptors. Nicotine stimulates the acetylcholine receptor then blocks it. Acetylcholine levels rise because nicotine has disabled the receptors, and so acetylcholine is in the synaptic gap not being picked up. Levels of the neurotransmitter noradrenalin also rise, which leads to better memory ability.

Commentary

Marks are likely to be given for mentioning nicotinic receptors in the nervous system. Then the more specific information about acetylcholine receptors is worth a mark, where it is said that nicotine stimulates then blocks the receptors. A further mark is likely for saying that acetylcholine is in the synaptic gap. It would be useful to say a bit more about synaptic transmission though the point about noradrenlin is also likely to be credited, so the answer should get full marks.

Examiner's tip

The question focuses on AO1, because knowledge is required. Biological detail is required for all four marks for this particular question and you can see that quite a lot of detail is needed. Note you can use any drug other than heroin, so prepare to answer this question using the other drug you studied, if it was not nicotine.

2. *Outline two reasons why researchers may sometimes prefer to use animals rather than humans for studies into the effects of drugs.* *(4 marks)*

Animals are used because they have a shorter gestation period so the effects of drugs can be studied across generations. Also, they are smaller and easier to handle.

Commentary

This is a well-focused answer but not enough for 4 marks. The comment about shorter gestation is good because it is explained and linked to drugs but it needs a little more for the 2 marks available. The second point might get a third mark but really it shows knowledge without understanding – it is not clear that the student knows why being smaller and easier to handle is a reason for using them.

Examiner's tip

When a question asks for two things to be done (such as two reasons given, as here), split the marks available into two and that will guide you as to how much to write.

8. *Evaluate the reliability and validity of one method using human participants that researchers use to investigate the effects of drugs.* *(6 marks)*

One method is using laboratory experiments. They are reliable because of the careful controls, which means they can be repeated and tested to see if findings are found again in the same conditions. They are, however, not valid because they take place in an artificial environment and so real-life behaviour may not be studied.

Commentary

This answer covers the main point but will not get the full 6 marks. There are likely to be two marks for the point about reliability and one mark for the point about validity. To get further marks examples can be used, reliability and validity could be defined, and other sorts of validity could be explored.

Examiner's tip

Strengths and weaknesses of methods can almost always be expressed in terms of good or bad reliability or validity. This question specifically asks about those two issues but if a question is more general and asks about strengths and weaknesses of a method, then using reliability and validity is a good idea.

Sport psychology (page 96)

1. *Questionnaires are sometimes given to sportspeople to discover how they feel when competing. Outline one weakness of this means of collecting evidence.* *(3 marks)*

One weakness of a questionnaire is that it may not gather valid data. The issue is that someone might say something on a questionnaire that they might not do or believe. This could be because of social desirability, which means they could say what they thought they should say, or they could be obeying demand characteristics, saying what they thought the researcher wanted because they guessed the purpose of the survey.

Commentary

This is a clear answer likely to get all 3 marks. It focuses on validity, explains why there is a problem, and then refers to both social desirability and demand characteristics, successfully explaining both terms.

Examiner's tip

Note that the first sentence sets the scene well for the explanation that follows but is unlikely to get a mark on its own. This shows that knowing the answer (that questionnaires may not gather valid data) is not enough; you have to say why the data may not be valid, for example.

4. Evaluate one study in detail from sport psychology. *(4 marks)*

Boyd and Munroe used a standard questionnaire that had been used before so had already been tested to make sure it was reliable. However, they did change the questionnaire for one of the two groups and using a slightly different questionnaire could have affected the data. They only looked at climbers who climbed indoors, which might not be representative of all climbers, so the findings may not be generalisable. Also, the track and field athletes did their questionnaires as a group and the climbers did it individually, which may have affected the results.

Commentary

This answer is likely to get all 4 marks. The comment about reliability is useful, as is the observation that changing the questionnaire might mean the findings would not be reliable after all. A third point is that there might not be a representative sample of all climbers and a fourth point is that the two groups undertook the questionnaire differently. The points are clearly expressed and show clear understanding.

Examiner's tip

If you are asked to evaluate a study in particular, be sure to make specific reference to that study at least once, such as when climbers are referred to. Make sure that your answer is sufficiently focused. However, you can also get general method evaluation marks.

5. Describe one key issue in sport psychology. *(4 marks)*

There is a tendency to categorise sports as feminine, masculine or neutral. In general, girls choose 'female' sports to participate in and males choose 'male' sports. Sport is not equally portrayed in the media, with female sports and female sportspeople being portrayed less.

Commentary

This is a clear key issue, the point that sport is 'gendered' in society. One of the studies in the course is Koivula's, who looks at how sport is gendered. This answer focuses more on the issue than the theory and some examples of how sport is 'gendered' are given, but the issue itself could be made clearer for a final mark. Three marks are likely.

Examiner's tip

When asked to describe a key issue, make sure you describe the issue itself and leave the psychology for any explanation of the issue that is asked for.

Clinical psychology (page 134)

1. Describe the procedure of Rosenhan's (1973) study. *(5 marks)*

Rosenhan aimed to test the validity of the DSM. He sent eight pseudo-patients to a variety of different psychiatric hospitals. They all said that they could hear voices in their head saying things like 'thud'. When they were admitted they had to act normally. Some took notes about how the staff interacted with them and the other patients. All the pseudo-patients were admitted for between 7 and 52 days.

Commentary

This answer gives quite a bit of detail for the 5 marks and focuses largely on the procedure as asked. The aim is not credited so the first sentence gets no marks. The results are not credited either, so the length of time the pseudo-patients were admitted for gets no marks. There is 1 mark for the idea of having eight pseudo-patients saying they heard 'thud' in their heads, and 1 mark for mentioning that they had to act normally and some of them took notes. So this answer gets 2 marks out of the 5 and shows how more detail is needed. The student could have added more about what the patients did when in the hospitals, or more about the instructions given by Rosenhan to the pseudo-patients, or their background.

Examiner's tips

These are AO1 marks as they ask for knowledge of the procedure.

Five marks are asked for so make sure you give enough for five clear lots of information.

2. Sarah has been referred to you, a cognitive therapist, for treatment. She is nervous about what the treatment entails, and asks you to explain it to her. Explain to Sarah what is involved in a cognitive therapy that you have studied. *(4 marks)*

RET is based on the idea that your disorder is caused by your faulty processing. Together we are going to look at how you process and think about various bits of information. Then I am going to ask you some questions about your thinking in the hopes of challenging your thought processes, and making you see that they are irrational. Once we have done this, we will replace those thoughts with more rational thoughts, which will help you cope better. This may involve some homework in the form of practising skills developed in our sessions in other situations. At no time do we focus on the past, which can be distressing for some clients.

Commentary
Choosing an appropriate therapy is very important and this answer successfully does that, but the marks are for explaining not for identifying a suitable therapy, so no marks for identification. The answer focuses on how the therapy involves the client and the therapist 'together', as well as mentioning processing information, which gets 1 mark. Asking questions and challenging thinking are also important features of the therapy, so another mark here (though 'making' the client see thoughts are irrational is perhaps not quite accurate). 'Replacing irrational thoughts with more rational ones to help coping' is relevant and useful so another mark here, and a fourth mark is given when homework is explained.

Examiner's tips
This answer is AO2 because you have to apply your understanding of a cognitive therapy to Sarah's situation.

Note that the answer mentions 'you' and clearly focuses on Sarah. This is important as an applied question like this will not be given marks unless the answer is 'applied' as well (at least once).

*3. Evaluate **one** cause of schizophrenia.* *(6 marks)*

I am going to evaluate the dopamine hypothesis. An excess of dopamine is thought to be responsible for schizophrenia. It has been found that schizophrenics do use L-DOPA quicker than non-schizophrenics. L-DOPA is used to make dopamine, so this suggests they make more dopamine. This is further supported by studies that have found that schizophrenics have more of the waste product of dopamine in their urine. Anti-psychotic drugs work by blocking dopamine receptors so not as much gets picked up.
As they do cure some of the symptoms of schizophrenia, it seems to be the cause. However, they don't work as well on negative symptoms, so maybe dopamine is not a cause of all types of schizophrenia. Depatie and Lal found that, when giving people a drug that mimics dopamine, they do not produce schizophrenic symptoms, suggesting dopamine isn't a cause. It can also be seen as a reductionist explanation as it only looks at our biology, it does not take into account our emotions, our family background or our thought processes.

Commentary
Choosing an appropriate cause is very important, and that is done here, so no identification marks but a good start. The point about using L-DOPA up more, which suggests making more dopamine, is a good evaluation point and gets 1 mark. The next mark is given for the comment about more waste dopamine, then another mark for the point that anti-psychotic drugs help (maybe not cure?) schizophrenia symptoms because the point is well explained. Another mark may be given for the elaboration point about anti-psychotic drugs not helping with negative symptoms as, although not well explained, this point is helpful and just about enough because the answer explains how the point links to the dopamine hypothesis. A mark is given for the named research evidence showing that 'giving' dopamine does not give schizophrenic symptoms, and a final mark for the point that there are other explanations.

Examiner's tips
This answer is AO2 because it asks for evaluation of a theory.

Note that 'just' saying the explanation is reductionist would not be enough on its own as 'reductionist' needs explaining to be a criticism of a theory.

Issues and debates (page 153)

3. What is meant by content analysis as a research method?
2 marks

Content analysis means gathering information from a media source such as a TV programme or newspaper. There would be a focus for the study such as how football crowds are portrayed. Categories would be drawn up initially so that instances of that category could be counted. Tallying would be used to do the counting. This means making a mark each time a category is fulfilled so that the number of times can be easily counted.

Commentary
There is enough here for the 2 marks. The ideas of focusing on a topic, using media sources, setting up categories and using tallying are all clearly outlined.

Examiner's tips
This is an AO1 question as knowledge and understanding are required. In a question asking for a definition, make sure you give enough for the marks. One way is to give quite a bit of information briefly (as is done here) rather than to give two clearly explained points.

(page 141)

3. *With reference to one contribution to society from the Learning Approach and one from the Biological Approach, evaluate those contributions.* (6 marks)

The Learning Approach has contributed the therapy of systematic desensitisation (SD) to society and the biological approach has contributed PET scanning as a way of studying brain processing and functioning. In SD the client is able to work with the therapist to build a hierarchy and learn to relax so there is co-operative working, which is more ethical than other treatments such as flooding. PET scanning is a useful method for studying the brain because there is little need for subjectivity. The scan generates computer images for interpretation but someone else can check the findings, which means there is reliability and objectivity.

Commentary

This answer is good because there is evaluation, which is what is required. The comment about SD being more ethical than flooding is explained when saying that the client has some power, so a mark would be given. The comments about PET scanning being reliable and objective get a mark as well and would get more if more were said about objectivity. Only reliability is explained really and a little more explanation is needed for 2 marks. More evaluation is needed, such as comments about when SD is successful (specific phobias) and when not (more general phobias perhaps). Ethical issues about PET scanning could be suggested.

Examiner's tips

This is an AO2 question because you are asked to evaluate contributions. If asked to evaluate, make sure you don't just describe.

(page 177)

2. *With regard to the AS approaches for your course, explain how one approach focuses mainly on nurture and one approach focuses mainly on nature.* (6 marks)

The Biological Approach focuses mainly on nature because it looks at genes and hormones and how they affect behaviour. The focus is on what the infant is like when they are born (and from conception) and examines inherited characteristics. An infant gets 50% of their genes from each parent and genes guide behaviour. It has been said that schizophrenia, for example, has links to specific genes or gene patterns. Hormones also guide behaviour and are part of our biology. For example, males are said to be more aggressive due to having more testosterone.

The Learning Approach focuses on nurture following Locke's idea that babies are born like a 'blank slate' (tabula rasa) ready to be 'written on' by experiences. Emphasis is on how stimuli from the world are associated with other stimuli to give responses that are learned. Classical and operant conditioning both emphasise how experiences lead to learning certain responses, for example operant conditioning explains how, if a behaviour is rewarded, it is likely to be repeated.

Commentary

There are likely to be 3 marks for each part of this question. The first two sentences about genes, hormones and inherited characteristics would give 1 mark as they go straight to a main point. The point about 50% of genes being from each parent, together with the example of schizophrenia, is likely to get another mark. If either of these points were explained more fully they might get a mark each. A final mark is likely to be given for mentioning testosterone and aggression, though more information would be useful. With regard to the Learning Approach a mark is likely for explaining about the 'blank slate' and the link to nurture. The sentence about learning responses to stimuli is better when the comment is linked to classical and operant conditioning and another mark is likely for explaining more about operant conditioning. The answer should just about get the 6 marks.

Examiner's tip

This question is AO1 as it asks for knowledge with understanding. Notice how the points have to be fully explained before a mark is given. Just knowing is not enough as you have to show the examiner that you also understand a point.

Glossary

Ablation: the destruction of a small, discrete area of the brain, usually done so that the function of that part of the brain can be understood.
Affectionless psychopathy: a lack of guilty feeling or empathy towards a victim.
Agoraphobia: a fear of open spaces; may cause panic attacks when in the open.
Amenorrhea: absence of at least three consecutive menstrual cycles in a woman of reproductive age.
Androgens: the hormones that make men 'male'.
Anorexia nervosa: a psychiatric illness that describes an eating disorder characterised by extremely low body weight and body image distortion with an obsessive fear of gaining weight.
Anthropomorphic: attributing human characteristics to (usually) animals, thus generalising results from animal experiments to humans.
Anxiety: the cognitive state of being worried or concerned over something, important in understanding why sporting performances can deteriorate
Anxiety hierarchy: used in systematic desensitisation, where the client confronts the phobic object throughout a hierarchy of exposure (least fearful at the bottom to most fearful at the top).
Arousal: a biological state when the body is prepared for action by changes in blood flow, heart rate and alertness levels.
Attachment: a strong emotional bond between a caregiver and child.
Attributions: ways someone uses to explain their own or other people's behaviour.
Bonding: the process of forming an attachment/loving relationship between caregiver and child.
Classical conditioning: learning to associate two stimuli in the same way so that the same response is displayed to both.
Cognition: mental processes, such as thinking, language, memory, perception and problem solving.
Cognitive interview: a type of police interview that uses special techniques to encourage witnesses to recall accurately.
Cohort effect: when a study is affected by the time, place or situation in which it was conducted. The participants all have similar experiences making them unique. This means that the study findings may not apply to anyone other than the cohort of participants studied.
Competent: the capacity to deal professionally with issues that arise during the course of a research programme.
Concordance: the percentage of agreement between two variables being studied, often used in twin studies to see the percentage of co-twins that have the variable being investigated.
Concurrent validity: a way of establishing validity that compares evidence from several studies testing the same thing to see if they agree.
Context dependency: when the location cues in certain behaviours or memories. Drug taking is often context dependent.
Contributions: 'contributions to society' refers to findings from psychological studies that are used to advise government policy or to help in, for example, understanding social interactions.
Covert: relating to an observation in which those taking part are not aware that they are being observed.
Criterion validity: how well a test or the results of a study can predict future outcomes.
Cross-sectional studies: where two or more conditions from the same time are studied, to make comparisons.
Culture-free: a test that can be used universally without culture impacting upon its results.
Debrief: the process of advising the participant what the true aims and nature of the study were and gaining their insights about the research process.
Deception: deliberately misleading or not informing the participant in research about the nature and aims of the research or some aspect of it.
Demand characteristics: behaving in a way that attempts to meet the demands of the situation.
Demographic mix: when the sample used in a study represents all ages, social classes, gender and educational backgrounds.
Dependent variable: the measured variable.
Depressant drug: a drug that reduces the ability of synapses to work effectively, so slowing down brain activity.
Deprivation: the loss of an attachment.
Despair: a stage of hopelessness after a period of separation from a caregiver, typically characterised by inactivity and withdrawal.
Detachment: resistance shown to a caregiver on their return from a period of separation, often characterised by not wanting to go to them and avoiding eye contact.
Detoxification: the process of removing poisons (toxins) from the body.
Diathesis-stress model: a theory that explains behaviour through a mixture of biological and environmental factors. A dormant genetic predisposition could be triggered by an environmental life event.
Dominant response: the behaviour that is most likely to occur.
Dopamine agonists: a drug that increases dopamine levels in the brain.
Ecological validity: a way of assessing how valid a measure or test is, that is concerned with whether the measure or test is like its counterpart in the real world.
Electro-convulsive therapy: a psychiatric treatment which involves inducing a seizure in the patient by passing an electrical current through their brain.
Ethical guidelines: a set of principles for the conduct of research designed to protect the rights and dignity of the participants, administered by the governing body for psychology in the country where the research is taking place.
Ethics: ideas in a society about what is right and wrong. People act ethically when they do what is right and avoid doing what is wrong according to social and cultural norms. In psychology, ethics involve treating participants – both animal and human – according to social views about what is right.
Ethnocentrism: the tendency to judge another culture by one's own beliefs and standards.
Ethological methods: where animals are studied in their natural environment, often through naturalistic observation or experimentation, and some aspect of the animals' environment is manipulated.
Etiological validity: the extent to which a disorder in a number of patients is found to have the same cause or causes.

Evolutionary: (here) the inheritance of certain characteristics and pre-programmed behaviour that aids survival. Attachment is a pre-programmed behaviour because closeness between a child and caregiver is essential for safety of the young.
Experimental controls: safeguards put into place to make sure that participant and situational variables are eliminated or held constant so as not to affect the results of an experiment.
Extraneous variable: a variable that may have affected the dependent variable but that was not the independent variable.
Extrinsic motivation: factors that encourage behaviour that come from outside the person, such as prizes.
Eyewitness testimony: the statement given by a witness about an event/crime.
Family therapy: a therapy that works with families and couples, focusing on family relationships and interactions between family members.
Functional analysis: used in psychotherapy, especially behavioural and cognitive therapies, to understand the causes of a behaviour, and sometimes to change that behaviour.
Galvanic skin response: slight sweating when aroused causes the electrical conductivity of the skin surface to change. It is measured by attaching an electrical sensor pad to the skin.
Generalisation: the transfer of knowledge gained in one situation (e.g. during a specific research setting) to another (e.g. real life).
Goal setting: a technique to improve performance by having small achievable steps to work towards.
Gradual exposure: used in systematic desensitisation on the anxiety hierarchy where the client is brought closer to the phobic object step by step.
Habituation: the process of becoming used to a particular stimulus such as a drug or even the ticking of a clock in the background
Hypothalamus: the body's regulator – this part of the brain controls many internal systems of the body.
Imprinting: a pre-programmed behaviour that creates a bond between an animal and its offspring to maintain close proximity, e.g. a duck will follow its parent.
Independent measures: an experimental design whereby each group involved contains different people. For every condition of the experiment, a different group of participants will be used.
Independent variable: the manipulated variable of an investigation.
Informed consent: an ethical guideline that requires participants to be fully aware of the aims and procedure of the research they are taking part in.
Insecurely attached: an attachment between caregiver and child that is formed by a lack of maternal sensitivity (avoidant or resistant attachments are formed due to a rejecting or inconsistent patenting style).
Internal working model: a cognitive representation of relationships formed from the first maternal relationship we have.
Inter-rater reliability: when more than one researcher assesses the same findings to ensure there is agreement with the results.
Interview: a data-gathering technique involving asking questions directly of participants. It can be unstructured, semi-structured or structured, and is usually conducted face to face.
Intrinsic motivation: factors coming from within a person that encourage behaviours, such as pleasure at achieving a goal.
Intrinsic reward: a reward that the person gets internally, such as feeling happy because an abnormal behaviour has been overcome.
Laboratory experiment: an experiment conducted in a controlled environment.
Latent content: the content of a dream that is hidden within symbols in the manifest content. An analysis of the symbols will reveal the latent content and thus reveal hidden wishes and desires in the unconscious.
Learned helplessness: a consequence of being unable to escape from a negative situation so the individual stops trying to escape, even when escape becomes possible.
Lesion studies: a study, usually conducted on animals, involving the deliberate damage of an area of the brain to test the effect this has on behaviour.
Longitudinal studies: studies where the same participants are studied over a period of time, usually to look for developmental trends.
Maladaptive: a behaviour that is not suitable for what is required.
Manifest content: the content of a dream that is clear and described by the dreamer.
Maternal deprivation: a child losing the attachment it had with its mother.
Meta-analysis: when a researcher collates all previously-conducted studies on the same topic and investigates similarities or differences in findings.
Modelling: a way of learning by imitating the behaviours of others.
nAch: need for achievement, the desire to excel and be better than **others.**
Negative automatic thoughts: a feature of CBT when someone is automatically thinking something negative (such as 'I never get anything right') that then guides their behaviour (such as them not doing anything).
Non-participant observation: when the observer is not a participant in the situation.
Object relations school: comes from Freud's ideas and refers to the idea that children develop according to their interactions with others and their ideas about others.
Oedipus complex: part of Freud's ideas about child development, where the boy fears his father whilst also feeling guilty about it. He identifies with his father, becoming his father, so that he can have the desired relationship with his mother and not feel guilty about it.
Oestrogens: any hormones produced in the ovaries. They have a role in female sexual development.
Operant conditioning: learning through the consequence of actions.
Overt: relating to an observation in which those taking part are aware that they are being observed, though they may not know why in great detail.
PET scan: Positron Emission Tomography, a type of functional brain scan that shows an image of a working brain.
Phallic stage: the third of Freud's psychosexual stages, where pleasure is focused on the genital areas. The child goes through the Oedipus or Electra complex, experiences castration fear or penis envy, and resolves the conflict by identifying with the same sex parent, so they 'learn' their gender.
Phobia: a fear that is strong enough to disrupt a person's life, so that they cannot do things they need or want to do.
Physical dependence: when the brain can no longer function normally without a drug supplementing the neurotransmitter levels.
Precocial species: animals that are mobile soon after birth.

Predictive validity: the extent to which results from a test such as DSM, or a study, can predict future behaviour.
Premorbid functioning: how well a person functions socially and interpersonally before a diagnosis of schizophrenia.
Privation: absence of an attachment with a caregiver.
Protest: the distress shown by a child when separated from a caregiver.
Proximity-promoting behaviour: behaviour that encourages the closeness of a caregiver, e.g. crying.
Psychoactive drug: a drug that changes the way in which the brain operates by altering the pattern of activity at a synapse.
Psychoanalysis: Freud's therapy, where the analyst listens to the analysand, such as about their dreams or using free association, to uncover unconscious wishes and desires, reveal them, and thereby cure the patient.
Psychological dependence: a perception that coping without a particular drug is impossible, leading to psychological symptoms such as cravings and irritability
Psychoses: mental health problems where the individual is not able to help themselves because they are not aware they have a problem or at least do not have the awareness to change.
Qualitative data: data consisting of words, text, ideas that are not reducible to numbers or quantities.
Quantitative data: data consisting of amounts measured by numbers (numerical data).
Questionnaire: a survey method consisting of a series of questions for participants to answer, usually written, often by post.
Rational Emotive Therapy: a therapy which focuses on resolving the client's emotional and behavioural problems. It is both active and directive, involving collaboration between therapist and client.
Recidivism: rate of criminal reoffending.
Reinforcement: the consequences of our behaviour.
Relaxation training: used in systematic desensitisation in association with the anxiety hierarchy where the client is taught to relax whilst being presented with the phobic object at the same time.
Reliability: the consistency of a method as it is applied to the participants, measurable by the ability to replicate the study and also by the consistency of the results found.
Right to withdraw: the participant's right to leave a research study at any stage and to take their data with them.
Schema: a packet of knowledge used to understand the world around us and new experiences.
Schizophrenia: a mental illness that causes people to lose touch with reality.
Securely attached: an attachment formed from a consistent and loving bond between primary caregiver and child.
Self-concept: how we view ourselves.
Self-efficacy: belief in one's own ability to achieve a particular goal.
Separation anxiety: the stress felt by a child when separated from a caregiver.
Sexual dimorphism: the difference in form, such as size, between males and females of the same species.
Situational variable: a variable in the environment/situation that, if uncontrolled, can have an impact upon the results of psychological research.
Social learning: learning by watching and imitating others.
Split-half reliability: a way of testing for internal consistency in a test by separating items into two groups and comparing the results with a correlation.
Stereotypes: classifying members of a social group as if they were all the same, and treating individuals belonging to that group as if no other characteristics were important. Often underlie prejudices.
Stimulant: a drug that increases the level of activity at synapses.
Strange situational procedure: a procedure that places a child in a strange situation to test how they respond. It is used to classify attachment type.
Structured observation: in which all data is collected by observation but the situation is not natural; it is set up or structured.
Sub-cultural factors: factors that may affect the behaviour of a specific sub-group in society. For example, teenagers behave according to their own values and rules, which do not apply to other groups in society.
Suitably qualified: with the right qualifications to do a specific job well (which might mean ethically).
Superordinate goal: a goal that members of more than one group have to work together to achieve, as the goal cannot be achieved without co-operation.
Synapse: a junction between two neurons where information can be passed from one to the other.
Systematic desensitisation: the gradual association of an undesirable behaviour with relaxation. Often used on phobics.
Test-retest reliability: a way of assessing the consistency of a test over time by correlating scores from two separate sittings of the test.
Token economy: a treatment that involves giving secondary reinforcement for desirable behaviour, that can be saved and exchanged for primary reinforcement.
Tolerance: where a drug user becomes used to a particular level of the drug so that more and more is required to maintain the effect.
Triangulation: taking data gathered from different research methods and pooling it to generate themes.
Turner's syndrome: when girls (who normally have XX sex chromosome pattern) do not develop normally and one of their X sex chromosomes does not develop sufficiently – so they are X not XX.
Unconscious: the area of the mind, according to Freud, that we cannot access, but that guides us strongly.
Validity: measuring what you claim to measure, and having findings about real-life situations and behaviours.
Ventromedial hypothalamus: part of the hypothalamus that appears to be the satiation centre; damage to this results in overeating.
Weapon focus: the close attention we give a weapon that results in a peripheral information not being remembered.
XX: females have one X sex chromosome from their father and one from their mother.
XY: males have one X sex chromosome from their mother and a Y sex chromosome from the father.

Index